£3·50

The Crusades

BY THE SAME AUTHOR

NOVELS

The Great Captains
The Golden Strangers
The Dark Island
Red Queen, White Queen
The Rebels
A Fighting Man
Jason

POETRY

The Black Seasons
The Exiles
The Haunted Garden
Invitation and Warning

VERSE PLAY

Carnival King

CRITICISM

Dylan Thomas: Dog among the Fairies

FOR CHILDREN

Legions of the Eagle
The Eagles have Flown
Viking's Dawn
Hounds of the King
Men of the Hills
The Road to Miklagard
The Children's Crusade
Ask for King Billy
Desperate Journey
Hunter Hunted
Don't Expect Any Mercy
The Bombard
Viking's Sunset
Red Settlement
Man with a Sword

ACKNOWLEDGMENTS

Grateful acknowledgments are made to the following authors and publishers for permission to quote from the works cited:

Ernest Benn Ltd: *The History of France* by Sisley Huddleston; Cambridge University Press: *The Kingdom of Acre* by Steven Runciman; George G. Harrap & Co. Ltd: *Primitive Races of Today* by J. W. Page; Lutterworth Press: *The Archaeology of Weapons* by R. Ewart Oakeshott; Macmillan & Co. Ltd: *Caliph's Last Heritage* by Sir Mark Sykes; Professor G. P. Wells: *The Outline of History* by H. G. Wells, published by Cassell & Co. Ltd

First published 1962 by The Bodley Head Ltd

This Edition published 1978 by
Souvenir Press Ltd, 43 Great Russell Street London WC1B 3PA

ISBN 0 285 62347 8

Printed and bound in Great Britain by
REDWOOD BURN LIMITED
Trowbridge & Esher

The CRUSADES

HENRY TREECE

SOUVENIR PRESS

Contents

Preface

To most of us, the word "crusade" carries with it the sense of noble and pure-hearted endeavour, the spirit of Christian adventure unpolluted by self-interest. In the imagination lives that figure of brave self-effacement, the idealised crusader, a red cross on his white mantle, his mailed hands clasped on the hilt of the sword which he had dedicated to Christ and the salvation of the Holy Sepulchre, a prayer always on his lips; a paragon who occupies a place somewhere between St. George and Sir Galahad—the prototype of European, and specially Nordic, heroism and chivalry.

But as we read more about the crusades this vision tarnishes; enquiry hardly bears out the truth for which we had hoped. Crusades and crusaders are seen to be different from what we had imagined; and finally we are led to agree with Sir Steven Runciman's masterly summing-up in *The Kingdom of Acre*: "The triumphs of the Crusade were the triumphs of faith. But faith without wisdom is a dangerous thing. By the inexorable laws of history the whole world pays for the crimes and follies of each of its citizens. In the long sequence of interaction and fusion between Orient and Occident, out of which our civilisation has grown, the Crusades were a tragic and destructive episode. The historian, as he gazes across the centuries at their gallant story, must find his admiration overcast by sorrow at the witness that it bears to the limitations of human nature. There was so much courage and so little honour, so much devotion and so little understanding. High ideals were besmirched by cruelty and greed, enterprise and endurance by a blind and narrow self-righteousness; and the Holy War itself was nothing more than a long act of intolerance in the name of God, which is the sin against the Holy Ghost."

Perhaps the only redeeming features of this "long act of intolerance" are the facts that it was inevitable because of the outside forces of history, and that its conduct often lay quite outside the wishes or control of those peoples involved in it. Superficially, it may be proved that at a certain date in the Christian era men stitched the red cross upon their mantles and set off to drive the Saracen from Jerusalem; but further thought soon shows that what we call "crusades" were relatively small journeys encapsulated within much older and greater ones; that men of the North and West had been journeying into the East to gain gold or land even before the dawn-world of the Hellenic Bronze Age; and that when all the folk-movement had died away, and the "crusades" had failed, men continued to push on towards the Levant, like lemmings taking to the seas in spring, but now under the banner of commerce and not of religion.

But at last, when the Eastern Mediterranean was finally closed by the Ottoman Turk and the tide of the Renaissance swept men and ideas back westward once more, we find that the Old World had gone for ever, that feudalism, the Church, the social classes had changed. Then men were left on the doorstep of the modern world, their faiths and institutions purged, ready to turn their eyes to the *New* World.

The crusades were not Pope Urban, or Emperor Frederick, or Bohemond, or St. Louis: they were *all Europe*, in the last death-throes of folk-movement before modern times. For most of the quarrelling hordes Christ was but another leader among many, the Sepulchre but another stage on an endless journey towards a vague fulfilment. Many scores of thousands "took the Cross," hardly knowing that it signified anything more spiritual than that their past sins would be forgiven them as long as they kept on the move. To them the men who lived beyond the boundaries of Germany or Italy were all "Saracens," to be slaughtered wherever they were found. To them, Constantinople herself was a vast, rich treasure-chest meant for their picking, its guardians exotic and strange, deserving a slaughter for which there need be no atonement.

An aborigine set down on the Arc de Triomphe to see Paris radiating outwards from him, her broad avenues lined with trees; her copper domes rising green above the clustered roofs, the noble towers of Notre Dame standing monumentally secure, might throw up his hands in a fearful wonder. His state of mind is not likely to be different from that of the average European peasant, whose world had been little more than a thatched hut, a square church and a squat fortress on the brow of a hill—until he came to Constantinople.

In the fourth century Constantine had merely created a great city; Justinian by the sixth century had made this city a dream. The great cathedral of St. Sophia had risen, a multitude of churches had been erected, palaces had been enlarged and decorated on a scale grander than anything the world had known before. The residential district had fine mansions for the wealthy, blocks of flats for the workers, colonnaded ground floors given over to shops.

An elaborate system of drainage was installed and immense underground cisterns constructed. One of the largest of these, the famous "Palace of Waters," was a vast subterranean hall, its roof supported by 420 pillars set in rows. Among all this splendour Justinian moved with his ex-actress Empress, Theodora, dressed in gorgeous robes, pampered, scented, painted like inhumanly beautiful dolls, not the common creatures of a world of sweat and toil.

It is not surprising that ignorant and illiterate swarms of "crusading" peasants or serfs, themselves escaping from a thousand years of Church-reiterated guilt, should behave so barbarously when all round them they saw their leaders, great or learned kings and princes, acting with treachery towards each other and with violence to all who opposed them. To the peasant, the red cross on his cloak was the promise of possible escape from hell-fire and certainly of escape from back-breaking slavery on his lord's land, with the possibility of a bag of gold thrown in to seal the bargain; to the nobleman, great or small, that same red cross was almost a guarantee of a kingdom. There is small wonder that the voice of Christ was too often unheard, and the land-claiming sword too often drawn.

How many men went out on these crusades? How many died in the various battles? How many stayed out in the East? And how many at last came back to their homes in Europe? We shall never know, for medieval chroniclers and historians were notoriously speculative and unscientific; they wrote from hearsay and not from fact.

But even if we had an accurate military census, it would help us very little to picture the *true* numbers of those who sailed or marched eastwards; great lords often took their wives and families, and each lady was attended by her numerous serving-women, cooks, musicians, scribes and pages. Each lord had his personal retinue. On a smaller scale the knights and even the foot soldiers did much the same; while the unattended ones and young bachelors chose from among vast companies of camp-followers, who trailed after an army on the march like a swarm of locusts. Priests, children, old men, tradesmen and beggars increased until a crusading army with its tents, and camp-fires burning, must have had something of the appearance of a vast and shambling shanty town. It is probable that an average army of this kind might consist of 5,000 cavalry and 30,000 infantry, including able-bodied male camp-followers.

When one comes to consider the non-military crusades like those of Peter the Hermit and poor Stephen of Cloyes who led the French children, the task of assessing actual numbers beçomes almost an impossible one. Since no true census was made on either occasion, and only an estimate given, it is unrealistic here to say more than that their numbers are probably heavily exaggerated.

The standing army of the Greek Eastern Empire numbered about 120,000 in the ninth century, of whom not more than approximately a sixth could be put into the field at any one place or time; while even the most mobile and best organised of Moslem armies are not likely to have exceeded 30,000. On the other hand, the Mongol hordes which rode into Europe in the thirteenth century are said to have numbered 660,000 men—made up of 160,000 true Mongols and 500,000 Turks, Finns and Slavs.

In this book, I have withdrawn from an unfightable battle and have quoted the figures given by original sources.

I also beg indulgence for leaving the highroad of history on occasions and for seeming to go down side-tracks. Byzantines, Templars, Assassins, Mongols, Mamelukes and Venetian merchants may, at first thinking, seem to be slightly alien to the crusades, as they are commonly taught; but here I see them as integral parts of a vast human pattern.

As a Christian, I am inclined to applaud the "crusaders" and to take some sort of stand against the "infidel" Moslems; but in quieter and less militant moments I sometimes wonder if the men who "took the cross" after the Pope's address at Clermont were in any respect the superiors of the "Saracens" they set out to destroy. Both Christianity and Islam are Middle-Eastern religious creeds and, at this distance and perspective of time, seem to me as of an almost equal worth. It is ironical that the conflict between the two creeds should have caused such a terrible waste of life, especially at a time when the majority of Europeans were still unconverted pagans.

In a different way, it is just as ironical that for most Europeans the very name "Saracen" soon came to mean "evil or diabolical"; whereas in fact it came from the Arabic word *sharkeyn* (through the Byzantine Greek *sarakēnos*) and simply meant "eastern people" as opposed to the *maghribe* or "western people" of Morocco. A "Saracen," then, was an Easterner—a Seljuk, Mameluk or Ottoman Turk, a Kurd or an Egyptian or a Persian. Instinctively "to hate the Saracen," as so many Europeans professed to do, is as unreasonable as it would be nowadays for a Chinese to say that he hated all members of the English-speaking world—which would include not only Britons and Americans, but also Canadian Esquimaux,

Australian aborigines, African Masai and Tongan Polynesians.

Finally, in a condensed account of the crusades, it is not always easy to put the emphasis where it properly belongs. Therefore, in order to provide some sort of central or unifying thread which may bind characters and events together, I have inserted at the end of the book a brief chronological summary of the major crusades.

HENRY TREECE

[PART]
ONE

1

The Turbulent Sea

The Mediterranean has often been called "the cradle of civilisation." For more than 4,000 years men looked on it as the centre of the world. Almost within an arrow's flight of the blue waters, from age to age have risen the great pyramids of Egypt, the high-gabled and many-roomed Palace of Cnossos on Crete, the tall and fluted columns of Athens, the domed graveshafts of Mycenae, the waterside mercantile villas of Alexandria, of Gaza and Tyre, of Carthage and Massilia, of Syracuse and Rhodes, of Epidaurus and Nicaea and Utica and Tarsus. . . . The high stone walls of Troy have gazed imperiously across the wine-dark Aegean, over the multitude of islands that we call the Cyclades; over islands with names like Lemnos and Lesbos and Tenedos and Scyros and Chios and Andros and Naxos. Proud galleys have rowed to fetch wine and marble and iron and copper from such places. Just as later the men of seven-hilled and many-columned Rome sent down the

Tiber to the island of Sicily for papyrus and oil and wine; or to Sardinia for lead and iron and sulphur; or to Corsica for wax and honey and pitch and slaves.

Wheat, cottons, linens, and papyrus were loaded and sent abroad from Egypt; oil, wine and aromatic herbs from the Greek colony of Cyrene; corn from Carthage; copper, iron, tin and silver from the many ports that lay along the southern edge of what we now call the Black Sea; corn, hemp, fish, hides, cattle, slaves, salt, honey, copper and silk from the Northern Scythian ports of that same inland sea.

It is impossible to keep track of the movements that men have made from century to century across and round the shores of the Mediterranean, carrying swords or account-books; often they have been those small-boned "dark-whites" such as the Egyptians, or Minoans of Crete, or the Phoenicians who originated in Crete and then set up their trading-kingdoms in what we now call the Holy Land, in North Africa, Spain and Southern France; and just as often they have been men of a more northerly race, who mingled their nordic blood with that of their brown-skinned victims—fierce fighters like the dreaded Hyksos, who imposed themselves on Egypt; the horse-riding Hittites; the fierce Hellenes who overran the old Minoan kingdoms and later, under the name of Achaeans, fought their cousin-Phrygians at Troy, in an attempt to break Trojan monopoly over the gold-fields that lay beyond the Hellespont.

Then there were the Philistines—descendants of Achaean-Greek cattle-chiefs from the Steppes—who found themselves a kingdom in Palestine (a name which comes from "Philistine") until, 200 years later, biblical King David of Israel routed them.

By the year 746 B.C. the Assyrian Empire, having absorbed Babylonia, was at its height. Both the great rivers Tigris and Euphrates lay within its grip; to the East this Assyrian Empire looked on to the Persian Gulf—to the West it embraced the whole of that Mediterranean coast we call the Levant, with all its cities, Tyre, Sidon, Gaza and inland Damascus and Ramoth-Gilead. Yet this power lasted only 140 years and fell when the northerly Medes and Persians allied against it and took the capital of Nineveh in 606 B.C.

At this time the mainlanders in Greece started to organise themselves and to look about them for still further conquests; they set up colonies in Gaul, Sicily, and the Southern Italian towns. From Colchis, at the eastern end of the Black Sea came supplies of gold and iron; from the barbarous steppelands of the north wagons rolled down into Greece, driven by half-wild Thracians bringing grain, linen, hides and metals; and from Tartessus in Spain (now Cádiz) came silver. Such a pugnacious display as the Greek merchant-princes put up around the Mediterranean shores and islands soon roused the enmity and envy of two great powers—Phoenician Carthage and the Persian Empire.

The Persians, now great imperialists who occupied even more territory than the Assyrians had done, including Greek Asia Minor, were anxious to avenge their defeat of 490 B.C. by the Athenians at Marathon, and in 480 B.C. under Xerxes, crossed the Hellespont and drove down southwards. Austere, disciplined, aloof, the Spartans had long disliked the gay, intellectual, democratic Athenians. Now at the pass of Thermopylae in August, the Greeks were for once unified against a common enemy, and gave battle.

In this campaign the Spartans were elected by the other states to take charge. For two days the Persian warriors stormed against the Greeks at Thermopylae, until they found a way of encircling the pass with a picked body of shock-troops named "The Immortals." Every Spartan at Thermopylae was killed, but the Athenian fleet was given time to regroup, replan and in September decisively to smash the Persian fleet at Salamis. That same month the Greeks, who also occupied the northern area of Sicily, decisively beat the empire-seeking Carthaginian fleet at Himera.

For a hundred years, led by Sparta and Athens, Greece dominated her part of the world. Athens rose supreme but her rivalry with Sparta soon became so intense that at last there broke out a great war between the two states which was destined to cripple Greece as a first-rate political power for ever.

Power passed from the hands of proud citizens into those of paid and often treacherous mercenaries; and then switched northwards suddenly, as is the way in history, beyond the boundaries of *true* Greece into the harsh mountainous area of Macedonia and among the warlike and semi-barbarous peoples of Philip the Great. In 346 B.C. he captured the already famous pass of Thermopylae and from that moment, however much she fought and protested, Greece was doomed.

After his assassination in 336, the task of "world conquest" fell to his son, Alexander, trained in Greek thought and one of the greatest military commanders man has known. His army was not immense—hardly more than 35,000 infantry and 5,000 cavalry—but with it he conquered Persia, Syria and Egypt. In this last country he founded the great Alexandria, was proclaimed by the priests as the son of Zeus and began, himself, to assume divine honours.

When he died of fever at Babylon in 323 B.C., this god-emperor, who had become by this time entirely Oriental in thought, behaviour and religious belief, was already planning a campaign westward through the Mediterranean to crush the commercial power of Carthage and to stifle the awakening military force of the new Roman peoples. Had he done this, then Europe and North Africa might well have come under the full force of Oriental religion a thousand years before it did indeed suffer the invasion of Mohammedanism, and it is inconceivable that there could ever have happened that bloody series of adventures which we call the crusades. As it was, Alexander's vast empire broke up into a number of separate units, out of which several powerful states were born. One of the most important of these was Egypt.

The next Mediterranean power to clench its hand about the inland sea was Rome. The Romans were not a particularly martial people, but they were deliberate, disciplined and persistent in all they did. Wherever he went, the Roman soldier intended to stay, to build roads and to set up fortifications. The speed of Rome's rise to power was unprecedented: only in 89 B.C. did Rome impose her rule over all Italy—but by 66 B.C., under Pompey, her power reached as far as the Caspian and Euphrates. The conquests of Macedonia and Carthage were ancient memories now. With Caesar's assassination would begin the line of Roman emperors, under his great-nephew Caesar Augustus—that same ruler who, in the New Testament, sent out "a decree that all the world should be taxed."

It was in this time of taxation, when Joseph and Mary went up from Galilee unto the city of David which is called Bethlehem, that a baby would be born whose power would become greater than that of any turbulent Spartan, sly Phoenician, cultured Athenian, conquest-drunk Macedonian or efficient Roman.

2

Gods and Goddesses

After 3,000 years of migration, conquest and reconquest, colonisation, trading-settlement and military occupation, the idea of any sort of racial purity among the Mediterranean peoples must be forgotten: any "Egyptian" might have as his ancestors Libyans, Cretans, Hittites, Macedonians and Romans—to name only a few. Any "Persian" might be part Indian, Greek, Jewish and Egyptian. A man living in Rome itself might have Etruscan, Greek, Carthaginian, Gaulish and Egyptian blood flowing in his veins. The dwellers along the sea coast of Palestine might well add Arabian ancestors to this collection of stocks. The islanders of Sicily must have been a complete amalgam of all Mediterranean peoples; and later on in history both Turkish and French blood were added to the mixture. What is certain is that by Christian times, most men living about the shores of the "Middle Sea" looked alike; that is, they had become Mediterranean "dark-whites" and it would have been difficult to distinguish, on appearance alone, between a citizen of Rome and one of Damascus or Alexandria.

Another factor which tended to give them a certain degree of basic unity was that (apart from the Jehovah-fearing Jews and the sun-god worshipping Persians) most Mediterranean peoples had sorted and selected from their innumerable deities and had settled down to worship only a few of them. The temples and shrines of the Ancient World—from the farthest shores of Western Europe to India and beyond, and from the frozen North down to the source of the Nile—had once echoed to the names of a great goddess in her many forms as mother, wife or maiden. She was everywhere, and all-powerful over men. Some of the earliest campaigns and voyages across the Mediterranean lands and seas, like that of the Achaean Greeks to Crete, had been at least partly concerned with destroying, or at least subjugating, this goddess and putting a god in her place alongside her on the temple-throne. But ancient superstitions die hard, especially when they are kept kindled among a subject-people and are taught in the secrecy of the home by mothers to their children. And when the military conquerors themselves adopt the alien gods they came to destroy, then the struggle is even more drawn out.

It is with no irreverence that I emphasise here that the idea of a virgin goddess was an old one in the Middle East centuries before Christ was born to Mary. In Asia Minor she was known in prehistoric times as Ay-Mari, Myrina, Marienna and Marian, and her symbol was the pure, white moon. And when this prehistoric goddess gave place to the real Mary, the mother of Jesus, most of the simple-minded people of the Eastern Mediterranean continued to confuse the two. In fact, this confusion became so intense by the year A.D. 323 that the Christian Roman Emperor Constantine forbade all worship of Mary in the Church.

Even so, the old dominance persisted; at the time of Mahomet, Moslems believed that *the worship of the Divine Mother* was the one great distinguishing feature of Christianity. At least two great military orders of crusaders fought under the banner of Mary, rather than that of Christ Himself. What is more, when the Crusaders did at last settle in the Holy Land, they found a number of "Christian" sects living under Moslem protection who worshipped Mary "the Egyptian" and used as their sacred symbol the scallop-shell of Greek Aphrodite who had once risen from the waves. From these clues, it has even been deduced that the "English" legends of Maid Marian and Robin Hood had their origins in pre-Christian times.

There are only two comments that I would wish to make here: that the many empresses of Constantinople did much to continue the domineering and often blood-thirsty traditions of the Ancient World, in the dual name of Christianity and goddess-worship; and secondly, that the Moslems, by whom women were regarded almost as slaves, while fully approving of patriarchal beliefs stated in the Old Testament, regarded Christianity, with its stress on the power of the Virgin Mary, as being a false and retrograde religion.

To the Moslem, in fact, Christianity led men's thoughts away from the true God and His stern prophets, away from Abraham and Moses and towards the corrupt goddesses of the earliest prehistoric world. In fighting against the crusaders, the Moslem Saracens felt that they were bringing a new and logical social order to an outworn and decadent world.

3

Constantinople

For 400 years after Christ's birth, the Roman, who had swept the Greeks from the stage like impatient young actors anxious to gain applause, marched here and there around the Mediterranean. By the time of Emperor Trajan in A.D. 117 they had "the World" in their military grasp: Britain, France, parts of Germany, Spain, Italy, Central Europe, Greece, Asia Minor, the Holy Land, Egypt and a band of territory a hundred miles wide along the entire coast of North Africa. Latin was spoken from the shores of the Caspian and the mouth of the Euphrates, to the rocky western coast of Wales.

It was not a peaceful area, nor was it entirely Christian, but the old gods were dying off one by one, and giving way to the Persian cult of Mithraism, a liberal religion based on sun-worship. By A.D. 230 Emperor Alexander Severus, to make quite sure he had neglected no god who might assist him, prayed to Apollonius,

Orpheus, Abraham and Christ in his private shrine, where *all* their images were set up!

But the empire was by now being attacked on every side by pagan barbarian peoples from Northern Europe and even from as far as China. To name but a few gives a little of the taste of the times: Goths, Ostrogoths, Visigoths, Vandals, Alans and the dreaded Huns. Rome tottered under their continued savage blows. Emperor after Emperor took sword in hand—and died defeated.

The year 303, when the legions had been momentarily victorious, marked "the last triumph that Rome ever beheld," as Gibbon puts it, "for soon after this the Emperors ceased to vanquish, and Rome ceased to be the capital of the empire." All this time Christianity, though often persecuted, made steady inroads into Roman thought, and when the Great Emperor Constantine transferred the capital of the empire from Rome to Byzantium (Constantinople), it was able to begin its evangelism afresh and on perhaps more congenial soil, nearer the Holy Land itself.

Indeed, the new capital stood at the cross-roads between Europe and the East. Though the men who founded it called themselves Romans for many generations, the effects of their almost Oriental environment soon changed them as much as Macedonian Alexander had been changed by his long campaign through the East, or as much as the later men of the First Crusade became changed when they settled down to make their new homes in Syria.

The men of Constantinople moved daily in a world whose customs, arts and religious beliefs were a composite of many earlier cultures—Ancient Greek, Classical Greek, Egyptian, Slavonic, Roman and Arab. The result of this peculiar synthesis is brilliantly summed up by Runciman, who says: "The Greek has a subtle and difficult character, not to be recognised in the picture that popular students of the fifth century B.C. like to paint. The Byzantine complicated this character with the strains of eastern blood in him. The result was full of paradox. He was highly practical, with an aptitude for business and a taste for worldly honours; yet he was always ready to renounce the world for a life of monastic contemplation. He believed fervently in the divine mission of the Empire and the divine authority of the Emperor; yet he was an individualist, quick to rebel against a government that displeased him. He had a horror of heresy; yet his religion, most mystical of all the established forms of Christianity, allowed him, priest and layman alike, great philosophical latitude. He despised all his neighbours as barbarians; yet he easily adopted their habits and their ideas. Despite his sophistication and his pride, his nerve was unsteady. Disaster had so often nearly overwhelmed Byzantium that his confidence in things was sapped. In a sudden crisis he would panic and would indulge in savagery that in his calmer moments he disdained. The present might be peaceful and brilliant; but countless prophecies warned him that some day his city would perish, and he believed them to be true. Happiness and tranquillity could not be found in this dark transitory world, but only in the Kingdom of Heaven."

As late as 1014 this Christian barbarism was apparent in the hideous punishment dealt out by the Emperor Basilius II to the Bulgarian army which he defeated on the Belasitza mountain. Having captured 15,000 of the enemy, he blinded most of them, leaving only one man in every hundred with an eye to guide his comrades home. There can be little wonder that later, during the First and other crusades, culminating in the sack of Constantinople by the crusaders in 1204, the uncomplex Europeans involved were so uncertain of the Greek temperament that they put them to the sword as being enemies evil as any Saracen. Nor conversely is there any wonder that the Slavs distrusted and ambushed the Christians under Peter the Hermit who straggled through their country in 1096, on their way to a Holy Land they never reached.

Constantine the Great, who had campaigned up through Gaul and into bleak Scotland, who had seen his soldier-father die at York and there had been hoisted on to his soldiers' backs and declared Emperor, was born in much the same area as Alexander of Macedonia, and had spent *his* early life as a soldier among the Persians. It is not surprising that when he became supreme ruler he turned away from the crude and tribal north to live in the luxury and richness of a city which he solemnly dedicated to the Blessed Virgin and to which he added such pagan relics as statues from ancient Greek shrines, and the Minoan serpent column from Delphi.

The richness of Constantinople, founded in A.D. 330, cannot be over-estimated. Again and again during the crusading period it attracted the men of both West and East, who tried to capture it for themselves. In the following century, while Rome darkened, foundered and perished, the bright if rather theatrical light of Constantinople burned clear, and though the subject of envy from such cities as Alexandria and Antioch, she turned her back on the West and South, and traded instead with Syria and Persia.

All the same, it was from a Syrian, Nestorius, Patriarch of the Orthodox Church in Byzantium, that the first great split in this new type of Eastern Empire came. At Ephesus in A.D. 431 Nestorius proclaimed a doctrine which laid emphasis on the *human nature* of Christ. He was inevitably outlawed, but his following in the East, supported even by the Persian King, became enormous, and soon Nestorius was sending missionaries as far afield as Turkestan, India and China, opening up the world still further. Other branches of the Christian Church, including the Egyptians and Armenians, also broke away from Byzantine ritual and went their own way. In this they were assisted by the immense wealth of the many Jewish merchant communities who saw the occasion as an opportunity to gain revenge on Rome. It is possible that Constantinople might have tried to bring these "heretics" back into the fold, but Pope Leo I in Rome forbade all true Christians to have any dealings with them, and, for the time being, the Patriarch of the Greek Orthodox Church accepted the Pope as his spiritual master.

It soon became clear that Constantinople was the target of envy from all sides: to the West this city, though it thought of itself as the last bulwark of ancient Greek and Roman glory, was a hotbed of idolatry; to the East it began to look like a rich storehouse to be plundered, much as the earlier Persians had tried to plunder Athens. In fact, during the reign of the Greek Emperor, Heraclius, the Persians under King Chosroes II made another effort to push their frontiers further west. Between 613 and 620 they reconquered Syria, Egypt and Asia Minor, entered Palestine and captured Jerusalem. They spared the Church of the Nativity only because a mosaic picture over the door showed the Wise Men from the East *dressed in Persian costume.* Sixty thousand Christians were murdered and 30,000 sold into slavery. The Holy Cross, which figured so constantly in the crusades later, was sent back into Persia as a gift to Queen Meryem.

It should be stressed here that the Persian entry into Jerusalem on April 15, 614, would not have been possible but for the help of the anti-Christian Jews, and that by this act alone they drew the hatred of the Christian West towards themselves. In 622 the Emperor Heraclius began what was in reality the First Crusade, although he did not call it such. To him, both Persians and Jews were the powers of darkness. Within six years he drove the enemy back beyond the Tigris, returned the Holy Cross to Jerusalem, and tried, though unsuccessfully, to convert the Jews to orthodox Christianity.

Letters of congratulation came to him from places as far afield as France and India; but among them also came a simple message of warning from an Arab chieftain who called himself the Prophet of God and who told Heraclius that if he were wise he would now embrace the new faith of Islam. The year 629 marked Mahomet's first appearance on the world stage, an appearance which was to start crusaders moving eastwards towards Jerusalem and Constantinople 500 years later.

4

Mahomet

The Arabs had always been mere nomads who claimed descent from the fathers of the Hebrew race through Ishmael. During the sixth century they had not known what their beliefs were; they had borrowed from the Jews, the Christians, and any other Oriental religions which seemed to give them some standard by which to guide their lives. Certainly they had a holy city, Mecca, and a sacrificial stone, in the Kaaba; both of which they associated with the Father of All, Abraham. But now in 629 they found something else—their first prophet, Mahomet, who had sent his warning to the Byzantine Emperor, Heraclius.

At this period Arabia was peopled by many undisciplined and independent tribes, some agricultural, some nomadic, and a few living in the merchant cities, which were strung like beads on a cord along the caravan-routes. Each district had its separate idols, and the most venerated of all was the Kaaba at the leading merchant city, Mecca.

For centuries Arabia had been the concern of zealous missionaries from among the Jewish, Christian and Persian peoples. The persistent Jews had, in fact, firmly established their own colonies in most Arabian cities, especially in Medina, and had, over the years, converted a multitude of otherwise disinterested Arabs to Judaism. Chosroes II, on the other hand, had maintained officials and tax-collectors in the Yemen, as though this area were part of Persia and nothing else. Previously the Yemen had been under the rule of the Abyssinian Christians for twenty years, while the princes of Yemen had either been Jews or had practised the Jewish faith for 700 years.

Yet, Arabia was of small importance. It was not a menace to any of the great powers: here and there, where water flowed, a small basically agricultural community subsisted, walled in for fear of the nomadic Bedouin; but even such famed caravan-towns as Medina and Mecca were of no great size. The first, whose inhabitants were Yemenites, had a population of perhaps 15,000, and the second was peopled by a recently-settled group of some 25,000 Bedouin who had given up roaming the deserts. It is of interest to consider the simplicity and poverty of Arabia and its peoples at this moment in history, for here lies the true motive force of the crusades, which were to set the Mediterranean world in a turmoil for another 600 years and were to give a sanction to such European folk-movements as had hardly ever been known before, or since.

Mahomet, born in poverty about the year A.D. 570, was probably illiterate, though not unattractive—as is proved by his marriage, at twenty-five, to Kadija, the widow of a rich merchant, much to the understandable annoyance of her ambitious family. That Mahomet was unconcerned with religious revolution at this point is illustrated by the fact that he named one of his children Abd Manif, the servant of the ancient Meccan god. Indeed, until he was forty, Mahomet seems to have let life flow past him, financially secure, dabbling in conversation and poetry, unwilling to disturb himself in any particular direction.

Sir Mark Sykes has guessed that, "in the silence of the desert night, in the bright heat of noontide desert day, he, as do all men, had known and felt himself *alone yet not in solitude*, for the desert is of God, and in the desert no man may deny Him." We know nothing of these trips alone into the desert. They would seem to be out of character. Yet it could be that on the occasions when he led his wife's camel-trains from water-hole to water-hole, down through Arabia, he had meditated under a hot sun, swaying rhythmically hour after hour, obsessed by the contempt of the powerful Jews for the multitude of Arabian idols, and by their vehement and only too frequent statement of belief that there was but One True God.

Such an obsession, in an otherwise unoccupied and semiliterate mind, could by repetition produce an effect like hypnosis, until, at last, the sufferer must give tongue to the "revelation" which obsessed him, which worked in his mind like yeast, if only to gain relief from its tyranny. To Mahomet it seemed that the archangel Gabriel had appeared to him in a sun-drunk vision, informing him of the unity of God, the necessity for righteousness, the reward of Paradise for the faithful, and the reservation of Hell for the negligent and evil. With a tolerance which may have been born of uncertainty, he allowed that the prophets who had gone before him, such as Jesus and Moses, were certainly divine teachers; but it was his conviction that he himself had been chosen to set the final seal on their doctrines.

To us today, with our vision made complex by thirteen centuries of religious discussion, philosophy, didactic literature and the findings of the various schools of psychology, Mahomet's words may seem naïve and elementary. His moral and religious doctrines were by no means sophisticated—yet they were infinitely better than anything which Arabia, the poor relation of the Mediterranean world, had known before. Moreover, they cut like an honest sharp sword through the corrupt practices and beliefs of the seventh-century Church of Byzantium, no less than through the decayed tradition of Persian beliefs in the sun-god, Zoroaster.

Constantinople, its shrines ablaze with gold and colour, seemed idolatrous to Mahomet; while the tradition of the Persian Zoroastrian Magi appeared to be little more than Mithraism or sun-worship. Looming darkly in the Eastern background was wilful Jahweh, the One God of Israel: a God to hold His People together, but one who demanded great sacrifices and punished all defection too terribly. He was not the God for the simple, fallible Arab, untrained to act concertedly after half a millennium of shiftlessness and inter-tribal contention.

Mahomet's words rang like the blows of a great hammer against this world of the decadent and the outmoded:

"Your lives and property are sacred and inviolable amongst one another until the end of time.

"The Lord hath ordained to every man the share of his inheritance and a testament is not lawful to the prejudice of heirs.

"The child belongeth to the parent; and the violator of wedlock shall be stoned.

"Ye have rights demandable of your wives, and they have rights demandable upon you. Upon them it is incumbent not to violate their conjugal faith nor commit any act of open impropriety; which things if they do, ye have authority to shut them up in separate apartments and beat them with stripes, yet not severely. But if they refrain therefrom, clothe them and feed them suitably. And treat your women well, for they are with you as captives and prisoners; they have not power over anything as regards themselves. And ye have verily taken them on security of God, and have made their persons lawful to you by the words of God.

"And your slaves, see that ye feed them with such food as ye eat yourselves, and clothe them with the stuff ye wear. And if they commit a fault which ye are not inclined to forgive, then sell them, for they are the servants of the Lord, and are not to be tormented.

"Ye people! hearken to my speech and comprehend the same. Know that every Moslem is the brother of every other Moslem. All of you are of the same equality."

Such words may lack the sublimity of certain utterances of Christ, yet they have a simple power all of their own; they strike at the very roots of social behaviour. In them, God announces himself as the protector of women and of slaves, as much as of warriors and merchants. All men are now equal, whatever their colour, their status, their calling—the black slave from Africa, the bejewelled Persian merchant. Mahomet certainly showed no discrimination of race in his own conjugal life: after the death of his first wife, he married, among others, an Egyptian and then a Jewess.

The truly important factor, however, in this new social-religion was that, in its original unequivocal statement of belief, it was incapable of being elaborated and twisted out of its direction as Christianity had been, in the separation of Rome from the Eastern Church and during the growth of Byzantium. Islam was a way of living *on this earth*—it was not a prophetic religion, as Christianity and Buddhism often were. Consequently it was not a religion of priests, of ecclesiastical subtlety and contrivance. It demanded no sacrifice, no ritual; it admitted no talk of Trinities, heresies, no misunderstandings of doctrine, no laying-up of wealth for the Church and its officers. Islam was *for all men*—the words of a practical God speaking to his children, telling them how to behave, pronouncing them brothers, holding them together as a family.

The Mediterranean world had known 3,000 years of spiritual confusion: a multitude of gods, of god-pharaohs, god-emperors, goddesses made flesh, priests who were God's mouthpiece, kings anointed by God, and emperors who interpreted Holy Writ to suit their secular ends. There had been blood sacrifice, incomprehensible taboo and ritual, the chanting and dancing of temple servants, the dark pronouncements of oracles. Now, for the first time in history, God had made himself clear through the mouth of a plain-speaking fellow, demanding no temples, no altars, no rich vessels and vestments, no blood; demanding simply surrender, for "Islam" means "surrender," just as "Moslem," from the same verb, means "one who surrenders himself."

Even so, not all Arabs were immediately prepared to make this act of surrender to the new code. Mahomet met with persecution and derision and in the year 622 was obliged to retire from Mecca. This was the *Hegira*, or Flight of the Prophet. He was almost murdered in his bed, but escaped and took to the caves while his pursuers ranged the desert, seeking for his tracks. At last, with his faithful friend, Abu Bekr, he reached Medina and safety.

He was joined by a few disciples who took a characteristically simple and sincerely-phrased oath: "We will worship none but the one God. We will not steal, neither will we commit adultery, nor kill our children; we will not slander in any wise, neither will we disobey the prophet in anything that is right." Mahomet's fame in Medina grew rapidly and his adherents multiplied. The men of Medina had long awaited some creed by which they could govern their lives. Soon Mahomet had an army big enough to allow him to think of reprisals against the Meccans who had driven him away.

Two incidents reveal Mahomet—despite his earlier rationalism and unambiguity of utterance—to be a true, typical Bedouin of the Bedouin; that is, a primitive man, uninhibited by city-born philosophy or ethics. In the sacred Arab month of Rahab, when all tribes acknowledged a truce, the Prophet commanded his followers to attack one of the Meccan caravans, which they did, shedding blood. Later, in 627, as his cause gradually approached victory, Mahomet demonstrated that cruelty was not incompatible with Islam. He attacked and breached a Jewish fortress near Medina, butchered the garrison of nine hundred men, and sold all the women and children into slavery.

Such acts of violence were later to be witnessed again and again, when the Western crusaders came within the Islamic orbit; and yet, curiously enough, the converse happened equally often—that Islam could show itself merciful, generous to the point of selflessness, when the hard-bargaining crusaders had come to expect nothing but the sword. Of this peculiar chivalry, the Kurdish "Saracen"

Saladin is the model, though there were many others cast in the same mould.

In the same year that Mahomet sent a message to the Emperor Heraclius in Constantinople, sternly advising him to embrace the new faith, the Prophet entered Mecca as its master, and as he set foot within the Kaaba, had the image of Manif smashed before him. With all Arabia now unified and converted to Islam, Mahomet died in 632, at the age of sixty-two. He had sometimes been vain, tyrannous, self-seeking; yet, by some unaccountable transfiguration, he had even more often transcended his mortal nature and had been empowered to launch a great religion in a decadent world. "Unlike Christianity, which preached a peace that it never achieved, Islam unashamedly came with a sword," says Runciman.

5

The Moslem Tide

For two years, Abu Bekr ruled as the first Moslem Caliph, or Successor of the Prophet, suppressing all rivals with a sword that had lost none of its keenness by the Prophet's death. The Arab armies flung back the demoralised Persians, advanced into Gaza and put its Christian garrison to the sword. From this time onwards, until the more tolerant twelfth century, the Saracens—as the multi-racial followers of Mahomet were to be called—offered the Christian world three alternatives: conversion, submission and tribute or death.

In 634 Abu Bekr was succeeded as Caliph by Omar, a man of immense force who desired immense movements of soldiery. Abu Bekr shrank graciously into the background, while Omar sounded aloud the brazen trumpet-call to all the Faithful. Christian Arabs, Jews and even Byzantines, flocked to the call. Islam inspired confidence, at least, and what did it matter to whom one paid taxes—Heraclius, the

Persians, or these new Moslems—if the taxes *must* be paid!

The Emperor Heraclius was short of manpower. He had disbanded many regiments after his long Persian wars, for the sake of economy. Now no one hastened to rejoin the colours and over the Eastern Empire spread the gloom of decadence. Constantinople seemed ready to lie down and die without a struggle.

On August 20, 636, on the banks of the Yarmuk near the Sea of Galilee, a decisive battle was fought in a blinding sandstorm. The Christian priests, parading sacred banners, pictures and holy relics, came forward chanting, to be greeted by the laughter of the emirs and sheikhs for whom such ritual held no further magic. As the armies clashed together, 12,000 Christian Arabs, all Monophysites, passed over to the side of Islam, wearied by the Emperor's lack of purpose and especially by the fact that they had not been paid for months. The Byzantine army had the river at its back. Retreat became a hideous massacre as the imperial forces flung down their arms and tried to escape across the Yarmuk. As the Arabs charged again and again, the river became choked with the dead.

At Antioch Heraclius heard news of this defeat and saw in it less the military supremacy of Islam than the vengeance of God, wrathful at his own incestuous marriage with Martina, his niece. Boarding a ship for Constantinople, he cried aloud, "Farewell! A long farewell to Syria!" In Jerusalem the Patriarch Sophronius began to repair the walls and to organise any citizens who would man them. As the victorious Arabs pressed on south to Jericho, Sophronius gathered together the holy relics of Christ and sent them by sea to Constantinople, so that they should not fall into infidel hands. After more than a year of siege

Jerusalem fell; though it should be noted that Sophronius surrendered only on condition that the Caliph Omar should come in person to take the city, for the Patriarch had faith in the religious piety of the Moslem leader.

Omar came from Medina where he had been busy organising military supplies, a distance of six hundred miles. He travelled on a camel accompanied by one attendant only. His provisions for the journey were a bag of barley, one of dates and a skin-bag full of water. When this man of the desert reached Jerusalem and saw his Arab captains waiting for him, dressed resplendently in silks and accoutred in their finest armour, he leapt to the ground and shouting abuse at their pride snatched up dung and stones to pelt these fine gentlemen into humility. Then, alone, he went forward to meet the Patriarch Sophronius, and to accept the surrender of the Holy City of Jerusalem.

The Moslem tide swept on: the Byzantine Empire was pushed completely out of Syria, Armenia was taken, the Persians were crushed at Kadesiah and Nekhavend and the Saracens rode as conquerors as far to the east as the Oxus and the Afghan hills. In 641 they took Alexandria and were welcomed by Coptic Christians there. Now the wheel had come full circle and the Arabs had recaptured within a few years all that the early Persian conquerors had taken over a thousand years before. In February, 641, the Emperor Heraclius died, leaving his wife on her insecure throne as Empress-Regent, terrified of shadows. As Runciman says, "Egypt was lost for ever. By the year 700, Roman Africa was in the hands of the Arabs. Eleven years later they occupied Spain. In the year 717 their Empire stretched from the Pyrenees to Central India and their warriors were hammering at the walls of Constantinople."

6

Haroun and Charlemagne

The Holy City of Jerusalem passed into Saracen hands in 638, but it was not until the late summer of 1095 that the need for the First Crusade was preached by Pope Urban II, at Clermont in France. What had happened in Europe during the intervening years? And especially what had happened during the generations immediately preceding the Pope's impassioned call to arms, to draw men's eyes once more towards the East?

Under the liberal and tolerant Moslem regime, most Christians of the lost Eastern Empire became indifferent to the claims of the weakened Emperor at Constantinople. Yet as time went on, the Saracen position both in Europe and the East became less secure: first, because the Franks, a dominantly Germanic people under Charles Martel, defeated and limited them; and much later, because a race of Mongoloid warriors, the Seljuk Turks, had established itself in the Saracen dominions of the East.

This uncertain situation clarified into a new balance of power, as Charlemagne of the Franks became the ruler over the greater part of Europe, established his military rights in the eyes of the Pope—and was elected Holy Roman Emperor, the barbarian latter-day successor to the Caesars, the acknowledged rival of the Emperor in Constantinople, and the assumed champion of Christianity in the East.

Then into this new Europe whose Dark Ages were ending and whose feudal system was in process of developing, drove the ruthless Northmen, whose descendants became the land-hungry Normans. They were a people every bit as restlessly ambitious as their Turkish counterparts, at the Eastern pole of this Mediterranean axis. The Normans, with papal connivance, destroyed the last remnants of Byzantine rule in Italy, and then turned their eyes towards Constantinople and the Eastern Empire itself, in search of new territories to acquire.

So the Eastern Emperor, caught between the millstones of two new and fierce warrior-peoples, one nominally Christian, the other Moslem, appealed for help from the Pope, to end the persecution of Christian peoples and pilgrims and to regain his own lost empire in the East. The Pope, seeing at last a chance to establish himself as leader over both Eastern Emperor and Patriarch, and over the Western monarchs of Europe, announced the First Crusade at Clermont in 1095.

Stated in this way the complexity of the Mediterranean situation is minimised: spiritual and cultural factors have been ignored. Yet the cynic, or even the practical man, reading the history of these times is almost driven to the conclusion that, on all sides, what moved men first—including popes and patriarchs—was a desire for power over others, symbolised in the acquisition of new territory.

The years between Omar's entry into Jerusalem and Pope Urban's call to crusade at Clermont, are the years of Europe's growing-pains; of the emergence of a new social, feudalistic code; of the antagonism between insecure Pope and decadent Emperor; of the rise to dominance of three peoples—the Franks, the Normans and the Seljuk Turks.

There can hardly have been any other period of 500 years in the whole of European history when so many conflicting factors jostled together so vigorously. It is little wonder that at times in the wars which followed, men sometimes lost sight of their avowed reason for stitching on the Holy Cross. Only too often they were puppets, pulled this way and that by new forces which they did not understand.

After the surrender of Jerusalem, the Christians in the East paid their poll-tax to the Saracens, at a lower rate than their own Emperor had once exacted, and went on with their almost uninterrupted worship, delighted at the lack of persecution. As for the heretics among the Christians, their hearts "rejoiced at the domination of the Arabs—may God strengthen it and prosper it!"

The fact was that the Arabs, unlike the Eastern Emperors, were realists, and liberal realists at that. They accepted a tax in lieu of military service, guaranteed the rights of belief of all whose religion was based on the Bible, and allowed each sect to live as a self-governing community within the Arab state. Christians were even allowed to build new churches, provided they did not overtop the mosques in height! In return, every non-Moslem was required to wear a recognisable "uniform" and not to possess a horse. There were strict laws against any attempt to convert a Moslem, or to marry a Saracen woman, though the latter was easily possible if the Christian man involved accepted conversion to Islam.

The immediate result of this Arab liberality was that Christians in the East tended to lose their national identity. Soon most men spoke Arabic, and after a while—with the exception of the Jews—a score of races mingled, all loosely called "Arab," though professing various religious faiths. After the Saracenic occupation of the Holy Land, Africa and Spain, European trade in the Mediterranean shrank to a minimum, with the result that European Christians left stranded in the Middle East tended still further to lose their identity and to adapt themselves to Moslem ways. It is worth noting that the leadership of Islam had fallen into the hands of a particularly broadminded family, the Omayyads, who held power for a century, and who positively encouraged Byzantine craftsmen, even to the extent of allowing them to create frescoes or wall-paintings showing the naked human body, a practice hitherto forbidden among the Arabs.

Generally Christians had never enjoyed such freedom in the East: taxes were low, business was good, administration was efficient. They had every reason to support their Saracen rulers. Moslem rule, social and political, was the best the Mediterranean world had known since the finest days of the Roman Empire. The peoples of what had once been that Roman world had suffered four hundred years of governmental oppression, lack of organisation, barbarism. Uneducated, unrepresented, many of them were now barbarians themselves—the descendants of the Huns, Vandals, Ostrogoths, Visigoths, Alans, Suebi and a dozen subsidiary peoples who had overrun the West, to smother its culture and destroy its institutions.

To this mêlée of primitive living came the Saracens, hammering in their simple and usable precepts, restoring order and faith in the worth and dignity of human life. It is pointless for the romantic to bewail their victory as being a barbarian swamping of earlier, more advanced civilisations. The fact is that Hellenic, Roman, Persian, Egyptian ideals had been destroyed long before Mahomet heard his angelic voices by the camp-fire in the desert.

The Omayyads did, in some measure, try to revive the glories of Greece in a Middle-Eastern world of poverty, oppression and religious apathy. Through Syrian translators they came into contact with Hellenic thought, and knew probably more of Aristotle than did the men of Latin Christendom. The keen and curious Arab mind, fresh from the brain-washing desert, learned avidly, and passed on what it learned with all the enthusiasm of the new convert. Moreover, Arab contact with the Jews, both in Greek-speaking Alexandria and Arabic-speaking Syria, revealed to the Omayyads a vaster field of learning than that encountered by any other single people before. Added to this, the Arab mind in its eastward wanderings came up against the challenge of Sanskrit literature, and of Indo-Persian works in science and mathematics. It is likely that at a time when the average European warrior baron, disdaining to read or write, employed a scrivener to set down his simple thoughts or to read to him his neighbour's brutish appeals and commands, the average Arab sheikh was well versed in philosophy, mathematics, history and the rules of grammar.

For almost a century the Omayyad family rose in power, carrying Islam as far as the Pyrenees and almost into China. But in 715, under Suleiman, the Saracens were thrust back by the Greeks from the gates of Constantinople, their shipping burned and their stranded soldiers butchered. The usurping Emperor, Leo III, an ex-general of the Isaurians of eastern Asia Minor, pressed home the counter-attack with all the savagery of desperation, calling to his aid the Bulgarian king. The Saracens, split by inner dissension among the caliphs and starved of supplies, were beaten out of Asia Minor. Their attempt to conquer France by way of the Pyrenees was met at Poitiers, or Tours, by Charles Martel, "The Hammer," who threw them back into Spain with such losses that after 732 they never again challenged Europe.

It is not long before we hear of an Omayyad Caliph who eats pork and mocks at the Koran; nor long before another great Arab family, that of Abbas, brings to a head a tribal feud which was old even before Mahomet was born. In 749 the Abbasids, with their black banner to replace the Omayyad white one, organised a revolution, declared the Omayyads usurpers, and hunted down and slew the last Omayyad caliph in Egypt. It is said that the first of the new Abbasid caliphs, Abul Abbas, was so thorough in his desire to extinguish the rival "house," that he gathered together all males of the Omayyad line and massacred them. The new Caliphate, anxious to wipe out any connection with their more liberal predecessors, then established their capital in Bagdad in place of Damascus.

The change of Moslem government was felt in the Holy Land by those Christians who had become used to Omayyad laissez-faire. The Abbasid movement turned its eyes *towards Persia and away from Greece* for its models, and its obedience to the Koran was so strict that for a time Christianity was only barely tolerated, except in Spain, where remnants of the Omayyad family lingered on. Nevertheless, in spite of occasional punitive raids on those

Eastern Christians who rebelled against Moslem regulations, and in spite of Arab dissatisfaction with certain Christian merchants who became over-prosperous, the Abbasids were not true tyrants. The Patriarch of Jerusalem, writing to the Patriarch of Constantinople, credited them with being just and with doing no great violence. This orthodox view may well have been expressed in the expectation that the letter would be intercepted, but it is certain that Christian heretics as late as the tenth century disapproved less of the Abbasids than they did of the established Church.

This religious confusion was also reflected by the usurping Greek Emperor, Leo III, who had defeated the Omayyads and whose family ruled Constantinople for over sixty years. Known as the Iconoclasts, or idol-breakers, Leo's family showed an immense, if barbaric, zeal in trying to purge the Orthodox Church of what they considered to be idolatry by smashing great quantities of the finest statues. Such passionate destruction was possibly due to the influence of Islam and certainly, in its sudden enthusiasm and its neglect of earlier orthodox traditions, it anticipated one aspect of Protestantism. The Iconoclasts, fervid almost to the point of revolution, not only cast down images—they rejected as violently the intervention of the Virgin Mary and questioned the celibacy of priests.

In 785, however, the Empress Irene restored Catholic orthodoxy, but it was too late: relations between the empire and the Pope were strained to breaking, and the new "orthodoxy" of Irene was suspect as being the old Iconoclasm in another guise. This is scarcely to be wondered at since earlier Irene, herself an Athenian, refused to take the oath of fealty to her Emperor-son, Constantine VI, and in 788, when he was eighteen and sufficiently old to make his own decrees, annulled his betrothal to Rotrud, daughter of Charlemagne of the Franks. In 797, after keeping the miserable wretch in prison until he went mad, she put out his eyes and then ruled the resulting chaos herself. In 802 her dynasty was overthrown.

It is at this point that two men emerge, one of the East and the other of the West, to focus in their achievements and beliefs what, in effect, became a new balance of power and culture in the Mediterranean world. They were the Caliph, Haroun-al-Raschid and the Holy Roman Emperor, Charlemagne.

Haroun-al-Raschid has been variously thought of both as a libertine and as a ruler enlightened beyond his time. Certainly of all Saracen rulers he was the most ready to co-operate with Europe—if only to create an alliance against Constantinople. With this end in view Haroun gave Charlemagne every encouragement to build churches in Jerusalem and to send money into the Holy Land without fear of its decimation by tax-gatherers. It is on record that Abbasid Haroun, delighted with the way in which Charlemagne had suppressed the rival Omayyad Caliphate in Spain, wrote to the Frank in terms of brotherly cordiality. The English historian, Gibbon, however, with a characteristic cynicism, assumes that this public correspondence was founded on vanity and that their remote situation "left no room for a competition of interest." However, that same historian goes on to say that Haroun sent Charlemagne a tent, an elephant, a water-clock and the keys of the Holy Sepulchre, the last gift seeming to indicate that the enlightened Saracen Caliph was not only on friendly terms with the Western monarch but regarded him sincerely as the protector of Christians and Christian shrines in the Middle East.

Haroun is important for yet another reason: in him is seen the last great triumph of the spirit of Moslem civilisation before the eruption of the Seljuk Turks, who 200 years later poured into the Middle East and with their new and sometimes barbaric concepts of Islam swept away all that had gone before, to provide the Catholic West with an entirely new set of problems which in the end precipitated the crusades.

It is therefore worth while to look more closely at the civilisation, now based in Bagdad and sharing many Persian ideals, which Haroun-al-Raschid, greatest of the Abbasids, controlled.

Sir Mark Sykes, in *The Caliph's Last Heritage*, provides a vivid and comprehensive summing-up of this society: "The Imperial Court was polished, luxurious, and unlimitedly wealthy; the capital, Bagdad, a gigantic mercantile city surrounding a huge administrative fortress . . . where schools and colleges abounded; whither philosophers students, doctors, poets and theologians flocked from all parts of the civilised globe. . . . the frontiers were secure and well garrisoned, the army loyal, efficient, and brave; the governors and ministers honest and forbearing. The empire stretched . . . from the Cicilian gates to Aden, and from Egypt to Central Asia. Christians, Pagans, Jews, as well as Moslems, were employed in the government service. Usurpers, rebellious generals, and false prophets seemed to have vanished from the Moslem dominions. Traffic and wealth had taken the place of revolution and famine . . . Pestilence and disease were met by Imperial hospitals and government physicians . . . Posts, Finance, Privy Seal, Crown Lands, Justice, and Military Affairs were each administered by separate bureaux in the hands of ministers and officials . . . The Imperial Palace and the entourage were equally based on Roman and Persian precedents. Eunuchs, closely veiled 'harems' of women, guards, spies, go-betweens, jesters, poets, and dwarfs clustered around the person of the Commander of the Faithful . . . Meanwhile the mercantile trade of the East poured gold into Bagdad, and supplemented the other enormous stream of money derived from the contributions of plunder and loot . . . This . . . produced a large and powerful moneyed class . . . who encouraged the arts, literature, philosophy, and poetry, as the mood took them, building palaces for themselves, vying with each other in the luxury of their entertainments . . . The Abbasid Empire was . . . constructed entirely by the fragments of the empires which Islam had destroyed . . . The Caliph had become a luxurious Emperor, or King of Kings . . ."

The situation and events surrounding Charlemagne are more complex because, unlike Haroun, he did not assume the control of a ready-made social and military system. His was the task of *creating*, against opposition from many directions, a European force which would both hold in check the aspirations of Byzantium and ultimately lay the foundations of that Western feudal system of government which would enable great armies of European knights and soldiers to move with some sort of unity against Islam.

The true greatness of Charlemagne lay in the fact that his ideas helped to bring about the downfall of the Dark Ages in Europe and the foundation of "modern" history. In the superstitious chaos of ninth-century Europe, he saw that the restoration of the old *Pax Romana*, of law and order and unity of belief over as wide an area as possible, was the chief need if Europe was not to sink back into the darkness of barbarism: and to him the spread of Christianity —by the sword, if necessary—seemed the best means for securing this peace and order. Though the Frankish Empire which he built up had to fall when other rulers and peoples rose, Charlemagne's concepts of government, law and administration have had a permanent effect on Europe, since they created a form of political monarchy, the effects of which have been seen almost to our own times.

Charlemagne was born in 742, the grandson of that Charles Martel who drove back the Saracens at Tours. He was of pure German origin, spoke German, and for the greater part lived in Germany, where he held his court at Aachen (later Aix-la-Chapelle), in the Frankish Rhineland. Here he concerned himself with building a great city, in which certain of his flattering courtiers professed to recognise a "second Rome." Apart from the royal palace, the theatre, and the great marble baths, soon rose the splendid basilica church, dedicated to the Virgin, a lasting and open tribute to the fact that Charlemagne—despite the uncertain temper and heathen beliefs of his barbaric Frankish ancestors—wished to proclaim himself as a champion of Christianity.

Eginhard, the chaplain, records that Charlemagne was a tall, flaxen-haired man with a long nose and a high-pitched voice. Together with these attributes, he had a domed head, a bull-neck and "a belly too prominent. . . ." Eginhard, however, is impressed by the fact that this monarch was never without his golden-hilted sword. Like Napoleon, Charlemagne was a man of immense energy both in love and in war. His indiscretions in the first, however, are counterbalanced by his careful planning of the second. He could not always discriminate between his numerous friends, but he was well aware who his numerous enemies were. Moreover, he knew his Bible and thoroughly enjoyed all the pomp of church ceremonial, to which he contributed generously.

Eginhard also reports that Charlemagne, himself the subject of so many poetic rhapsodies, "used to keep his writing-book and tablets under his pillow, that when he had leisure he might practise his hand in forming letters . . . but he made little progress in an art begun too late in life." His correspondence with his Islamic counterpart, Haroun, was naturally dictated to, or supplemented by, a professional scribe.

Crude though his own efforts were, Charlemagne respected learning and listened attentively to the carefully-disguised lectures which his priestly tutors gave him. Anxious not to be outdone in religious discussion, he even added a word—"*filioque*"—to the Nicene Creed, thereby giving as much importance to Christ the Son as to God the Father, an emendation which at the time was skilfully disguised by the current Pope Leo, but which was later, on a question of doctrine, to split the Eastern Greek Church from the Latin Roman establishment. By the use of that word "*filioque*" ("and the Son") the Roman Church indicated its belief that the Holy Ghost proceeded both from God the Father *and* Christ the Son; while the Greek Orthodox Church still adhered to the doctrine that the Holy Ghost proceeded directly and entirely from the Father.

Though this is a point which might exercise the theologians intensely, the common man, shouldering his axe in the later crusades, would care little beyond that the Greeks had "denied Christ"—a sufficient reason to the peasant mind for regarding Greeks as near-heathens and

Constantinople as the home of "Unbelievers." Undoubtedly on a number of occasions the European crusading footmen were unable to distinguish Greek from Saracen, which resulted in many unfortunate massacres.

The Pope, having found a king like Charlemagne, who enjoyed building such cathedrals as Worms and Cologne and who was also an enthusiastic and successful military leader, was anxious not to let him go. Nevertheless, Charlemagne's career was not an easy one; in fact, he had been King of the Franks for thirty years before the astute Pope Leo III felt inspired to crown him Emperor of the Holy Roman Empire at Rome, on Christmas Day, A.D. 800.

During those thirty years Charlemagne had been at war almost constantly, proving the new unity and superiority of the Franks against all comers. And wherever he conquered, he evangelised, so that after a while the rise of the Frankish Empire in the West became associated in men's minds with the revival of the Church in the West and many there were who began to look on Charles and the Pope as joint rulers, temporal and spiritual, over all Europe. For a while, however, Charles's conversions by the sword lacked permanence, and he had to retrace his steps annually to remind certain barbarous tribes of their vows, with force. This was especially true of his Saxon cousins, who needed much weaning away from the groves in which they worshipped horses' skulls nailed to trees—a relic of the ancient days of the Aryan plains-folk.

In 773 Charles began his greatest drive by wiping out the old Lombard kingdom of Northern Italy and by assuming the title of King of the Lombards and Patrician of the Romans. From this conquest the Pope received as tribute a great increase of territory and power, while

Charles established himself in the papal mind as a "Roman." Then followed the push against the Saxons, folk of heath and marsh and forest, in the low-lying country about the mouths of Ems, Weser and Elbe; a territory which had proved too difficult for the Romans themselves in the days of Augustine and Tiberius and was almost too difficult for Charles.

The Saxons accepted Christianity in 776, but while Charles was campaigning in Spain, establishing a strategic frontier along the Ebro and shattering a Moslem pride already frayed by dissension within the Islamic ranks, they began their pagan practices once more. Charles returned and baptised them by the thousand, making them accept Christianity almost as a sign of military submission. Three years later, when the fires were once more lit in the oak-groves and the broken crosses were trampled underfoot, he had to go back again, and this time forcibly "transplanted" 10,000 families to France and butchered many other thousands in cold blood.

This was the sort of language the Saxons understood. They "accepted" Christ once more—long enough for Charles to turn and ride down against the Slavonic tribes beyond the Elbe; and, at last, to break through the huge skull-decked fortifications of the Mongol Avars in Hungary. When the proud khan of this savage race had bowed the knee before Charles and had accepted baptism from him, there was no doubt in the European mind that here was a man to outrival the Emperor of Constantinople himself. Everywhere he was regarded as having waged a holy war, not one of kingly aggression—against Saracen, Saxon, Avar, Slav and Lombard. So when Pope Leo III hailed Charlemagne as Roman Emperor he was merely making vocal an accomplished fact—especially since

Charles himself had released Leo from the dungeon into which the previous Pope's relatives had cast him and had restored him to the papal throne by sheer force of arms.

On Christmas Day, 800, after mass in St. Peter's Church at Rome, Pope Leo III saluted Charles as the Holy Roman Emperor and placed the many-sided crown upon that round flaxen head. The fact that Leo himself fell upon his knees to pay homage to the new Emperor did not lessen Charles's anger. According to Eginhard, Charles angrily declared that the Pope had outwitted him and that he had had no suspicion that Leo had intended to give him the crown. For his part, Pope Leo was clearly determined that if the papacy must be controlled by a secular master, he should be a Roman Emperor whose interests were clearly bound up with Rome and the papacy, and not merely a barbarian King of the Franks. So was the Pope's position assured. In his eyes Irene was a priestess of the old cult, savage and sacrificial. Her predominance must be avoided at all costs.

It appears that Charles was not happy to receive his crown from a pope he had himself established. Indeed, one of the few pieces of advice Charles gave to his son and successor, Louis the Pious, was that he should crown himself and not allow a pope to do it. Louis did not follow his fighting father's counsel. His meek nature forbade such an act of recklessness; and the Empire of Charles, having flared out in a Neo-Roman blaze for a while, subsided into a gentle glow of disintegration, precipitated in the early stages by the feminine intrigues of his power-hungry wife, the Empress Judith, whose anxiety to establish something like a matriarchal rule turned both Roman Church and nobility against her. It was not long before the papacy, raised from the dungeon by Charlemagne, felt itself powerful enough to disclaim any subservience to the emperors and to act in its own spiritual rights as their master and not their servant.

The shrine of Charlemagne in the chapel of his palace at Aachen has a sculpture showing him dedicating the church to an imperiously-crowned and finely-robed Virgin Mary. The epitaph on his tomb begins: "Within this tomb lies the body of Charles the Great . . . *the orthodox emperor*." Once a life-sized effigy of Charles stood above the tomb; but in A.D. 882 foraging Northmen chopped it down with their axes. The splendour was already tarnishing a little.

There is this to be said, however, in conclusion, that Charles had shown an interest in the holy places of Jerusalem and, with the collusion of Haroun-al-Raschid who, like Pope Leo, regarded the Frankish Emperor as a bulwark against Byzantium, had sent money to the Church there. In the eyes of most Christians in the Holy Land Charles *had* supplanted the emperors of Constantinople as the head of the Orthodox Church.

After the death of Charlemagne in 814 at the age of seventy-one, this Frankish dominion in the East faded and was soon almost forgotten except, as Runciman says, "for the hostels that Charles had built and the Latin services held in the Church of St. Mary of the Latins, and the Latin nuns serving in the Holy Sepulchre. But in the West the episode was never forgotten. Legend and tradition exaggerated it. Charles was soon thought to have established a legal protectorate over the holy places, and even, in time, himself to have made the pilgrimage thither. To the Franks of later generations their right to rule in Jerusalem had been acknowledged and endorsed."

The decay of Charlemagne's Frankish Empire, however, under his successors, left the Pope without a champion. The Saracens had taken Sicily, Byzantium was rising again, and, almost worse still, the rebellious Roman nobles, led by two women, Theodora and her daughter Marozia, openly flouted him. These women took and held the great tomb of the Emperor Hadrian which had been made into a fortress and was known as the Castle of Saint Angelo and there they contested and finally destroyed the temporal power of the Pope. Theodora had been the mistress of Pope John X (928), but her daughter, Marozia, captured and killed him. She then made her own illegitimate son Pope, as John XI. Her grandson, John XII, followed him, to lead a life of such obscene perversion that in 962 the new German Emperor, Otto—who was no saintly man himself—crossed the Alps and degraded him. Once more an emperor had risen above a pope—a type of struggle which became almost a medieval pattern of behaviour as time went on.

Now there was insecurity and decadence both in West and East: only among the native Christians of the Holy Land did the true spark of religious enthusiasm still burn, and that rather uncertainly.

7

Europe Before the Crusades

During his last years Charlemagne had kept his large empire at peace for the most part. The Northmen were his only really troublesome enemies; but by concluding treaties with the Danish kinglets, by building fortresses along his northern frontiers and by floating a powerful fleet in the North Sea, Charles managed to protect his territories and to keep the Danish freebooters in check. This he also did in the Mediterranean, where the Arab raiders were less formidable than the brutish Northfolk.

But though Charles beat the Vikings off, his successors could not. Before long these sea-wolves were the dread of every coastal and riverside town in Northern Europe; and soon they even passed through the Straits of Gibraltar, to ravage the coasts of Southern France, Italy and the Mediterranean islands. In 881 they struck at the very heart of Charles's Empire, burning Maestricht, Liège, Cologne, Bonn and even imperial Aachen. The Holy Roman Empire could not stand against such attacks and its disintegration rapidly set in. By the end of the ninth century the imperial title was but an empty dignity in an "empire" which now consisted of little more than a number of decentralised kingdoms misruled by contentious knights.

These bloody-handed Northmen, or Vikings, which means "Travellers," were of that same North-Central Aryan stock which had produced Goths, Visigoths, Angles, Saxons and Jutes and, at a much earlier stage, the first "Hellenic" Greeks! In the ninth century they carried little learning with them, except a belief in Odin (much like Zeus), a great love of horses when they could find them, an immense thirst, and an incomparable skill with the axe; which last attribute commended them to those unprotected kingdoms they visited, inducing the weak kings to employ them as royal guards.

Their evolution of the long, flattish, shell-like ship with its high prow and single sail produced a standard of seamanship unequalled since the great trading-days of the Cretans and the Phoenicians. And, driven from their own Scandinavian lands by the shifting of the herrings' feeding-grounds and also by their domestic system of splitting up the dead father's land among his sons, which, in a polygamous society, left too little for each individual to live on, they set forth to find new homes. An impoverished people, their dreams and stories abound with references to some vast rich place that their heroes find. "Miklagard," it is often called: "The Great City."

Some of them sought this Miklagard in England, Scotland, Ireland, France; some in Iceland and even Greenland. Still others, taking the overland route southward down the rivers of Europe, came at last to Constantinople; and there indeed they found their gold and their palaces, so commonly that they even confused this city with Asgard, the home of the gods. The Saracens saw them appear on the Caspian Sea and gave them the name "Russians." In Spain, the Moorish Arabs were less polite and called them "the flail of Allah."

After the Viking attacks on Constantinople, the Greeks became so impressed by them that the Emperor, who called them Varangers, or Varangians, persuaded them to stay peacefully and form his own royal guard. This appealed to most of them, and once they had settled, Vikings became surprisingly obedient to the law. They either married a Byzantine wife and took life as it came, or stayed long enough to make their small fortune before returning up the Dnieper, across the Baltic, and so back in triumph to the rude village which had given them up for dead.

The importance of these disruptive Northmen in helping to promote the crusades is enormous and has perhaps never been fully stressed. These sea-rovers drove large masses of the hitherto stable European population to seek new homes elsewhere, to migrate south-east, and so brought the furthest Mediterranean within the limits of the European horizon; they opened, or reopened, a trading-route (not again closed for 400 years) through Russia to Constantinople, the *Austrvegr*; they showed pilgrims another route, through the Western ocean and the straits of Gibraltar, the *Vestrvegr*; and another over the Alps to the Apostolic city, the *Sudrvegr*, which linked up with the Italian ports and so with the East. This last became the main pilgrim route from Central Europe to Jerusalem, and the frequency with which it was used is shown by the visitors' book of Reichenau monastery, which records ten thousand names of pilgrims within two years.

It is ironical that one of these Northmen, Olaf Trygvasson, the first Christian King of Norway, died fighting for the Greeks at Svoldr in 1000, after making the journey to Palestine, and was even canonised as St. Olaf by the Greeks. His half-brother, Harald Hardrada, was wounded in the same battle and retired to Constantinople, where he was appointed Captain of the Varangian guard. In his ten years' service he visited Sicily, North Africa, Palestine and Egypt, before returning to Kiev and eventually himself ascending that throne of Norway which Olaf had once occupied.

Equally important as this concept of Viking and Norman territorial expansion was that of feudalism. Eighth-century Europe was a shattered civilisation, lacking law, education and roads. The barbarians—Goths, Huns and their fellows—had played havoc with the unified pattern of the Roman Empire, and though here and there small pockets of cultural resistance existed, mainly in hilly areas, Europe was largely given over to the harsh hands of tribal chieftains and adventurers, whose simple and single object was to live on their pickings from a disorganised and distracted people. In such a situation the European sufferers lost the Romanised concept of a unified and central government, of being members of a vast family, and to ease their distresses looked round for any leaders who would act as their protectors and spokesmen.

This, of course, is a process as old as history itself. It had happened in ancient Greece, and much later in Gaul. In Britain the Celtic chieftains had imposed themselves on the bronze-making tribes already living in the island, and in return for protection, had required of them oaths of loyalty against all later invaders. By the time the first

Romans set foot in Britain, there was already an active, though crude "system" of society with a kinglet at the top of each tribe, his warrior-aristocracy beneath him; and lower down the scale a caste of technicians, workers in iron, who provided these adventurers with the weapons which made them supreme. Lowest of all were the weavers, the herdsman, the crop-growers, whose work though essential to life had not that glamour which attaches to the man who uses weapons, or even of that man who makes the sword for another to wield. The priests, or Druids, had their own laws or taboos sanctioned by powers to which they alone had access. Often these men came of kingly families themselves.

Basically there was nothing new in the primal concept of feudalism. The later form differed from the earlier mainly in its complexity, the nature of the oaths of loyalty taken, and the responsibilities or duties of one social grouping to another—and these oaths were based on regional custom rather than on any written law.

Professor G. B. Adams, in his article on Feudalism in the *Encyclopaedia Britannica*, says: "The foundation of the feudal relationship proper was the *fief*, which was usually land, but might be any desirable thing, as an office, a revenue in money or kind, the right to collect a toll, or operate a mill. In return for the fief, the man became the *vassal* of his lord; he knelt before him, and, with his hands between his lord's hands, promised him fealty and service. . . . The faithful performance of all the duties he had assumed in homage constituted the vassal's right and title to his fief. So long as they were fulfilled, he, and his heir after him, held the fief as his property, practically and in relation to all under-tenants as if he were the owner. . . ." Originally, of course, such a system was intended to produce stability within a social unit, though later it was to become an oppressive force to those in the lower ranks of the hierarchy.

Viking attacks and the collapse of Charlemagne's Empire after his death caused a protective European feudalism with such force that it lasted, in its more complex forms, from the ninth to the fifteenth centuries. It has been said that in the feudal state private law usurped the place of public law. It is arguable, however, that after Charlemagne such public law no longer existed and that this "private law" was all which stood between some form of civilisation and complete and chaotic barbarism.

Certainly for a time after Charlemagne the kings were without authority, administration or trustworthy armies. The constant attacks by Northmen made life insecure and uncertain. To ward off such blows, even the loss of liberty to an overlord seemed not too high a price to pay. The feudal regime was forced by necessity and in the beginning the people willed it—even if later they found its duties onerous, especially when their overlords forgot their patriarchal duties and inflated their privileges.

In his *History of France* Sisley Huddleston comments pointedly on this dictatorial aspect of feudalism: "The seigneurs themselves soon became veritable brigands. From the peasants they extorted heavy payments, and generally the condition of the dependents was miserable. The serfs were attached to the soil. They could not leave their village; they could not marry without permission; their children belonged to their masters. They could not bequeath property—everything went to the seigneur. The freemen could go where they pleased, could marry and bequeath their property, but upon them were laid formidable charges. They were bound to work on the land of the seigneur without remuneration. They were bound to pay tribute in cash and in kind. They were bound to grind their corn in the mill of the seigneur, to bake their bread in his oven, to press their grapes and their olives in his *pressoir*—and naturally they had to pay for all these operations."

From this picture, it can be seen that both serfs and freemen had every reason to move eastward under Peter the Hermit in 1096, in a vast Peasants' Crusade. They had the papal assurance of Urban II that all their past sins and debts would be forgiven them. Moreover, during the period of their crusading they would be free from the inhibiting force of the seigneurs: they would be their own men. That they would *belong to Christ*, their newly-assumed seigneur, many of them soon forgot or did not even realise. For so many of them this new Seigneur, Christ, whose feudal commands were issued through His steward, the Pope, was giving them leave to make their fortunes and to throw off their yokes. All men whose language they did not understand were "Saracens"—Hungarians or Greeks—to be pillaged and butchered light-heartedly in the vague name of God.

Elsewhere Sisley Huddleston considers the crusades with relation to feudalism in another light. "Those Crusades, which began in 1096," he says, "helped the French Kings in that they served to break up the power of the feudal lords. The lords were obliged to abandon their prerogatives to raise money for the far-off expedition. Further, in their absence, they were often impoverished. They learned, too, to respect their humble comrades in arms. . . . The intellectual horizon was widened, and the social consequences of the crusades were altogether incalculable."

It can be seen, then, that the feudal system had both

its good and its bad aspects: good, in that it gave new backbone to a decaying Europe; bad, in that it came to cause oppression. In the military, crusading sense, its effects and functions were equally varied. Feudalism was good, practically, in that it allowed the seigneurs to raise great armies quickly and assured their loyalty once in the field; bad, from the seigneural viewpoint, in that the experience of new customs and the acquisition of new freedoms turned the minds of the land-enslaved serfs towards independence, and finally towards rebellion against the very system which had previously given them some degree of uniformity and social power.

It seems appropriate, at this point, to consider the societal habits of the Saracens against whom the first of these feudal crusaders marched. And here we see, perhaps with some surprise, that there is no great difference—certainly among the upper reaches of Oriental society.

In his chapter on the herders of Arabia in *Primitive Races of Today*, J. W. Page says: "The unit of Bedouin society is a group of related families who claim descent from the same paternal ancestor. The members of such a kindred group wear cloaks and head gear of a distinctive design and decorate their saddles and bags in a distinctive way. One or more such groups form a camp-unit under a chief or Sheykh, who is a member of the most influential kin in the camp. The camps unite to form a tribe for the defence of its pastures. Such an organisation partly counteracts the tendency to split up into small groups. . . . Descent is in the male line, and is most carefully reckoned. A man's kinsmen, in the restricted sense, are defined in relation to himself alone; they are his paternal ancestors to the third generation, other descendants of these ancestors to the third generation from each, and his own descendants in the male line to the third generation." A man's property passes to his sons, the eldest receiving a larger share, while his widow receives one camel and his daughters two each. Any camels a woman owns pass, on her death, to her husband and sons, her kin having no claim."

Patriarchal government, or the rule of the father, still persists among the Bedouin. They are never ordered to do anything by their chief but just follow his example voluntarily. This, however, necessitates a certain amount of obedience and submission to the sheykh who is their leader. "A Bedouin does everything out of necessity, never by command or compulsion."

It is this respect in which Arab society differed most strongly from that of their Western opponents—though basically the results were the same, even down to the fact that below the camel-riding soldiers or "knights," was a class of slaves, often Negroes imported from East Africa. These were the serfs of the Saracen world; just as the smiths and their families, who largely came from Iran or the valley of the Euphrates, were the "freemen." And, as in Europe, neither class might marry into the other; that is, not marry officially, in church.

It would be unwise, in any consideration of the early patriarchal feudal system, to assume that women in general were highly esteemed by the Western seigneurs, apart from their uses as menials, cooks, or bed-mates. A lord might fight for the honour of his own wife or daughter, and would certainly restrain their illicit relations with other families, when he could, as is shown by those metal "crusaders' belts," riveted about a noblewoman's middle before her lord left home; but to him women of low degree were hardly more than cattle. Out of feudalism grew the concept of chivalry—but this did not mean, until much later times, simply courteous behaviour by men towards women. Chivalry was, at its beginning, a code of general behaviour among *chevaliers* (horsemen), or lords. And often the requirements of this code, in combats between knights, were anything but gentle and courteous.

There is, of course, much to be said for feudal groupings in that type of war which calls for simultaneous independent attacks on a number of fronts. Their great disadvantage was a lack of completely unified command which might sometimes result in dissension and a consequently disastrous withdrawal of certain sections at a vital moment.

In the midst of this political and racial chaos, the only stable factor seemed to be the Church; yet even here there was dissension, since the Eastern Empire had for many generations been at variance with Rome. There were, to be sure, serious doctrinal differences; but beneath them all it was clear that the true motivating force was political and territorial jealousy; for though because of Saracen conquests the territories of the Eastern Empire had sadly shrunk, Constantinople still kept her arrogance, founded on the dream of her ancient glory. It was unthinkable that the Greek Church could accept the primacy of Rome with its upstart and often licentious Popes.

In 867 the Macedonian adventurer Basil, bodyguard and drinking-companion of the effete Greek Emperor Michael, in typical Byzantine fashion murdered his master and founded a dynasty which was to survive by its ruthlessness for 200 years, a dynasty which would have no dealings with the West. This was an important break in the traditional military alliance, that is, a break in the temporal sense.

The break in the spiritual sense came just before Michael's assassination when, in 866, a Synod at Constantinople made certain declarations opposing papal orthodoxy. The Patriarch of Constantinople declared against the universal celibacy of the clergy and equally against the Roman doctrine of the "procession of the Holy Ghost from Father *and Son*." In themselves, these words may seem to lack dramatic force; yet they gave sanction to the rapidly-growing feudal armies of Europe to regard Greek emperors as imposters, the Eastern Church as being hardly of better worth than Islam itself, and Constantinople the rich and golden as a perpetual and never-failing source of pillage and rape. The Synod of 866 was responsible for more misunderstanding between peoples, more death, and more destruction of artistic masterpieces than any other single council the world had known.

This is not to say that the blows of disintegration fell entirely on Constantinople. The papacy had been once indebted to Charlemagne, and he to the papacy, in an unstated pact of mutual aid; but during the century and a half that had elapsed since Charles had gone to his tomb at Aachen, France, Germany and Italy began to seek their own destiny, uncontrolled by papal authority. For a time, indeed, it seemed that the papal throne was little more than the prize of certain noble Roman families and factions. It is said that money was sufficient to buy a seat on that throne; and it is certain that on one occasion there were at least three men who simultaneously claimed the papal title as of family right.

It is at this point that the celibacy of the clergy became important, especially with regard to the monastic movement at Cluny. The sole conception of this order was of a church universal, united, disciplined by a solitary head, and free from the demands of all secular, feudal powers. Celibacy, in the Cluniac sense, strengthened unity, made ecclesiastics single-minded and left them free of domestic encumbrances. In shaking off woman, they shook off also the distractions which go with the raising of a family. The man who can so deprive himself must be strong in his belief, must be dedicated; and so this Cluniac movement became the nucleus of a church within the Church, a spiritual striking-force, a spear head, ready to be directed by the right hand when such a hand could be found.

By a strange twist of history, this church militant was stung into action, was lent support and even given a powerful leader by the descendants of those very heathen against whom the priests along all European seaboards had once chanted so vehemently, "From the fury of the Northmen, Good Lord deliver us!"

These Normans, who had settled in France under Rollo the Ganger (called so, it is said, because his legs were so long that no horse could lift him high enough off the ground to keep him from walking!), in carving out their own duchy had become a sharp thorn in the flesh to all French monarchs. Coming from the harsher north to an easily exploited land these rovers had at first flouted law and church, and then, at the moment when rebellion had come to be accepted as normal for them, had swung about, awkwardly as ever, to conform in a manner unknown in Europe since the great days of Caesar.

Rollo, head of the Seine pirates, had ravaged his way through France, Friesland and England before establishing himself at Rouen, where Charles the Simple, King of the Franks, ceded the whole of Normandy to him, in return for

Rollo's oath of fidelity. That was in 911; in the following year, for good measure, Rollo not only accepted Christianity but also took the baptismal name of Robert, so as to merge even more completely with his Frankish neighbours. Moreover, having divided his Dukedom of Normandy among his faithful followers, he imposed strict laws upon his new subjects, to restore law and order.

These Normans gradually blended with the French, whose language, manners and habits they adopted; and soon they even surpassed their Frankish neighbours in religious zeal, without in the meantime having lost their love of fighting and their zest for adventure. Though their numbers were too small for them to form a nation they soon made themselves felt as a military force within the European feudal system. Wherever there was fighting and hire-money to be had, there would be found parties of Normans waiting to be signed on. Their ambition and greed for pillage was unbounded; they were born warriors, fierce overlords, turbulent vassals. Yet in all matters to do with Church discipline and the requirements of piety they were punctilious in the extreme. Had the Pope but understood this new people he would have grappled them to his heart much sooner, and with much greater profit to himself and his Church.

But before this could happen the inevitable misunderstanding had to arise: Robert Guiscard, nicknamed "The Weasel," head of the Norman family of the Hautevilles and, next to William the Conqueror, the most famous Norman in history, in 1046 led his many brothers and their war-bands into Italy, where it seemed there were easy pickings to be had for any young brave with a sword and a horse. The first of the militant Cluniac popes, Leo IX, misinterpreting these northern wanderers, entered into an unwanted alliance with the Greek Eastern Emperor in an effort to crush the Normans; but at Civitate in 1053 Robert Guiscard's men not only defeated these strange allies with comparative ease—they also captured the Pope.

However, this defeat turned out to be more useful to the Pope and the Church than any victory could have been, for the victorious Normans, declaring themselves the new champions of the papacy, flung themselves at Leo's feet in reverence while Robert Guiscard, smiling up into Leo's puzzled face, announced himself as the Pope's vassal for all time. Defeated Leo found it difficult to do anything but pardon him: no fool, he realised that each could be invaluable to the other, as did his successor, Pope Nicholas II.

Later an alliance was struck and Robert Guiscard, the head of the Hautevilles, received the Italian dukedoms of Apulia and Calabria as papal fiefs. Furthermore, he was promised the island of Sicily as a similar fief—as soon as he could recover it from the Saracens. This he did after a long struggle and then, still hungry for power, went on to threaten the Greek Empire itself. Joined by a strong contingent of Moslems from Sicily, he crossed from Brindisi to Epirus and in 1082 captured the Byzantine city of Durazzo.

Two years later, drawn back there by a political situation too complex to summarise, Norman Robert Guiscard besieged and took Rome itself, leading his contingent of Saracens through that city with all the air of a conquering Caesar. When he died, in 1085, Robert was master of Sicily, Southern Italy and many lands to the east of the Adriatic, which had formerly belonged to the Greek Emperor; a Norman backed by Saracens! Only ten years later, with such a formidable spearhead waiting to be directed towards the Holy Sepulchre, Pope Urban II called for the First Crusade to take place.

It has happened often in human history that if a powerful military force emerges, another follows it in quick succession, as though to preserve a relatively stable equilibrium. In this way the Greek states had once counter-weighted the Persians; and later, the Romans the Greeks. While the Northmen were becoming absorbed in France to become Normans, and then pushing their way down to the Middle Sea to fulfil their turbulent military destiny, certain Eastern peoples, equally warlike, and equally desirous of gaining territory and wealth, were thrusting westwards—like the Normans, towards the centre of the Mediterranean world, Constantinople.

From the area beyond the Caspian had come the questing Avars, closely followed by the Turkish Magyars, often raiding as far west as the Rhine, to be kept in check only by the constant vigilance of the Franks and Germans. The originally Turkish Bulgarians, moving south, had set up their kingdom under Krum between the Danube and Constantinople, gradually to merge with the Slavonic peoples. For generations they seemed likely to form an alliance with the Saracens.

The Hungarians, battered into subjection by the King of Germany, and Otto, the first Saxon Emperor, were not converted to Christianity until A.D. 1000 and were always liable to break out and destroy their masters. Again, close on the heels of the Bulgarians and Hungarians pushed the Turkish Khazars, and behind them once again the Patzin-aks, another Turkish nation more akin to the savage Huns than to any other folk.

But of all the races of Turkestan to make this instinctive drive against Constantinople, the strongest were the Seljuk Turks who burst with a cataclysmic force into the decadent fragments of the first Moslem Empire and forcibly established themselves as "Protectors" of the Caliph of Bagdad. Orthodox Sunnites, they lacked the restraint which had governed the Abbasid Saracens for so many generations. Now, with the Caliph of Bagdad no more than a frightened puppet in their power, the Seljuks swept into Armenia, driving the Greeks before them. In a short while the Seljuks had grasped almost the whole of Asia Minor, had set themselves up at Iconium and had taken possession of Nicaea, on the very threshold of Constantinople. So was founded the Turkish Sultanate of Roum—the very name of which must have echoed ironically in *Roman* ears. In 1076 the Turks entered Jerusalem itself.

At last, with the Normans threatening his western frontiers, the Patzinaks his northern ones, and the Seljuk Turks gazing across the narrow waters at him from their kingdom of Roum, the weary Greek Emperor, Michael VII, appealed to Rome for military assistance. This appeal brought no reply. In 1081 Michael was replaced by the Emperor Alexius Comnenus, an astute and extremely able man, who also knew only too well that without Western aid he would never recover his lost dominions in Asia. He was cynical enough to realise that if he could persuade the feudal Europeans that they were fighting a *Holy* War, for Christ and not for Alexius Comnenus, they might perhaps march against the Seljuk menace. So in his appeal to the new Pope Urban II, Alexius stressed that the Seljuk Turks, now in possession of the Holy Sepulchre, were subjecting European pilgrims to persecutions which the earlier, more liberal Arabs, had never indulged in.

Now Pope Urban listened to the Greek Emperor's appeal with an unusual interest. By answering such a cry with all the forces that feudal linkage could command, the Pope knew that he could then definitely assume the character of Christendom's leader in the eyes of the world. He knew also that such a conflict would end the bickering among European princes and would usefully employ the warrior-energy of the still turbulent Normans. Moreover, Urban saw that such an enterprise might bring the Greek Church and the Eastern Empire into a state of subjection for all time. Such a success would leave the Latin Church supreme in its influence over Syria, Palestine and Egypt. It was an opportunity not to be missed. The envoys of Alexius were formally received at a Church Council held at Piacenza in 1094: in the following year, at Clermont in Auvergne, Urban called upon the Christians of Europe to avenge the Holy Sepulchre.

His appeal, spread by the priests of every town and village, reached the ears of all, not only of the educated. True, there were many faithful and devout souls, of every degree, who suddenly flamed with the desire to expend themselves for Christ and the Church; but equally true, among the great princes and the nobles there were many who saw their chance to make a vast fortune; and the merchants of Genoa and Venice understood with a most mercantile understanding that while the obdurate Seljuks maintained their barrier there could be no more trade with Bagdad and Aleppo and Egypt.

As for the common folk, the simple souls who crowded the lanes and market-squares to listen to the words of Peter the Hermit, whose beard flowed like that of an old Hebrew prophet as he sat, dressed in sacking, on a mule—what was in their minds? An escape from hell-fire for their sins? An escape from their feudal overlords, who worked them to an early grave and enjoyed their wives and daughters in the name of seigneurial privilege?

Many of them, illiterate and hardly articulate, may have sensed the glory of God from Peter's staring eyes, his pointing finger: but there were many, many more who, in the last two years, had seen famine and then plague sweep down through Central Europe from the North Sea to the Adriatic. They had lost their families, and sometimes their overlords. There was little for such men to eat if they stayed in their villages—but there might be much to enjoy if they followed this man on the mule, who spoke their own language and who seemed confident that God had spoken to him direct, telling him what he must do and even which roads he must follow to find the now-darkened Sepulchre.

8

The Men Who Went Crusading

The men who went crusading at the command of Pope Urban after Clermont were a cross-section of eleventh-century feudal Europe—the bishops, knights, barons, peasants and kings. And I place the king beside the peasant here to stress a certain point—that a king was of no more divine or delicate origin than the men who sweated in the manorial fields.

In the most ancient eras a king was a chosen or elected scapegoat in periods of hardship, and something of a privileged brigand in times of prosperity. Often he was selected from the lowest, slave class of his community. Often, as in the case of the Assyrian and Babylonian kings, he was a man of physical courage and warlike skill, willing to die for his people, and obedient to the priests. Others cast aside their crowns when the victories were won and became humble priests themselves. Only in such limited and mystic areas as Egypt or Crete were kings thought to be godlike and different by nature from the common men about them.

In the barbaric tribal world which followed the downfall of Rome and became feudal Europe at last, the Venerable Bede wrote of the early Saxons that "they have no king, but several lords who rule their nation; and when any war happens, they cast lots indifferently, and on whomsoever the lot falls, him they follow and obey during the war; but as soon as the war is ended, all those lords are again equal in power."

Such a lord was the Saxon Cerdic, who reached the shores of Britain in A.D. 495 with only five small ships at his command—being little more than a sea-going pirate-chief—but who had the hardihood to hack out the Kingdom of Wessex for himself and his sons, and so to provide Queen Elizabeth II of England with an ancestor. Three hundred years after Cerdic's landing a Holy Roman Emperor was proclaimed, whose ancestors had been hardly more than palace officials serving under petty kinglets, but who had been able by the power of their swords to elevate themselves to thrones of their own. This was the great Charlemagne.

King Harold of England, who reigned in 1066, had much the same sort of background. Son of a turbulent warlord, besides being nephew through his mother to the Danish King Canute, his most pressing claims to kingship lay in the facts that his sister had married the previous English king, Edward the Confessor, and that the parliament of the day, the Witan, had elected him at a time of military emergency, over the head of the true successor, Edgar Atheling, who was a mere boy and untrained in warfare.

Harold reigned less than a year, if leading armies up

and down a land disordered by numerous powerful earls—who even dictated whom their king should marry—may be called reigning. In Harold we see the last agonies of the dying Viking world; yet he is important in our story, if only because his quarrel with Duke William of Normandy caused the invasion of 1066 and the setting-up of a new type of monarchy, which brutally unified the country but which also, and with finality, established in England that Continental form of the feudal system that enabled a king to call with immediate results upon a large army for such adventures as the crusades.

Duke William did not himself go crusading—he died in 1087—but he is typical of that Norman vigour and rapacity which had earlier sent his fellow-countrymen into Italy, Sicily, and even to the gates of Constantinople. The type of government which he set up in England and Northern France did not change in its essentials for almost a hundred years, by which time the crusades had become firmly set as a spiritual and military habit in the European mind.

It is worth considering the nature of Duke William, since he serves as a prototype of what an eleventh- and even twelfth-century king was like. "Stark he was to men who withstood him; so harsh and cruel he was that none withstood his will; all men were obliged to be obedient, and to follow his will, if they would have lands or even life." That is how the *Anglo-Saxon Chronicle* describes him, and justly.

Some of this ruthlessness may have come to him from a parentage typical of this time; he was the illegitimate son of Robert the Devil, Duke of Normandy, and Arlette, the daughter of a tanner of Falaise. Through his youth and early manhood William had to put up with the nickname,

"The Bastard." A man of violent temper, he avenged all insults with extreme severity. He was not the sort of man who would concern himself too greatly with the rights or well-being of the common man; and it is just as obvious that, after any experience of rebellion, William would set his mind to the task of limiting the power of his own barons, most of whom were as well-born as he.

Like most other rulers of the eleventh century, William himself officially had an overlord; in this case, young King Philip "the Cross" of France, a dissolute, lethargic and crafty youth who, though possessing little control over his feudatories, had an immense capacity for turning their baronial feuds to his own advantage. This he was forced to do because he was only one among several French princes, each one as powerful as he, who ruled their own principalities. Duke William learned much from his overlord's weakness, and determined that once he came fully to power he would not allow himself to be cornered by *his* feudatories in the same way. Moreover, Philip had yet another point of fallibility; he lacked that piety, real or assumed, which other lords put on, and which might have condoned his immoralities in the eyes of the clergy and have persuaded them to form a strengthening alliance with him.

At this time the French monasteries were nurseries not only for learning, but also for the most zealous and often the most bigoted form of militant Christianity. Abbots and bishops were frequently great landowners, proud and self-sufficient, obeying only the Pope—and then only when his edicts and their wishes ran together. To have the Church on his side was of immense strategic importance to a duke, count or king. Duke William was fortunate in this respect; he had a powerful churchman in the family—

his own half-brother, the Bishop of Bayeux; a man who, like himself, gloried in the acquisition of broad territories and lived the life of a great baron rather than that of the humble priest.

However, there is an ambivalence in the Continental royal attitude to the Church which is worth noting: though a king might desire the Pope's support, he would often protest against the Holy Father's commands and would even fight for the right to elect his own bishops and abbots, so as to have feudal control over the Church within his own territories. When William was contemplating his seizure of the English throne, however, he did what any astute European military leader would have done—he sent Gilbert, Archdeacon of Lisieux, to Pope Alexander II to ask for papal blessing on the enterprise, promising that in return for such a blessing he would bring the distant English Church more closely and firmly under the authority of Rome. The result was that Alexander sent the duke a consecrated banner and declared him to be the lawful claimant to the English throne, made vacant by the death of Edward the Confessor.

When the invasion did take place, William, like any other virile monarch of his day, was in the forefront of the battle at Hastings. It is reported that he always rode where the fighting was thickest, that he dealt great slaughter both with sword and mace, and that he had three horses killed under him. By his side he had many armed priests, including Odo of Bayeux, who came dressed in warrior's mail and swinging a leaden mace, so that "as a good Christian he might shed no blood," and who for his help was later granted vast estates in conquered Saxon England.

Duke William was not only a brave fighting-man, he was almost the sole strategist of the invading Norman force, for in the eleventh and even the thirteenth century a king was expected to instruct his soldiers where and how they must attack. It was William who had previously decided where the battle should take place, and how he should attract the rival Saxon King Harold to this particular place by burning up the houses and fields in the area. It was William who ordered the feigned retreat which drew the over-confident Saxons down from their fortified hill-top; and William who then commanded his archers to let fly volleys of arrows.

Once more we see how closely the duke allied himself with the Church and with God; his arrows were to be a divine weapon of retribution—and swearing his usual oath, "By the Splendour of God," he vowed to build Battle Abbey on the spot where this conflict raged *if he were given the victory*, a promise which he duly carried out. For William, as for many kings and dukes of his day, God was a fellow-warrior, a wrathful and militant deity. And when, at the end of that fateful year of 1066, he sailed back to his Dukedom of Normandy to put certain affairs in order, he left his new kingdom of England in charge of his priestly half-brother, Odo.

Between 1069 and 1071 William sent an army into the north with strict instructions to leave all the land between the rivers Humber and Tyne a desert. When these hard-bitten feudal forces had finished, northern England was a wasteland; uncounted thousands of Saxons died by the sword, butchered in their homes or in the fields; those who escaped the sword starved to death; and those who did neither, literally sold themselves as slaves to any Norman who would put bread into their mouths.

After this clearance was effected, Norman barons had become lords of more than half the manors in England.

Even then William was not entirely satisfied; he intended to establish himself as a feudal monarch without any fear of contradiction, either from the conquered Saxons or from his own restless war-lords. So he saw to it that every baron or land-holder of any sort to whom he gave territory held that land *directly from the crown.* Moreover, when allocating these grants of land, he made sure that the favoured lords should have their several manors or holdings *in different parts of the country,* so that no powerful magnate could consolidate his holdings and build up a little kingdom within a kingdom, as had so often happened under Philip in France.

In King William we see feudal monarchy at its most stern, but also at its most efficient. To him his kingdom was much like a great farm, for which account-books must be kept. His particular ledger was the Domesday Book, compiled in 1085, in which he caused to be recorded how much land was cultivated and how many men lived on it. He knew who had previously held this land, exactly which crops were grown on it, and what those crops would fetch in the current market; how many fish-ponds there were in his kingdom; even the number of ox-teams.

For his own pleasure he laid waste thousands of acres in Hampshire to form a deer forest, which he called "the New Forest." It is an amazing fact, however, that during his reign he only had one man sentenced to death—the Earl Waltheof—and that for the most heinous of crimes, in William's mind, of leading a revolt against authority. In effect, he was the Chief Justice of England. He also fulfilled the functions of Foreign Minister and Minister of Trade; and it was by his command that Jews and Flemish merchants were allowed to settle in England and to develop trading-communities which later brought to its shores the produce of the Saracen East.

His hold on the Church was no less complete. Soon after his accession to the English throne, he deposed the old Saxon Archbishop of Canterbury, Stigand, and appointed Lanfranc, his own candidate. William's policy, like that of other European feudal monarchs who came much later, was to make the Church a separate department of the government, with the archbishop as a sort of regent, acting on the king's behalf only. So he did the amazing thing of refusing to allow the Pope to excommunicate or even to send letters to the Norman clergy *without his own express consent.* This attitude had the obvious result of splitting up the allegiance of churchmen, whose loyalties were often given to the nearest and physically most potent master—the king on the throne in London and not the Pope on the throne in distant Rome.

Historically, the Church had always been a military power, or possessed implied military connotations, long before Pope Urban commanded the bishops and priests to join with the warriors and go crusading against the Saracen infidel in 1095.

The concept of the warrior-priest who was required by kingly law to possess a helmet, mail shirt, sword, lance and horse, is clearly seen in the *Chanson de Roland*, which records the heroic deeds of the Franks against the infidel Moslem in the time of Charlemagne. Before the great battle Archbishop Turpin addressed the Frankish leaders in these words: "Barons, the Emperor Charlemagne gave us our task, and we must die for our king. The Saracens stand before you and you must fight them with all your might. So, confess your sins, ask God for pardon, and I will then absolve you to save your souls. If you should chance to die today, then you will be holy martyrs and will win a place in Paradise, each one of you." At this point, the barons fell before him on their knees and, having blessed these ferocious warriors, the Archbishop commanded them to strike the enemy *as a penance*, much as King Louis the Pious commanded his soldiers, towards the end of the crusades. Such incidents tend to stress the twelfth-century comment of the Bishop of Rennes, that St. Peter brought two swords to Christ—one for the clergy and the other for the knights.

A militant frame of mind was not surprising in the eleventh century, when the Church and its lands were ruled mainly by Norman bishops and abbots who were often the brothers of those warrior-barons who ruled the rest of the land. These lords sat side by side in the Great Council of the realm, which, after the Norman Conquest of 1066, replaced the Saxon Witanagemot, or Parliament of the Wise. There is perhaps little wonder that such Churchmen became lax and worldly-wise on occasions, or that by 1075 the reforming Pope Gregory accused them of self-seeking and forbade them either to marry or to accept investiture from any earthly monarch. Neither, considering the warlike breed from which these Churchmen sprang, is there any wonder that many of them flatly ignored the good Pope's decrees. Such a one may have schemed for lands and revenues, may have hunted with kings and barons; in his mansion or castles may have gorged himself with meat and drunk too deeply of wine, may even have had his own wife or mistress.

But the common priest was most probably a frugal man of dedicated devoutness. Often originating from the peasant class, he was used to a hard-working life, such as that recommended by St. Benedict in A.D. 529 in founding the largest and most learned order for centuries to come. To the primary vows of obedience, poverty and chastity, he added one which prescribed manual labour for seven hours each day. The Cistercians, who came into being about fifty years after the Norman Conquest, were also hard workers, mainly on the land. In fact, these monks were largely responsible for bringing back into cultivation those districts in the north of England which Duke William had wasted in his determination to stamp out any further Saxon revolt. Like the Benedictines, these Cistercians built for the glory of God. Such abbeys as Fountains, Rievaulx, Tintern and Beaulieu, though now ruined, show in the magnificence of their conception that though, like all human bodies, the Church might often be corrupt, it was at its finest moments capable of such flights of beauty and imagination as to be an inspiration to any man with eyes that sought for truth.

The importance of monasteries and their monks can hardly be over-stressed; indeed, many present-day towns owe their origins to the clusters of huts which, in the eleventh and twelfth centuries, grew up about the monastic buildings, while the monks themselves not only gave education to all who required it, but also acted as doctors to the sick, and providers of food and money to the destitute. Furthermore, they were the only artists of their time and specialised in fine penmanship and pictorial illustration of the Gospels. In this respect, the monks kept alive the artistry of the greatest imperial ages of Rome and Greece. The Irish monasteries as early as the seventh century were producing illuminated manuscripts of the rarest beauty; one of these, *The Book of Kells*, can be seen today in Trinity College, Dublin. It is a glory of design, colour and gold; and the fact that its interlaced decoration closely resembles both Byzantine and early Arab work serves to show what a binding cultural influence the

Church had upon the Mediterranean world. The fact that Norman monks tended to break away from the stiff and ritualistic early designs, towards miniature paintings and drawings of worldly figures and scenes, does not lessen their importance as artists in the general sense.

However, in the main, theirs was a very practical form of Christianity; they founded hostels along the routes taken by pilgrims and at the foreign shrines themselves. Sometimes these were of a special sort, such as those for the old and infirm, or for those unfortunates who had already been to the East and had contracted that most dreadful of medieval diseases, leprosy. Many monasteries were vast—like towns themselves, often full of pilgrims, knights, common soldiers, merchants and wandering beggars. The monks were dedicated workers, able by their selflessness to establish most of the habits which helped to civilise England, and to counter the influence of the baronial war-lords.

Such good works demanded wealth to sustain them. If bishops and abbots are at times condemned as "worldly," and their powers compared with those of the barons themselves, it is well to remember that as Shakespeare wrote, "Nothing will come of nothing." To supply with food one refectory of an abbey where a thousand monks and needy visitors might sit down to dinner required that the abbot should be something of a territorial magnate.

In writing of the eleventh and twelfth centuries it is impossible to get very far without using the word "baron"; yet its meaning is only infrequently understood. Philologists are at variance when it comes to explaining this word; in Latin it used to mean a man, usually a warrior, as opposed to a woman; in Celtic it meant a hero; and in the ancient German tongue it meant a bearer or carrier, a chieftain's messenger and confidant. The words "lord" and "earl" are equally confusing, largely because they changed their essential meanings by the end of the Middle Ages.

At the time of the First Crusade, however, a baron was simply a tenant-in-chief owing military service to the king, whether he held one manor (or fief) or a hundred. A lord was anyone who had jurisdiction over a manor, whether as a tenant-in-chief or as a mesne tenant of a baron. The term "lord" was not a title of honour, but a description of a man's legal status; just as today the lord of a manor or a Scottish "laird" are likely to be commoners and not peers. The terms "baron" and "lord" did not become specifically titles of honour until the fourteenth century. So when we speak of "the barons" of the early Norman period, before Parliament had taken on a definite shape, we usually mean territorial magnates whose holdings were large enough to allow them to attend the king's Great Council.

The term "earl" in Saxon times had simply meant "a free man, one of gentle birth." Danish King Canute raised the status of an "earl" until it corresponded to the Danish title "jarl" or nobleman. Under William the Conqueror the "earls" were still further elevated and the title was allowed only to the greatest territorial magnates. The earl was powerful *not* because he held that high rank but because he was a great territorial magnate. And after 1075 all the earls were of Norman blood.

A baron, then, was basically a territorial magnate, not necessarily noble; an earl was a nobleman, but was also a territorial magnate; and both held their land from the king himself who, in theory, owned every inch of it from coast to coast, together with the trees that grew on it, the fish that swam in the rivers, and the birds that flew in the air.

The twelfth-century King Henry II who, like most Normans, delighted in hunting and falconry, laid down very strict laws concerning the creatures which ordinary folk might not hunt. Members of any rank in the baronage, which of course included those clergymen who held *fiefs*, might hunt such creatures by reason of their special licence; but lesser folk were forbidden to do so under pain of mutilation.

It has been said that the Saxons lived in mean houses, but ate well; while their eleventh- and twelfth-century overlords lived in great houses and ate frugally. This distinction may be a true one; the difference in eating-habits was perhaps not so marked as idealistic historians have made it. The fact is that both Saxons and Normans lived off the land, eating and drinking just what that land provided, no less and no more.

In Saxon times, the peasantry ate a gruel of ground beans flavoured with herbs, a pottage of venison occasionally, roast duck, bacon and cabbage (the bacon being fresh in summer and salted in winter), cheese made from the milk of sheep or cows, and rye or barley bread. They drank a weak brew of barley beer, and occasionally mead concocted from honey. The peasantry under the Normans ate much the same food—though any venison or rabbits which found their way into the pot would now leave a guilty taste in the eater's mouth. Also, their mead was now made from the honey of the wild bee and not from that of the hive, which was more carefully watched by the master. A Norman peasant ate salt meat once a week; the salt being of the grey variety, obtained from boiling sea-water in iron cauldrons. But he does seem to have eaten more fish such as cod, obtained under the carefully organised Norman fishing-code. He was allowed a goose at Michaelmas and a roast pig for Christmas. As for the overlords, both Saxon and Norman, they fared much the same, but added the flesh of deer, duck, pig, sheep and cow to their diets in a less limited quantity.

In days of famine—which occurred perhaps half a dozen times in a man's life—all ate the same: bread made from roasted and ground acorns, and pottage made of grass. Famine made no distinction between baron, thegn and serf. It was fear of such famine and the difficulty of obtaining winter fodder that caused both Saxon and Norman to slaughter most of their cattle in the autumn and to salt them down so that they lasted until the next spring.

By the mid-twelfth century, the baronial castle had changed from being a crude wooden fortress, erected hastily on a strategic hilltop. Now made of stone, it not only had its "shell" keep within its two encircling walls, but also its separate great hall, kitchen and chapel—besides its private withdrawing room for the baron and his lady. And when such crusaders as Richard Lion-Heart came home, having seen the intricate planning and the military impregnability of certain Byzantine fortresses, Norman castles began to be things of awesome splendour. Richard's own castle of *Château Gaillard* was said to have been the finest fortress and home any man of that time had ever seen.

In times of peace, the twelfth-century baronial castle must have seemed a bedlam of noise and activity, which went on for most of the day. Blacksmiths would be shoeing horses; squires would be burnishing helmets, swords and shields; swordsmiths would be retempering blades; archers would be practising at the butts; foot soldiers would be competing with each other at quarter-staff play; the baron's horses and hounds would be exercised and his men-at-arms drilled; knights would be jostling with each other in any space they could find, using wooden cudgels instead of swords. There would be a great blowing of trumpets, a beating of drums, a baying of hounds, a lowing of cattle, a neighing of horses, a screeching of falcons; the laughter, shouting, singing of rough men occupying themselves like vigorous animals.

There might, in some dim courtyard, be also the groaning or screaming of men; not necessarily from whipping, branding or mutilation (though these were always possible) but because of that peculiarly Norman institution of Judicial Combat, by which common men had to settle their differences. Each contestant had his head shaven, was given a wooden shield and a sharp-pointed tomahawk-like pick of horn, and was bundled into the enclosure to fight for his life, watched carefully by the baron who administered the law. Such combats might end quickly if one of the contestants was old, or lacked pugnacity and skill. But sometimes the gruesome exhibition would drag out the length of a day, until the more battered man gave the traditional cry, "Craven!" He was then judged to be in the wrong and, if the matter under judgement was a grave one, was hanged without delay.

In any case, most activities of the European common men of this period would seem brutish to the modern eye. Though scholars read their books and played chess, knights rested from their jousting by playing draughts, and ladies embroidered as they listened to a wandering troubadour singing Provençal ballads of love—ordinary men enjoyed such bloody pastimes as bear-baiting and bull-baiting, or cracked their ribs at wrestling or at that curious form of early football in which whole communities took part. Such folk, so used to hard knocks and empty bellies, were not likely to fear the Saracen any more than they did their own rude fellows or their merciless overlords.

But, brutal as village life may have been in these days, siege-warfare was worse, whether at home or abroad. In the East, soldiers first came across the horrors of Greek fire—a mixture of flaming asphalt and crude petroleum; they also learned what it was like to topple from the *Beffroi*, an immense wooden tower which was dragged up against the wall of the castle to be captured. The *Beffroi* had a drawbridge of its own, which, at a given signal, was lowered to let the soldiers run across to the enemy's battlements high above the ground. Under the baron's care were other, missile-flinging, siege-engines—the *mangonel*, *trébucket*, *scorpion*, *perrier*, *arblast* and *espringale*; quaint and even poetic names for machines which had so bloody a purpose.

The knights are the typical "crusaders." True, they might not themselves have instigated any particular crusade, but they were always, by reason of their nature and essential function, in the forefront of every battle. These knights were not cultured and courteous noblemen; instead, they were, as Ewart Oakeshott says in his *Archaeology of Weapons*, "Tremendous bullies overflowing with energy and martial fury . . . who, though Christians, were as ferocious as their opponents." (The earliest knight was any able-bodied free man who owned a horse.)

But when their enemies, the Danes, Slavs and Spanish Saracens, were overwhelmed, the feudal nobility still remained, "invincible with its terrible cavalry, impregnable in its castles, and as much of a menace as its foes had ever been. The problem of every monarch and prelate was how to find something for it to do before it tore Christendom to pieces. The solution was given at the Council of Clermont in 1095, where Urban II proclaimed the crusade which fired the imagination of the whole of France . . . and sent knights, burghers and peasants off, aflame with holy zeal, to rescue Jerusalem from the hands of the Heathen. So the Church found a job for the unemployed brigandage of Europe." A similar point of view is also expressed by Professor Arnold Toynbee, in *A Study of History*, when he lumps together the crusades with the Spanish Inquisition, the English slave trade, the plantation slavery in the American South, and the genocide of Jews by Nazis, as all belonging to the "catalogue of Western atrocities."

But there are two sides to every penny. The Church, while seeing that this unemployed brigandage of Europe became gainfully occupied overseas, at the same time sowed the seed of a different concept of knighthood, which was to flourish during the next three hundred years. Pope Urban, the instigator of the First Crusade, issued a general command that all boys of good family should take an oath before a bishop, *on reaching the age of twelve*, to defend the oppressed, the widows and orphans, and especially to care for all noblewomen. At this date in history, 1095, then, the twin ideals of nobility and chivalry enter into knighthood.

Five years later the Church created an order whose members were half-priests and half-soldiers, the Knights of St. John, whose task was to provide protection and lodging for Christian pilgrims to the Holy Land. This ideal so caught the fancy of young men of good birth that, in 1123, a second order formed itself—the Knights Templar. They, too, were priestly and well born, but they knew that no war could be prosecuted without money; and to obtain this they went to lengths which were neither holy nor noble.

They were members of the Church, men of God, and yet they were also a military body of a ferocity and political ambition which can only be matched in our own times by the hardened French paratroopers of Algeria. By becoming the bankers of the Eastern Mediterranean, the Templars took on a function which had previously been regarded as the prerogative of Jews and burghers. Moreover, they numbered in their ranks men of lowly, though free birth, who served as foot soldiers, grooms and general servants —the sergeants. Even kings, such as Richard Lion-Heart of England, admired these knights; and other kings, such as Philip IV of France, so feared their powers that they wished to wipe the Templars completely out of man's memory.

The *average* European knight of the eleventh or twelfth centuries was not cast quite in this mode, however. He was born into a Western world which, about A.D. 1100, had France as its ideal: the France which produced the First Crusade, the first drama, the first song of the first troubadour, the first city-charter, the first window-panes and the first tournament! This France gave the world such literature as the *Gesta Francorum* and the *Chanson d'Antioche*, in which it is made clear that God had chosen the French to be His champions in the holy wars against Islam.

The knights of France, and their close relatives in England, set courage above all things, a courage bound up with loyalty to God, to the liege-lord who held the fief, and to chivalry. Above all, the knights' duty was to defend the Church. John of Salisbury may have said that "the knighthood is the armed hand of the state," but Vincent de Beauvais, a Frenchman, comes nearer to their intended function when he says, "The use of an organised knighthood lay *in protecting the Church*, attacking disloyalty, reverencing the priesthood, avenging the wrongs of the poor *and keeping the country in a state of quiet.*" They were the policemen both of church and state and, as such, inevitably grasped for themselves privileges which the lesser ranks of society dared not aspire to, either in Europe or in the East.

Before the First Crusade, French, English and German knights were almost entirely dedicated to the practice of war. If women were ever mentioned in the *chansons* of that period, it was only as aloof and depersonalised puppets. But, by about 1100, the poets of Southern France so swamped their lyrics with references to the warmer aspects of love that soon dreams of women began to dominate the minds of the knights, leaving the Church and loyalty to the liege-lord to take a second place. Knights now looked on war as a glorious way of winning the favours of a selected woman—as well as of acquiring a fortune or a territory.

The word "*amoureux*" now occurs more and more frequently in documents. At this stage of knightly development, it is "love" which makes life gracious and civilised—and not mere church discipline, or loyalty to one's king. "No man makes a good fighter, unless he has been in love," wrote a poet of the time. But here it is necessary to to say that "knightly love" of the twelfth century was not quite the distant yearning that Tennyson shows in *Lancelot and Elaine*. To come even within reach of understanding it, one had better forget that Queen Victoria ever reigned! The love and chivalry of which the troubadours sang and for which the knights fought lay outside matrimony. Indeed, it became the ideal of the warrior knight to make love to the wife of another, unsuspecting lord. Not for the knight the constant ties of marriage; his must be a freer life.

When Pope Urban commanded young knights to care for noblewomen, he had not intended his instructions to reach so far. It was the poets, the troubadours of Southern France, who gave the instructions which led to the Age of Chivalry proper, or improper. And naturally the Church frowned on the illicit practices of the knights and their chosen ladies—but not, as Ewart Oakeshott says, "so much because it was immoral, but because it diverted the attention of the knighthood from its task of fighting the infidel and of recovering the Holy Land."

Yet though twelfth-century knights were often murderous, superstitious and adulterous, such was their respect for ceremony and symbolism that every aspirant to knighthood paid homage to the final and overriding power of the Church. The young knight-to-be was bathed in holy water, dressed in a pure white tunic, girt with the belt of chastity, and was required to pray all through the night, his weapons lying before the altar. When morning came he would hear mass, make his confession, and the priest would then dedicate the young man's sword to Father, Son and Holy Spirit, naming it as the weapon which would strike against Christ's enemies and would defend the Christian faith. After this the knight's sword would be girded on him by his sponsor (perhaps another, older knight), on the battlefield, who gave the aspirant to knighthood a blow, or *colée*, across the shoulders with the flat of a sword, or with the fist), and he would take his vows—never to deal with traitors, never to give evil advice to a lady, never to forget the Church festivals and fasts, and never to omit hearing a daily mass. Cynically, one is driven to consider that though the last two vows are clear and absolute, the first two might be, and were, capable of a variety of interpretations.

Tournaments, though often condemned by the Church as a cause of drunkenness among the crowds, and immorality among the ladies who watched them (and ended up half-naked, having stripped off and thrown various articles of clothing to their chosen *chevaliers*), were almost a necessity to knights of the twelfth and thirteenth centuries. They were a battle-school for military training and, moreover, the main source of revenue for most young knights who depended on prize-money or ransoms for their living. The tournament was, together with hunting and hawking, the knight's principal means of exercise, and was regarded the length and breadth of Europe with the greatest seriousness. And although the Church often placed tournaments under a ban, men of the knightly class did not take these bans too much to heart. As Aucassin says, "to Hell go . . . the goodly knights who have died in tourneys and in the great wars . . . And there go also the fair courteous ladies who have two loves or three besides their lords; and there go also the gold and the silver and the rich furs; and there also go the harper and the minstrel and the kings of the world."

At various times monarchs such as Henry II and Edward II joined with the Church to put down this shedding of blood—but at other times the kings, and Richard Lion-Heart was one, granted licences to barons to hold tournaments in certain places. Lion-Heart did this to gain revenues for his crusades; Richard II, much later, did it in the hope that his champion, Thomas Mowbray, would put an end to his cousin Henry Bolingbroke, a royal baron who was threatening the throne.

The fighting-class of knights who took part were professionals, like boxers or footballers today, whose business was fighting and whose swords had such names as

"Gagnepain" or "Breadwinner." Some of them were knights errant, or wandering warriors, who hired out their swords to the highest bidder. Their dedicated and ritualistic fury caused them to be invested with a mystique which roused fear in the common people.

It is probable that the armour worn by a Norman knight in 1066 would have been much the same as that worn by his Saxon opponent. It is just as likely that their great-grandfathers and their crusading great-grandsons had worn or would wear almost exactly the same type of armour. And so did the Saracen knights, except that they covered their iron with a linen coat (which crusaders soon learned to do, also) because of the sun's heat on the metal, and often wound a length of cloth round their helmets for the same reason and also to distinguish themselves by this "turban" from their opponents.

In effect, a knight (or king, or baron) of the First Crusade would wear a conical helmet with a projecting and protective nose-piece. His coat of mail, or *hauberk*, would be made of leather or strong linen, on to which were sewn many flat rings of iron. It would have elbow-length sleeves, would fall just below the knee, and would be divided between the legs so as to make riding more comfortable. Under the *hauberk* was worn a long tunic of wool or linen, with sleeves down to the wrist. The knight's legs would be covered with thick stockings, or *chausses*, usually made of linen, and cross-gartered with leather thongs. Some knights, following the fashion set by Duke William at Hastings, might even wear *chausses* of mail. The shield would be of metal, would reach as high as the knight's shoulder, and would be roughly kite-shaped: that is, rounded at the top and coming to a point at the base. It was made in this shape so that a knight might use it on horseback to cover all of his left side, when he was using a lance, from neck to ankle.

Also following the Norman fashion introduced in 1066, it became usual for a knight to be clean-shaven, and to have his hair cut very short, or even to have his head shaven above the ears and high up the neck. Often he would wear a hood or leather cap-piece to prevent his iron helmet from chafing his head; and, when off-duty temporarily and not needing his helmet at all, he might wear instead a cap of soft felt of any colour except yellow, which was worn only by Jews at this time.

An ordinary soldier or sergeant would be dressed similarly to a knight, though his *hauberk* is likely to have been less elaborately made, and he would be forbidden a knightly sword. His weapons were most probably the dagger and the lance, though, in the heat of battle, there would be nothing to prevent him from picking up and using any weapon which came most easily to hand.

Knights rode well-bred "Great Horses" (*destriers*), halfway in power and size between a shire-horse and a modern hunter. Ordinary troopers or sergeants (that is, men of common and not noble families) rode Rounseys or ponies of no particular breeding. Foot soldiers, such as archers and pikemen, were not mounted at all, but were *infantry*. This word, rather like the Saxon word "ceorl" or churl, originally meant "simple" or even "childish," and is, in a way, indicative of the conquering Norman's attitude towards a subject race. The infantry, or simple footmen, were regarded by the knights as needing fatherly care (as well as punishment) when necessary. They were seldom given military tasks of the first importance, unless all the knights were crippled or wiped out. Their function was to "mop up" after the first shocks of the knightly charge, to follow the Great Horses and to finish off the unhorsed enemy while the knights pressed madly onwards.

Knights fought as naturally as bull-terriers do, with immense fury, and yet with little animosity after all was over. They died without complaint; they treated their defeated enemies well and only demanded what ransom they thought was reasonable. Their behaviour on the battlefield may not have been in accordance with what we call the rules of fair play—for their object was to destroy the enemy at all costs and in any manner available; but at least they followed their calling without self-recrimination or self-pity.

During the Crusade of St. Louis in 1250, the Sire de Joinville records how the Christians were hard-pressed by a vastly superior force of Saracens. At the point when all seemed lost, a knight staggered to Joinville, his face slashed open and his nose hanging down over his lip. "Sir," this knight said, "if you think that neither I nor my heirs will incur reproach thereby, I will go and seek help from the Count of Anjou, whom I see yonder in the field." Joinville answered that this would be an honourable action to take and would show no cowardice; but before the knight could do as he had suggested, he fell dead.

Such were the men who rode against the Moslems, to gain military fame, land or treasure. They may not have been modelled in the mould of Christ, but they were an essentially sharp weapon in the hand of the Church. It has been objected that these knights despised all who were not of noble rank or not, like themselves, dedicated to the act of war. Yet it is equally true that the average English knight by this period had become greatly concerned for the welfare of all who fought under him, infantry or grooms; villeins from the fields of his native parish.

Ewart Oakeshott, whose insight into this period is invaluable, says, "In this country [England] the lower classes were far more independent and less down-trodden than their Continental fellows, while the average English knight from the twelfth century to the fifteenth was a simple country gentleman, looking after his land and his tenants, serving in the county courts, on juries and inquests, or doing his work as Sheriff or in Quarter Sessions. When knight and yeoman went to war together, there was a comradeship between them which was found nowhere else in chivalric Europe."

However, the duty of a knight to his people was sometimes appreciated outside England too, as is shown by Sire Joinville of Champagne, who spoke with his cousin before he sailed to Egypt with St. Louis. Said the cousin, "You are going overseas. Now take care how you come back, for no knight, whether poor or rich, can return without shame if he leaves in the hands of the Saracen the meaner folk of our land, in whose company he went out."

It is not easy to get an over-all picture of these "meaner folk," whether in England or France, however, since their exact social status and nature has never been fully settled by historians. Always, in the story of Western mankind, it has been the custom of a conquering warrior caste to use the conquered as workers or slaves, in the home or on the land. The Roman settlers in Britain used the conquered Celtic folk as their tied manual labourer-slaves. From the Roman *villa* we get *villanus*, or slave farm-worker, and in eleventh-century Norman times *villein* or *villain*. A century or so later these *villeins* were known simply as peasants—or folk who lived in the country, unless they had got themselves into the growing towns to become burghers—who pressed solidly for personal and political rights and charters, to become entirely free citizens. But the situation in the eleventh century is in fact so confused that further examination of it is essential.

William the Conqueror had decreed that his new kingdom should be *governed under her old laws*. But in the preceding "Saxon" England, with its entire population of 2,000,000 beset by many invaders, social status had seemed to vary as the occasion demanded. By 1016, when Danish King Canute ruled England, this flexibility had largely disappeared. In the new state, every man had his job and his definite fixed position.

The lowest order was that of the slaves; but here it must be stressed that in late Saxon England of the eleventh century, slavery was a quite benevolent institution and that, under Canute, there were more entirely free men in the lower orders of English society than there had ever been before in Christian times. An English slave would have sufficient food, a warm home to winter in and, if he could profit by it, instruction by monks in reading and writing. What is more, he was not required to place himself in danger by bearing arms in battle, and he could always rely on the protection of his master. As a "free man," hiding among the hills or in the forests away from the settled communities, his dangers and discomforts would have reduced him to a state of brutishness and have brought him an early and perhaps violent death.

Less than a lifetime after Canute's social system, the Normans had overrun England and for a hundred years they imposed on it a way of life which was much more oppressive, being based on the Hitlerian concept that the true function of every man was to serve the state itself, the most privileged members of which were the military men —the barons and the knights. Under William of Normandy life in the country became far less pleasant than it had been before. With the ruthless persistence of the conquering war-lord, William had made an almost complete and detailed record of the land he had acquired, which enabled him to reallocate the estates to his Norman warriors. Most of the old English lords were dispossessed, and their places taken by Normans, who wanted to extort everything they could get from their underlings. So it came about that great numbers of those who had been thegns or free tenants, merely bound to render some services in return for their land, became serfs or villeins, bound for ever to the often cruel and humiliating service of the new Norman lord. In the old days serfs had been few, but now they multiplied, since if they refused serfdom, they were driven from the land which fed them, into starvation and even outlawry. So tenants who had once been on terms of good will with their old English lords now looked upon their new Norman masters as enemies and robbers.

Saxon ceorls, who once had been permitted to improve their station by hard work and become "gentlefolk," were now condemned for ever to be "churlish."

The new courts were administered by Norman judges; the new laws were Norman laws; the new priests—of any substantial rank—were Normans. If an Englishman was murdered, no questions were asked. If a Norman was murdered—and often this was the churl's only way of ridding himself of a tyrant master—heavy penalties were exacted on the whole Hundred, or legal district in which the killing happened.

To recapitulate briefly: in 1016 all men had a fair amount of freedom and independent status; in 1066 the English lost most of that freedom; in 1095, when the First Crusade was preached at Clermont, peasants (serfs, villeins, and any others tied for life to the land by their conquerors) were only too willing to evade their masters and, *with the blessing of the Church* in Rome, which was never too anxious to allow the kings and great barons overmuch man-power, to rush headlong away from slavery at home under the pretext of killing "Saracens," and of bettering their own miserable lot.

A villein was *almost literally tied to the land* and could not take leave of absence from his Norman lord's manor unless given permission to do so, or unless his lord required him to go to the wars, or his bishop commanded him to make a pilgrimage. On the average Norman manor, he was given about thirty acres to cultivate and to live off. However, for three days in every week he had to leave his thirty acres and work without wages on the land of the manorial lord. In the spring he had to leave his land completely until he had ploughed four acres for this lord. After which, he had to lend the lord two oxen for a whole week, probably at a time when he most needed them for his own ploughing.

The fact that a villein was commanded to deliver to his lord one hen and sixteen eggs each year has been cited as evidence of Norman leniency, and indeed, that *is* a trivial payment in itself. But the offering did not stop there: every villein had to chop and prepare a wagon-load of good burnable wood for his master—which might not come from any of the hunting forests so beloved of the conquerors. A villein might have to journey far afield to get such wood, and all the while his own land (unless it was very different from our own) would be producing a fine spate of weeds or its crops shrivelling from lack of irrigation. Moreover, such wood-gathering had to be done in preparation for winter frosts and draughts—that is, roughly speaking, after the lord's harvest had been gathered in by his villeins and at a time when they wished to turn back to their own land. And, if this was not enough, the villein's own crop of wheat was subject to a tax, both from the lord and from the Church. Two sheaves in every ten went to these masters.

The manorial lord's power did not stop there. It went right into the home. If a villein wished his daughter to marry, consent had first to be obtained from the lord, who would seldom allow her to wed outside his own manorial boundaries, since that would mean loss of labour. As a seigneur, the lord also had the legal right to lie with her on the first night of her marriage. It is thought by humane historians that this "*droit du Seigneur*" was not always insisted on. What is certain, however, is that once a marriage had been celebrated, the villein-father was required to pay to his lord a wedding-fee of one shilling, the present-day equivalent of twenty pounds or fifty-six dollars.

And if this villein still had enough hardihood and belief in the future to send his son to school at one of the monasteries, he was then legally bound to pay the manorial lord sixteen shillings (about three hundred pounds or 840 dollars), because an educated lad would for ever be lost to the land as a labourer. It was permitted, we are told, for a villein to buy himself free only if he was able to save enough money to satisfy his manorial lord.

In the event that this picture seems too bleak, it should be stressed again that in eleventh-century law, the law of the conqueror, *every acre of land belonged ultimately to the king*, and then to his baronial henchmen. The ordinary folk, who had been the ceorls, *owned* nothing. At a period when the entire population of England was one-quarter of the contemporary population of London alone, there is little wonder that men took up the sword to avenge their losses.

And if it is suspected that the eleventh-century peasant English might have evaded oppressive taxation, then one only has to read this entry made in the Domesday Book: "The Land of William of Braiose. The land is of three ploughs. The whole extent of arable is three ploughlands, though it was only assessed (by its previous owner) at two hides. There is one in the domain (William manages one ploughland himself), and five villeins and cottars with two ploughs (there are two ox-teams in the domain). There is a mill of eighteen shillings-worth and a fishery of fifty pence-worth." This is the precise and searching eye of the conqueror who wishes to be certain of the exact extent of his spoils.

And, when those spoils were fully counted, it was found that the parts of England which the census-makers could safely cover amounted to 5,000,000 acres under cultivation, on which now lived 300,000 families. The total population of England was 2,000,000; of which only 9,000 were land-owners or clergy. Of the vast remaining rest, about 30,000 were freeholders or yeomen, such as followed the war-crazed knights into the field bearing pikes or bows; 200,000 were villeins or worse; and 25,000 were *bondsmen or landless men*—which is much the same thing as calling them slaves, though without those essential *human rights* which Canute's honestly-termed "slaves" enjoyed under a benevolent though equally foreign monarchy.

At my reckoning, this Domesday census accounts for about 264,000 men *out of a total population of* 2,000,000. Let us say that each man had a wife, and that each of these pairs raised an average family of four children—a generous estimate in an economy which subsisted only just above starvation level and in a country which was largely ignorant in medical matters: then this estimate accounts for *just over half* of the total assessed population. We are left with the astounding fact that, in England alone, there must have been a floating population of something like a million souls, and the complete continent of Europe, with its far greater area, must have contained at least four times this number—that is, 4,000,000 nameless ones.

In 1096, ten years after the census, according to Albert of Aix, Peter the Hermit led 40,000 peasants towards death in the Holy Land. In 1212 the boy Stephen of Cloyes led 30,000 child "crusaders" unwittingly into slavery. The magnitude of these figures appals our minds today; yet, set against the possible totals of landless and hopeless populations of those times, such numbers are still small ones. And the bait held out by the unknown East was rich beyond all impoverished dreaming.

[PART]
TWO

9

The Council of Clermont

In April, 1095, such a great shower of meteorites fell over Europe that Bishop Gislebert of Lisieux interpreted them as a sign from God, asking for a crusade to the holy places of the East. Seven months later, in November, 1095, Pope Urban II called a solemn Council at Clermont in Auvergne.

The gathering was immense despite the cold season of the year: there were more than two hundred eminent prelates, knights and barons from mid-France, and so many thousands of others that tents and shelters had to be erected for them in the open fields. From a scaffold in the market-place of Clermont, Pope Urban stirred the hearts of his vast and clamouring audience: "Hitherto," he said, "ye have waged unjustifiable warfare, slaying each other and sometimes wielding mad weapons for the sake merely of greed or of pride, whereby ye have earned everlasting death and the ruin of certain damnation. Now we set before you wars which have in themselves the glorious reward of martyrdom, and the halo of present and everlasting fame."

Simply to remind the peasant-folk who crowded the square that for years the barons had seemed intent on annihilating each other would not have been sufficient inducement to send them off on a holy war; but Urban, with consummate craft, found another way of touching each man's heart. "The end of the world is near," he cried. "The days of Antichrist are at hand. If, therefore, when he cometh, he shall find no Christians in the East, as at this moment there are scarce any such, then there will be no man to stand up against him." Then the Pope went on to promise God's pardon of all past sins to the confessed soldiers in the proposed war, to assure all who died in this venture of a martyr's crown, and to protect by the most solemn curse the family and possessions of all crusaders, whatever their social degree. And Constantinople was to be the gathering-place of all crusaders.

It was as though a great weight had been lifted from the minds of those who heard him. They laughed aloud with hysteria and shouted that this was God's will. Then they set to and sewed the red cross upon their garments without delay. Sensing success, Urban deputed the leadership of this venture to his legate, the Bishop of Le Puy, and set the time of departure for August 15, in the following year, 1096, by which date the harvests would be gathered in, and all the princes ready. The multitude dispersed, to carry the glad tidings from town to town through France and even as far away as Scotland and Denmark, in a frenzy of excitement which surprised even the Pope himself.

It is necessary to consider what factors, apart from the undeniable power of Urban's oratory, had so inflamed the minds of those who listened to his words. In the first place, at a national level, East and West had been expanding towards each other by trade and war since the fall of the Roman Empire, and had now come to the point when they felt the need to test each other's metal. Lower down the scale, moreover, and to keep the people in check, the frightful nightmare of the Antichrist and of the Day of Judgement had been preached from every pulpit in Christendom. Families of churchgoers for the past century had heard this warning, until the sensation of imminent disaster had become second nature to them, until whole generations were hag-ridden with the image of unavoidable damnation. Again and again, common men sought the opportunity to become clean, to stand well in the sight of God and His prelates. This desire put a weapon in their hands and, wherever they found opponents, they attacked and converted them—Lombard, Slav, Norman, Magyar and Saracen—hoping to bring them to Heaven as a ransom for their own souls.

Guibert called his history of these times *God's Dealings through the Franks.* The French had become a unified people who, by deciding on a crusade, had proved their identity, their Christian courage and their desire for salvation. Here, it is even possible that the turmoil and vigour needed for a holy war, or a war of any sort at all, was largely provided by a new race—the Normans, who in England and Southern Italy had suddenly found themselves capable of expressing their warrior pride and strength, and now looked for a more rewarding goal.

The pattern for such a venture had already been set for them in the tenth century, when the Orthodox Greek emperors had regained wide territories from the effete Mohammedans. Though the enemy they were now to meet had changed. The newest hordes of Islam, the Seljuk Turks, were no more decadent than the Normans who yelled for their blood at Clermont. Central Asiatic nomads, they were as hard and as crafty as their ancestors, the Huns, had been. In less than a lifetime, these nomads had moved from the howling steppes to the very borders of Egypt in search of their own national fulfilment. By 1071 they had captured Jerusalem and, though the Greek Emperor Romanus had turned on them his army of 100,000 men, the Seljuks had routed them by their mobility and single-mindedness, so closing the land route to the Holy Sepulchre for all pilgrims. The merchants, whose trade with the East was in process of developing, suffered no less than the Church. For years Greek emperors had appealed to the West for help, and not always on grounds of religion. It was inevitable that sooner or later a Western people would evolve which would see the potentialities, religious and mercantile, of such a movement eastwards.

There was yet another basis of conflict. The world of the Seljuk Turk was one of a small warrior aristocracy lording it over a multitude of easily-dominated peasants or workmen. The West had, by the eleventh century, begun at least to outgrow this primitive stage. In most European towns and villages, individual men had begun to regard it as their personal right to improve their conditions wherever they might. On the religious side, the difference between East and West was even greater. While the Seljuk Turk regarded all Christians as polytheists in their worship of the Holy Trinity and in their kneeling to graven images, the Christians firmly believed, with a conviction produced by generations of reiteration, that no unbaptised person could escape the dreadful fires of damnation. To Europeans, all Moslems were damned: to kill them was to act as God's instrument and to hasten God's judgement upon them. Ironically, this feeling of the Frank against the Moslem Turk was also extended, largely because of doctrinal differences, against the Greek Christians.

It is probable, however, that the greatest inducement towards this war was an economic one. The Seljuk Turk by capturing Asia Minor and the Levant, had turned the Mediterranean into a cul-de-sac, and the swiftly-growing race of Western merchant-adventurers, whose sheer political force cannot be over-estimated, could not tolerate such a limitation. It is impossible to visualise these merchants in the sedentary terms of today; they were men of action, fighters, often unprotected or unguided by law, custom or morals. To gain trade and a good bargain, they were prepared to kill or to be killed. There were no half-measures among them. In this respect, they resembled all the other soldiers of fortune at that time—from the young noblemen who possessed little more than a sword and a horse, to the half-starved, work-weary peasants.

Again, at the lowest level, there were many thieves and murderers who escaped block and gallows only on condition that they redeemed themselves by spilling heathen blood. Such men would know no mercy, whatever the colour of their opponents' skin, and Christian though they might be, could hope for little understanding from the majority of the crusaders who were soon to meet them.

There is one other factor which should be mentioned, and that is the eleventh-century love of pilgrimages. Relic-worship had by this time grown to such an extent that no Christian altar could be considered completely hallowed unless it were surrounded by a heap of saintly or at least martyred bones. By his inflammatory words at Clermont, Pope Urban gave sanction to a repetition of such an act of relic-gathering, of expiation by the robbery of martyr-tombs. To save his soul, the man of eleventh-century Europe would have stolen anything to avoid the hot flames of Hell which, the priests had told him, licked his legs at every step.

10

Peter the Hermit

Of the many priests and preachers who spread the word of Pope Urban through Europe, Peter, a hermit of Amiens, was the most astounding. His hypnotic effect upon the simple countrymen of Northern France went beyond religion and into the realm of hysteria. With a linen smock pulled over his monkish robes, his hair shaggy, his eyes rolling, he wandered barefooted among the crowds, promising indulgence for all sins, the words pouring from him in a torrent of passion. The peasants noted with awe that he neither ate meat nor drank wine. They looked on him as a more-than-mortal man, and even plucked hairs from the tail of his mule to keep as holy relics.

Wherever Peter preached, men flung down their tools and vowed to follow him to Jerusalem, via Constantinople, at whatever cost to themselves and their masters. The result for a time was economic chaos in France. As Abbot Guibert of Nogent said, "Each pilgrim was so bent on raising money, come what may, that he parted with his goods, not at his own price but at the buyer's. So all men bought dear and sold cheap." They "bought dear" because the supplies they needed for their journey were wanted by everyone, they "sold cheap" in their anxiety to be rid of their now unwanted possessions; and this among a group of northern peasants, whose only rivals in frugality before had been the poverty-stricken Highlanders of Scotland.

Pope Urban had fixed the day of departure for August 15, 1096; but the princes who had to equip themselves would not be ready; although the peasants with their few belongings were. They had sold all and they must set out without delay or starve, now.

Peter the Hermit elected to lead this People's Crusade, accompanied by a knight, Walter the Penniless, and a German monk, Gottschalk, who had inspired the German peasants just as Peter had done the French. Guibert's half-amused account of their setting off from Cologne on the thousand-mile journey has the simplicity of great tragedy: "You might see a marvellous and most laughable sight, a troop of poor folk with two-wheeled carts drawn by oxen whom they had shod after the fashion of horses, bearing their few possessions in these little carts, while their very children, as soon as they came to some walled town, would ask again and again if this were Jerusalem . . ."

The general lack of military preparation for this exodus can be deduced by the fact that the vanguard led by Sir Walter had only eight horsemen to 15,000 foot soldiers when they started off. As the horde rolled on, however, 3,000 horse joined them, under the command of a few laughing noblemen, who were more concerned with gaining loot than access to the Holy Sepulchre.

It seems that not all the pilgrims themselves were aware of the nature and seriousness of their journey. One group of German peasants was led by a goat and a goose, two creatures sacred among their forefathers, and as they marched, these peasants sang the old pagan songs. This frightening crowd now totalling 40,000 men, women and children were not long to be kept in check by a handful of knights. Suddenly it occurred to them that Jews were as much the infidel as were Saracens—and had not Pope Urban himself despatched them to slaughter infidels wherever they found them? So, as the vast rabble moved through Europe, they massacred Jews wherever they could find them—in Verdun, Trèves, Mainz, Speyer and Worms. When the Archbishop of Cologne flung his palace open to the Jews, the furious peasants broke down the doors with their axes and butchered all inside. In that terrible affair alone, it is recorded that 10,000 were slaughtered.

When the Bishop of Speyer, motivated by gifts of money rather than by purely Christian compassion, took the Jews of his diocese under his special protection, the pilgrims were for a time baffled: but they succeeded in catching twelve of these "infidels" and beheaded them, having first offered them the unacceptable alternative of becoming Christians. The example set by such "Christians" appalled the unbending Jewish followers of Jehovah; but when they protested, the pilgrims took and publicly raped the prettiest Jewess they could find, as positive proof of their new spiritual power. It is some consolation to know that the Bishop of Speyer, anxious to give value for money, captured some of the pilgrims concerned and cut off their hands.

So like a great tide of blood, the crusaders and pilgrims moved eastwards and after a month reached

Hungary. Here the nature of the country brought its own dangers, by its rivers, marshland and vast areas of ancient forest. The towns there were little more than huddles of thatched huts, for the Slav population of 1096 were largely nomadic cattle-raisers who set little store on fine building. What shelter they had, however, they were willing to share with the pilgrims. It was here, according to Guibert, that "the undisciplined crowd, finding the country very rich in all foodstuffs, began to riot in revolting self-indulgence against the kindness of the inhabitants."

It was the custom of the Hungarians to heap their successive wheat harvests in towers set about the fields. The crusaders, now intoxicated with arrogance, set fire to these wheat stores, assuming from the quiet behaviour of the Hungarians that they must be a timid race. For a while no woman was safe: peasants who in feudal France and Germany had been compelled by priest and lord to lead the most moral lives, now indulged in an orgy of rape.

When one group of pilgrims reached the town of Moysson, they rushed forward to pillage it, as had now become their general custom. Peter the Hermit called out to them to behave like true Christians; but having tasted power, they mocked and ignored him. This time, however, their assault did not succeed. Ambushed, and attacked on all sides by the furious citizens, the peasants were butchered or driven back into the swollen river to drown. Those who escaped from this particular battle, dragged themselves back to France starving; figures of mockery among their own countrymen after their months of the most futile bloodshed.

Another wave of these crusaders pressed on through Hungary, to find all roads and villages now closed to them, and death lurking behind every bush and in every ravine.

At Semlin, Peter the Hermit and his followers found to their horror that the city walls were now decorated with the armour of certain knights who had ridden in the vanguard with Walter the Penniless. Roaring with baffled rage at this, the pilgrims broke into the town and slaughtered 4,000 Hungarians. News of this massacre travelled before them through Bulgaria and soon every man's hand was against them. They were killed at night as they slept by their fires, and the wells along their route were defiled by the rotting carcases of sheep. Suddenly this crusade turned into a War of the Peasants—French and German against Bulgarian; and the latter had never been renowned for their gentleness.

Of a total of 300,000 crusaders who had started off in such haste, only a third survived the first stage of the journey. Those who struggled on into Constantinople were like walking corpses, brutalised beyond all measure and no longer Christians of even the most primitive sort. Behind them a trail of bones reached back to the Rhineland and to France.

Guibert reports that remnants of this tattered army fed into Constantinople all through July of 1096. The Emperor treated them kindly, allocated them lodgings in the outskirts of the city, and threw open the markets to them freely for all commodities they needed. But, seeing their unsoldierly state, he forbade them to cross the Bosporus into Seljuk Turkish territory where, he warned them, they would only too easily be massacred by the superior forces of the enemy. For a time, this contented the crusaders; but when they had eaten and rested, they began to interpret the Emperor's words as a reflection on their manhood. Once more they went mad, setting fire to palaces, stripping churches of lead and murdering all who tried to reason with them. Most of them had now forgotten why they had ever come to Constantinople; all they remembered was that Pope Urban had offered them pardon for all their sins, and that their leaders had promised them loot.

The Greek Emperor, with characteristic Byzantine subtlety, refrained from punishing them as he might have done. He took the other course and immediately commanded them to cross the Bosporus and conquer the Turks of Kilij Arslan. Like men in a dream, 100,000 peasants crossed the straits to Nicomedia, where on landing they began to quarrel among themselves, the Franks separating from the Germans, Lombards and Italians, who then chose as their leader one Rainald, and marched forthwith into the Turkish kingdom of Roum.

Here they came upon the apparently deserted castle of Exorogorgon, which they invaded like a swarm of locusts, once more congratulating themselves on easy victory. Shortly afterwards, at Michaelmas, the Turks crept up and examined the trap they had laid. It was nicely full, they decided, and so surrounded the city walls in great strength, knowing that Exorogorgon's wells had long been dry.

For eight days the crusaders suffered the torments of that damnation they had always feared, until at last their elected leader, Rainald, went out of the city with a handful of his friends, and surrendered all in Exorogorgon, on condition that his own party was spared. The smiling Turks accepted his offer and gave him a place in their army. After which the occupants of the besieged city were either slaughtered or sold into slavery. Those unfit as slaves were used as targets in archery practice.

Meanwhile, the French peasants who were left behind at Nicomedia, had got so out of hand that Peter the Hermit would have nothing more to do with them and handed over his leadership to Walter the Penniless, in the hope that this soldier would know how to discipline the ragged horde. By now they were an army of fanatics, and Walter knew that the only discipline they would obey was that of war. He decided to attack the city of Civitot (Hersek), if only to give these men something to occupy their minds. Halfway there they were ambushed by the Turks. The battle was a short fierce one and ended with Walter and 17,000 of his army being killed.

Peter the Hermit, broken in spirit, had already turned back to Constantinople. The crusaders who escaped from the shambles of the battle fled like senseless beasts—some to drown in the sea, others to starve among the rocks or in the forests. By October of that year the Turks had tracked down and beheaded or enslaved all they could find. A few sorry remnants of that immense army were allowed by the Greek Emperor to cross over into Constantinople once more, where he disarmed them contemptuously. So ended this strange prelude to the First Crusade with an undoubted and encouraging victory to the Turks.

Anna Comnena, the daughter of the Greek Emperor, who wrote a sardonic chronicle of these times, records that the victorious Turks created a monument to celebrate the occasion. It was a "mountain of bones, most conspicuous in height and breadth and depth;" the last remains of those power-drunk peasants, who had once plucked the tail-hairs of Peter's mule to keep as relics, and had dreamed of recapturing the Holy Sepulchre without the aid of kings and lords.

11

The Crusade of Princes

The befuddled fanatics who shambled to their frightful deaths after Walter and Peter the Hermit were one thing; the army of princes and great noblemen who formed the true striking-force of the First Crusade were another. These noblemen should have started out on August 15, 1096, but partly owing to careless organisation and partly because of their high-born arrogance towards all authority, they delayed their departure and did not reach Constantinople until May, 1097.

These 600,000 trained fighting-men, both horse and foot, had one ideal in common—that of destroying the Turkish menace and of gaining estates. At the same time, if possible, they intended to satisfy the requirements of the Pope that the Holy Sepulchre should be opened up again to visits by European pilgrims. However, they had no general leader. Indeed, so various were their languages and backgrounds that no single commander could have gained the confidence and obedience of such a mixed force. The result was that this immense army split into four great divisions, each under its own chosen general.

The first group, of Southern Frenchmen and Italians, rode out under the papal legate and Count Raymond of Toulouse; Gibbon describes the latter as "a veteran warrior, who had fought against the Saracens of Spain. . . . His experience and riches gave him a strong ascendant in the Christian camp, whose distress he was often able, and sometimes willing, to relieve. But . . . his eminent qualities were clouded by a temper, haughty, envious, and obstinate; and, though he resigned an ample patrimony for the cause of God, his piety, in the public opinion, was not exempt from avarice and ambition." Raymond's army marched down through Italy, crossed by boat to Dalmatia, and then continued its route through mountainous Albania.

The second army, composed of 70,000 northern Frenchmen and Germans, was led by Godfrey de Bouillon and his two brothers: Eustace, Count of Boulogne, and Baldwin, Duke of Lorraine. Their route followed the Danube, much as the luckless peasants had gone under Peter the Hermit, and so through Hungary and Bulgaria. Of these three brothers, Runciman observes that the middle one, Eustace of Boulogne "was an unenthusiastic Crusader, always eager to return to his rich lands that lay on both sides of the English Channel." The youngest one, Baldwin, had no estates; he had been destined and trained for the Church, a calling for which he had neither the vocation nor the temperament. He was taller than his immense brother Godfrey. "His hair was as dark as the other's was fair; but his skin was very white. While Godfrey was gracious in manner, Baldwin was haughty and cold. Godfrey's tastes were simple, but Baldwin, though he could endure great hardships, loved pomp and luxury. Godfrey's private life was chaste, Baldwin's given over to venery. Baldwin welcomed the crusade with delight. His homeland offered him no future; but in the East he might find himself a kingdom. When he set out he took with him his Norman wife . . . and their little children. He did not intend to return."

Gibbon reports that "Godfrey was the first who ascended the walls of Rome; and his sickness, his vow, perhaps his remorse for bearing arms against the Pope, confirmed an early resolution of visiting the Holy Sepulchre, not as a pilgrim, but a deliverer. His valour was matured by prudence and moderation; his piety, though blind, was sincere; and, in the tumult of a camp, he practised both the real and fictitious virtues of a convent. Superior to the private factions of the chiefs, he reserved his enmity for the enemies of Christ; and, though he gained a kingdom by the attempt, his pure and disinterested zeal was acknowledged by his rivals." Of all the landed warriors who made this first attempt against the craft and power of the Seljuk Turk, it seems that Godfrey de Bouillon was the most moderate and the least self-seeking. In him one sees the early model of chivalry.

The third army, however, which took much the same route as that of Raymond of Toulouse and the papal legate, was the main one and contained the majority of the northern French contingents, but few "English" Normans. Appropriately, it was led by princes of the highest degree—Hugh of Vermandois, brother to the King of France; Robert of Normandy, eldest son of William the Conqueror; Robert, Count of Flanders, a country rich in royal blood; and Stephen, Count of Chartres, Blois and Troyes, who, according to Abbot Guibert, owned as many castles as there are days in a year.

It is difficult for the modern mind to understand the rich dream which this venture unfolded before the eyes of the knights who undertook it; men whose homes were often little more than gaunt stone towers, their inner walls blackened with soot, their floors covered with urine-sodden rushes which were changed once a year in spring; men whose pallisaded courtyards were knee-deep in mud and manure by mid-winter; whose solid and hide-draped beds provided the only privacy available in a keep swarming with servants, grooms, soldiers, dogs and even horses; men who bathed infrequently and then communally, outside, in great wooden tubs, when they had returned from prolonged hunting-trips which left them ragged, filthy and verminous; their matted hair to be combed and oiled by the women of the castle; men who knelt piously on saints' days in their squat square-towered churches, but celebrated the evenings with drunkenness and promiscuity among the stable-straw with any woman who could be forced or persuaded; men who blasphemed "by the body of the Virgin," and held crossed-fingers before any addle-headed old woman who might be a witch; men who, if they were younger sons or beggared by too many daughters needing dowries, were often pledged down to mail-shirt, sword and horse with any Jewish moneylender who would allow them credit; men who gained what they might in ransom-money from the tournaments held up and down Europe; who gorged on spiced roast meats in times of plenty—but managed on pig-meal, horse-fodder, and bread made with bran when, as happened once a decade, famine stayed through the winter.

For such men, a vast treasure store lay ahead which

would make all their previous plunder look insignificant. Never before in recorded history had the possible gains looked so tempting and so easy of achievement. There is little wonder that this army of princes cantered down through Italy with high-spirited merriment and minstrelsy.

A fourth army, which in the end gained rather more glory than the others, joined this great movement almost as an afterthought. One of the greatest warriors of his times, Prince Bohemond of Tarentum in Southern Italy (the son of an equally famous warrior, Robert Guiscard, and a man who had already defied the Greek Emperor in two campaigns), was besieging Amalfi when the other groups had started on their journey. Suddenly his force of Normans and Italians became so infected by the crusading wanderlust which they sensed about them on all sides, that they begged Bohemond to raise the siege and travel further afield, where the pickings would be greater.

Bohemond, of whom Gibbon wrote, "It is in the person of this Norman chief that we may seek for the coolest policy and ambition with a small alloy of religious fanaticism," made up his mind on the spot. The siege of Amalfi was forgotten and Bohemond's army, already formed and prepared for battle, took the old Roman road down the Appian Way to Brindisi, and so across the Adriatic to Durazzo in Bulgaria.

Though he had entered middle age, Bohemond was still tall, broad-shouldered and narrow-waisted. His skin was clear of all blemishes, and his cheeks were fresh-coloured. His bright yellow hair was clipped shorter than was the Western custom among noblemen, and he was clean-shaven. This last feature came as something of a shock to the Byzantine eye, for both Greeks and Armenians regarded the beard as a necessary demonstration of a man's virile dignity. Comnena, the Greek princess, said that Bohemond had something hard and sinister in his expression. This, together with his undoubtedly handsome face, appealed to her; it was part of the tradition she knew—beauty with an underlying note of cruelty.

It is of this army that we have the most realistic of all records, that of the anonymous warrior who wrote the *Gesta Francorum.* This knight tells how he "took the cross" at Amalfi in 1096 and lived to storm Jerusalem three years later. The last action he describes is the Battle of Ascalon in 1099—but before that, like many other poor knights who possessed but one horse, he had that killed under him and thenceforth had to march alongside other impoverished foot soldiers.

His simple story throws an interesting light on his master, Prince Bohemond: "The warlike Bohemond . . . began to inquire curiously what weapons they (*the other Crusaders*) bore, what token of Christ they displayed on their march, and what was their battle-cry. . . . Then Bohemond, moved by the Holy Spirit, bade men cut the most costly of his mantles, which he expended forthwith in crosses, down to the last fragment."

His army, landing in Bulgaria, marched down the valley of the Drino, where their commander issued grave instructions: "Sirs, beware, for now we are all God's pilgrims; wherefore we must be better and humbler than we were before, and do not plunder this land, for it is a Christian country; and let no man take more than is needful for him to eat, with God's blessing." During the Christmas of 1096, Bohemond's army camped at Kastur, where they kept up their prayers and feasting for some time.

However, the Bulgarians, who had already had some

experience of crusaders when Peter the Hermit's rabble had stolen and raped their way through the countryside, were not anxious to assist this new army in any way. The result was the obvious one: in spite of Bohemond's earlier fine words, his soldiers took all the oxen, horses and asses they needed. One can assume with a fair certainty that there was a repetition of rape—though this time by more courtly exponents.

It is hardly surprising that the Bulgarians of Pelagonia, in the next stage of the journey, fortified their towns against this new army of pillagers. "But we assailed them on all sides and soon had the upper hand," innocently says the author of the *Gesta Francorum.* "Wherefore, we set fire to it, and burned the town with all that dwelt therein, to wit, this congregation of heretics."

So, congratulating themselves on what was a tragic act of brutality, the crusaders crossed the river Vardar, only to be met by the Greek Imperial army. By this time the Emperor was out of all patience with "crusaders" of any sort. In his place, it is unlikely that any monarch would have acted otherwise; for years he had appealed to the West for a small army of 10,000 to set against the expanding Moslem communities on his doorstep and now when such help came, it appeared utterly self-seeking and brutalised. The Turkish enemy to the East was bad enough, but to be caught between two millstones was unthinkable. So the Emperor attacked Bohemond with all the ferocity of which his army was capable.

While the battle was at its height, Tancred, Bohemond's cousin and lieutenant, plunged into the icy February waters of the Vardar and swam across, accompanied by 2,000 picked warriors, to aid his relative. The surprise arrival of this romantic young firebrand won the day for

Bohemond, who was now able to rout the Emperor's forces. These were later found to consist mainly of Turkish and Patzinak mercenaries.

The Patzinaks, a fierce and basically Mongolian people, had once terrorised vast tracts of Central Asia and had held lands along the Dnieper as far north as Kiev. In defeating them, therefore, Bohemond had proved that his own crusaders were not inferior to anything they would be likely to encounter further east, among the Saracens. It was in a mood of high confidence, then, that Bohemond entered Constantinople, to find the city already swarming with crusaders, most of whom had been attacked at one point or another by the angry nomads of Central Europe.

The political situation in Constantinople was extremely precarious at this time, with four great crusading armies more or less in control of the city, consuming its food-supplies under the shallow pretext that ultimately they intended, by destroying the Seljuk Turks, to render service to the Emperor, Alexius. Greek Alexius, long-experienced in all the chess-moves of policy, was under no illusions about the services these foraging princes were likely to render him. In the plainest terms, he well understood that once they had crossed the Bosporus and had moved down through Nicaea, Dorylaeum and Antioch, their main concern would be for their own welfare and future.

All the same, he was subtle enough to persuade all the leaders except Tancred, who scorned him, to swear homage and to promise that the land they captured in Asia Minor should either be restored to him or held in vassalage under him. It cannot be doubted that these oaths were taken in a spirit of lightheartedness by the princes, and that their intention was merely to adapt themselves to the requirements of the moment, nothing more.

Bohemond's army struck out towards Nicaea but found the going hard, in an almost impenetrable jungle. When at last they reached the Turkish capital city they were almost starving and a loaf of bread cost them as much as a fair-sized flock of sheep would have done in their homeland. "But when the noble Bohemond came," says the *Gesta Francorum*, "he ordered great plenty of victuals *to be brought by ship* . . . and the whole Christian army was in great plenty." For this, they had to thank the Emperor Alexius, who sent a Byzantine contingent to keep them supplied with food and guides.

At this point there was gathered about Nicaea the greatest number of soldiers that had ever yet been put into the field. They mined the walls of Nicaea and then lit fires in the holes so that the principal tower fell; but night came on before they could come to grips with the Turks. By dawn, the following day, they saw to their amazement that the enemy had worked through the darkness and had rebuilt the ruined wall so strongly that entrance was impossible that way.

Nicaea, the capital city of the Seljuks, lay across the direct route to Jerusalem and was so heavily garrisoned that its destruction was essential if the Christians were to maintain contact with the Holy City. After three weeks of stalemate, the crusaders planned their attack for June 19, but on the dawn of that day they woke to find the Byzantine flag fluttering from all the city's towers. During the night, Alexius, who already knew all the secrets of this city, had sailed a flotilla of boats across the Ascanion Lake and had conducted a surrender treaty with the Turkish garrison.

So, after a siege which had lasted over seven weeks in all, the Emperor issued orders that all Turkish inhabitants of Nicaea should be given safe conduct to Constantinople.

Although on the surface this move appeared the usual medieval one of gaining hostages, many of the crusaders suspected that Alexius was once more providing himself with military reinforcements, so that later he might bring force to bear on his fellow-Christians. This move was set down by Western chroniclers as yet another example of Greek cunning. In the whole of human history there can scarcely have been so little trust between allies. On July 1, however, came an event which turned the warriors' minds away from politics. It was the first truly important battle of the crusades, fought at Dorylaeum.

Setting out from conquered Nicaea, the crusaders had become separated, owing to their poor system of liaison. Bohemond's men were suddenly aware that they were surrounded on all sides by Turks in immense numbers. While the Frankish knights charged again and again at the enemy, the foot soldiers hurried to erect tents and fortifications. So hard-pressed were the ambushed crusaders that Bohemond sent riders through the attacking hosts to Godfrey de Bouillon, the Bishop of Le Puy, and the noble Count of Toulouse, saying, "If they wish to fight today, let them come like men." Their reply seems typical, in such a situation, of inter-rivalry and envy. However, good sense prevailed at last and the other princes rode to relieve Bohemond. Now the entire weight of the crusading force had had time to assemble, and the Turks, with their allies, faded away. The crusaders reckoned that they had defeated an army of 360,000 Turks, Persians, Saracens and Africans.

"We pursued and slew them the whole day long," says the *Gesta Francorum*. "And we got much spoil; gold and silver, horses and asses, camels and sheep and oxen, and many other things." However, the chronicler pays a tribute, first of its kind, to the infidel Turk: "What man is so learned and wise that he can describe the prudence and warlike skill and courage of the Turks? Certainly, if they had always been firm in Christianity and had been willing to confess the articles of our creed, no man could have found stronger or braver men, or more skilled in warfare; yet, by God's grace, our men had the upper hand."

12

Antioch

There is little wonder that the more intelligent of the crusaders soon came to respect the Seljuk Turk as a soldier. Like the Normans themselves, he came of long generations of fighting-stock; he was prepared to use the peoples, Armenians or Saracens, among whom he settled —just as the Normans used Italians or Saxons to their own advantage; his religion, too, though noised about in public, was easily neglected to give room to the more urgent necessity—that of conquest.

Basically, the real difference was in military strategy. The Norman attack was usually launched by quite heavily armoured knights on strong horses. They charged in a tight-packed unit, sweeping all before them with their lances and using swords or axes at close quarters. Their successes depended largely upon this initial, and in many ways invincible, charge. Footmen took over, with bows and pikes, only to give the cavalry time in which to re-form;

or as followers behind the horsemen, to mop up the area already enfeebled by the charge.

The Turk, on the other hand, was a more subtle fighter. On his light and mobile pony, he slid to right and left, avoiding the shock of the heavily-armoured charge; he then used his long-range bow and arrows from the saddle as his opponents were carried forward by their impetus. Afterwards, when he had succeeded in splitting the attacking force, his method was to move away, deceiving the Franks who galloped after him, forcing them to separate in rocky defiles or on rising ground, so that he could turn on them at his leisure and pick them off at a range beyond their lance-point.

Though these tactics had been used by the Normans at one time, as was shown at Hastings, it is interesting that in the East they reverted to that form of solid attack on a broad front which had been established as a method of warfare by the Romans, and which was to continue, almost as an article of faith, until the Battle of Crécy in 1346.

Between Dorylaeum and Antioch, about 500 miles, the crusaders fought no other pitched battle against the Seljuks. Here and there, the Turks commanded towns and cities, but had never made any attempt to subjugate the native population of the countryside, as the Normans had done earlier in England. The Saracen form of invasion was a mobile one in which they passed through a country, only establishing strongholds at different places as they went. Consequently the crusaders were able to press onwards through Cilicia, often receiving help from the native Christian inhabitants and hardly ever fearing a night attack as they lay in their tents.

It is important to remember, however, that the Turks themselves were not unified. Their Emperor, Soliman, having lost his own stronghold of Nicaea, had tried to gather together a crushing force of Turkish noblemen and generals; but each had found himself a province or kingdom and was reluctant to leave it to throw in his lot with rival families. Therefore, Soliman's plan was to wear down the crusaders, in a series of minor engagements, and by trying to turn all towns against them or to starve them out, in desert country.

For a little while, the labours of this forced march at the height of summer were eased when the crusaders reached the rich country near Iconium—but their relief did not last long, for soon the army moved southwards across a desert and through the Taurus range. To the already exhausted knights, this must have seemed a torment beyond the power of body and spirit to withstand. They began to beat their breasts with grief and were willing to sell their shields, their coats of mail and their helmets for a few pence, if only to be rid of their intolerable weight. When there were no buyers, these thirst-crazed soldiers of Christ flung weapons and armour into the deep chasms that lay beside their path. But, at last, this stage of the nightmare ended, and they came down from the mountains to Maragh, where they were welcomed by those Christian inhabitants of the city who had made preparations for the liberating army of Bohemond.

For a while the crusaders rested, eating and drinking and regaining the strength they would need in their proposed assault on the city of Antioch, which lay further along the valley, and which, at this time, must have seemed a prize second only to Jerusalem in their eyes.

One can picture the crusaders gazing on Antioch in much the same hypnotic manner as their sea-drugged ancestors, the Vikings, had stared at Byzantium. This was the place where they had been told all dreams would come true, and the dread of death shrank backwards into the desert for a while; the place where woven silks embroidered with gold would dazzle the eye; and transparent veils of muslin daze the senses. In the shops, or bazaars, there would be things so beautiful that the men of the West would stand awestruck before them, tongue-tied to describe them.

As the crusaders approached this city, a nuisance force of Turks made a flanking attack, appearing from nowhere and disappearing in clouds of dust when the Franks turned savagely against them. Then for a time all was quiet. The crusaders surrounded the city, enjoyed the fruit-trees, vines and grain-pits which they discovered, and prepared for a siege of some length.

Their intentions, however, were already known to the large Turkish garrison within the walls of Antioch. Every day Armenians and Syrians would make their "escape" from the city and run for shelter to the crusaders' tents with frenzied stories of their ill-treatment by the Saracens. Then, just as regularly, when these refugees had been fed by the guileless Europeans, they would disappear again—to take what military intelligence they could gather back to their Turkish allies and masters. It must be remembered, at this point, that the ordinary Armenian knew little of the Frank, except that he was a bloody-minded adventurer who professed an obscure form of Christianity, whereas the Armenian knew the Seljuk Turk from long and intimate experience.

Inside Antioch, the Turkish commanders weighed the potentialities of their wretched-looking besiegers and then began to make a series of small-scale attacks from all possible angles. Daily sorties also came from the nearby

Turkish fortress of Harenc, until at last Bohemond decided that he must wipe out lesser plague-spots with all brutality. The prisoners he succeeded in capturing from Harenc were dragged within sight of the walls of Antioch and beheaded.

As the siege dragged on towards Christmas, food supplies among the crusaders ran out, for they had now exhausted the generosity of all surrounding Christian peoples. The result was that Bohemond and the Count of Flanders led a force of 20,000 foragers to pick up what they could from outlying districts. They came back empty-handed to find that during their absence the Turks of Antioch had received word of their project and had made a terrible surprise attack on the weakened siege-army, whose minds had been set on the feasts they were about to enjoy and not on any further torments they might endure.

"Then the Armenians and Syrians, seeing our men had come back empty-handed, concerted together and secured the mountains and places that they knew, curiously inquiring and buying corn and victuals, which they brought back to our army, where there was terrible famine." Outside Antioch, the Armenians and Syrians undoubtedly drove a hard bargain with the hungry crusaders, many of whom were forced to die since they had no money left at all by this time.

It is interesting to note that old Peter the Hermit returned to stand before the walls of Antioch; though, when the suffering grew too great, he slipped quietly away—only to be pursued and brought back by the redoubtable Tancred, he who had once swum a river in winter to relieve his comrades. There is a wry comment in the *Gesta* at this point, almost as though the realisation of their wickedness and un-Christian plundering had been at last understood by the crusaders: "It was for our sins that God sent us this poverty and misery; for, in the whole army, you could not have found a thousand knights who had first-rate horses." Another blow was struck at the besiegers when the Greek Emperor's envoy, Tatikios, left them with a promise to bring back food supplies—but never returned.

Now the Turks of Antioch, encouraged by their Armenian spies, were able to come out as they wished to make surprise attacks, even at night—a time when medieval armies usually ceased hostilities, because of the uselessness of long-range weapons such as javelin and bow, and the necessity for close hand-to-hand fighting when the advantage, in the dark, did not necessarily go to the better swordsman. At last, during a particularly bloody engagement, in which the crusaders were being attacked strongly from the rear, Bohemond gave a great berserk roar and called on all to stake their lives on a last desperate effort. He and his constable, Robert Fitzgerald, another Norman, led the counter-attack so ferociously that their pennons soon fluttered among the densest body of Turks, who, taken by utter surprise, began a terrified retreat back to Antioch, but, unable to pass in one body over the iron bridge before the city, were massacred there in great numbers.

The coda to this incident is significant: the ubiquitous "Armenians and Syrians, seeing that the Turks were utterly defeated, went forth and lay in wait in the defiles, and slew or took many of them. Thus, by God's will, our enemies were overcome on that day; and we recovered much, horses and other necessaries, whereof we had some need." But this engagement was not a decisive one: the indefatigable Turks—like no opponents the Normans had met anywhere else except, perhaps, in England, under such guerilla leaders as Hereward the Wake—came out, again and again, from various gates to harry the crusaders, and once killed over a thousand of them at one sortie.

Once again Bohemond turned and drove the audacious Turks to their death on that narrow iron bridge outside Antioch, "driving and hurling them into the river, so that the waters of the rushing stream seemed all red with Turkish blood. And if any one of them strove to creep by the piers of the bridge, or to swim and come to land, he was wounded by our men who lined the whole river-bank." The chronicler records that this battle cost the Turks twelve emirs and 1,500 soldiers, and no longer did the walls of Antioch echo with Turkish laughter, "by day or by night, as had been their wont until now."

The next day the Turks came out of the city at dawn and buried all the men they could reach, just outside Antioch, with their weapons, armour and jewellery. But the crusaders, seeing this, ran forward and dug the corpses up again, throwing them into a common pit, after decapitating them and sending their heads in great bundles on the backs of horses to the sea for transportation to the Emir of Cairo, with whom Bohemond was trying to negotiate an alliance, on the strength of the constant quarrels which were always flaring up among the Moslem leaders. Then, while the Turks were wailing at this desecration, the crusaders built themselves a fortress to stop food supplies from entering Antioch any longer.

Typically, Tancred volunteered to man this fort with his own warriors, leaving the other crusaders to forage for food and drink in the surrounding country; but a curious note creeps into the chronicle here: "So they promised him forthwith 400 marks."

The grim siege lasted seven months and was ended with typical Norman ruthlessness and craft by Bohemond;

who got in touch with Firuz, one of the besieged Turkish emirs known to be tired of the whole affair. He was promised all safety and honours if he would betray the city. Bohemond's necessary condition was that when Antioch had fallen he should be made prince of that city.

It seems likely that the other crusading princes would have put an end to this ambition, but for the fact that spies brought the sudden, frightening news that the Emir of Mosul, Kerboga, was already on his way to relieve Antioch with at least 200,000 men, fully armed and desperate to fight the Christians. The bickering among the crusaders ended only just in time. Firuz opened the city gates one night and gave the Christians command of the outer wall.

With a savagery which one has come to expect on such occasions, the crusaders massacred all they could find in the houses and streets. The lucky ones escaped into the inner citadel on the hill. Three days later, Kerboga of Mosul arrived with his 200,000 Moslems and effectively crushed any attempt by the crusaders to make a sortie against him; trapping and killing them on the bridge before the main gate of Antioch, just as Bohemond had twice trapped the Turks themselves.

13

The Holy Lance

At this point the courage of many crusaders broke. Hundreds of them escaped over the walls of Antioch by night and fled down to the port of St. Simeon, spreading the news that the whole Christian army was in defeat, and commanding the waiting sailors to set course immediately for Europe. But this retreat never took place. Before the ships could get under way, a large detachment of Kerboga's Turks got aboard and burned and plundered to their heart's desire.

Back in the city of Antioch, food had now become so scarce that the crusaders ate their horses and asses. They were almost without water, the streams being situated largely on the high ground of the inner citadel still held by the Turks, or outside the city walls where Kerboga guarded it. This hideous situation lasted for nearly a month, and left the crusaders almost too weak to make an attack outside the city. Bohemond the tireless, however, did what he could inside Antioch, burning nearly "2,000 buildings, churches, and houses," of the citadel and setting up siege-engines to take it finally.

One of the principal crusading leaders, the Count of Chartres, retired with a great force and galloped to the Greek Emperor, who had followed the crusaders. His confused tale was that the main crusading army within Antioch had perished, at which the emperor's immediate and typically face-saving reaction was to order a complete withdrawal of Christians from the Holy Land. This he followed by the command that every corner of Bulgaria should be laid waste, so that when the Turks did finally follow the retreating Greek army, they would have no supplies to draw on. This moment formed the crisis of the whole crusade; yet a crisis which was resolved in an almost childlike manner quite out of keeping with the high events which had gone before.

Inside besieged Antioch a certain humble priest named Peter Bartholomew professed to have seen a vision in which Christ warned the crusaders against having further intercourse with Moslem women, on condition of which He would once again help Bohemond's army. Swearing before the papal legate that this was true, the priest roused such enthusiasm in the leaders that Tancred swore a solemn oath to proceed to Jerusalem even if he had only as few as forty knights to follow him.

Peter Bartholomew then had an even stranger vision to report. He alleged that St. Andrew had appeared to him repeatedly, to tell him that in the Church of St. Peter in Antioch was the actual Roman lance which had pierced Christ's side as he hung from the cross. This holiest of relics, said St. Andrew, would assure victory to whichever side carried it into battle. The priest's dream caused the revival of a great deal of tumultuous discussion among the weary crusaders, and in the end a group of men agreed to dig in the Church of St. Peter. By nightfall they unearthed a lance-head very similar to those used by the Normans themselves.

At first there was some doubt in the minds of the diggers, who suspected that the priest had planted the spear himself to support his story; but when the great body of crusaders were shown the Holy Lance, they immediately accepted it as a token of forthcoming victory with great rejoicing. Whatever the facts of the matter, the crusading army prepared once again to fight under Bohemond. They even sent an arrogant message to Kerboga, ordering him to become a Christian, after which they would "allow him to return unmolested, bag and baggage, from whence he had come."

Kerboga made the ironic counter-offer that he did not wish to become a Christian, but that should the crusaders decide to adopt the Moslem faith "not one of you shall serve henceforth on foot, but ye shall all be mounted knights, even as we are." Kerboga's alternative, as reported back to Bohemond, was a choice between death and spiritual slavery.

For three days the crusaders made processions from church to church inside Antioch, confessing their sins, giving alms and causing masses to be celebrated. After that and with the papal legate himself carrying the Holy Lance, the crusaders marched like sleep-walkers through the main gates, now convinced that their relic would bring them victory.

At first the Turks attacked them from all sides, but soon even Kerboga realised that these Europeans had reached a point of ecstasy when death itself seems a negligible occurrence. That day many crusaders, in a frenzy produced partly by enforced fasting and partly by their faith in the Holy Lance, positively welcomed death, provided that they could take a Turk or two into the darkness with them. It is recorded that many Christians rode through a barrage of arrows, without knowing that they had been wounded by them.

This hypnotic berserk attitude seems to have unnerved the Turks. And here the course of events becomes confused, for many of the crusaders, looking up towards the mountains, cried out that they could see countless soldiers riding on white horses and carrying banners, galloping down to assist them. These, they felt certain, were led by St. George and were the reinforcements of Christ which had been promised to them.

In hot climates and under conditions of great stress it is possible for hysteria to spread rapidly. The emotions liberated by this vision were transmitted to the Turks, who swung their horses round and tried to gallop away. The crusaders clung to them, slashing and clubbing without retaliation, until the retreating Saracen army became quite demoralised. Those who could, fled from Antioch. What followed had now almost become a formula: "The Armenians and Syrians of those parts, hearing that we had conquered the Turks, hastened to the mountains to cut them off; and they slew all that they could catch."

The victorious crusaders now re-entered Antioch, to find that the inner citadel had surrendered on hearing the news of Kerboga's rout. The Count of Toulouse immediately announced himself as the Prince of Antioch, but proud Bohemond, the supreme commander, tore down the count's banner and set up his own on the highest tower of the citadel. The Moslem Emir, together with many others who had stood out against Bohemond, now agreed willingly to become Christians. With extreme and chivalrous forebearance, Bohemond allowed all others who wished to remain Moslems to leave Antioch unharmed.

As for the Holy Lance, the papal legate who had carried it was now dead, and the relic had passed into the hands of the Count of Toulouse. This did not please the Normans, but no one dared snatch such a relic from its holder in the way Bohemond had snatched down the banner. The Normans, descendants of the Vikings in their craft and guile, went about its acquisition in another way by saying that the whole thing was a trick and that Peter Bartholomew, the priest who had described his vision, had himself buried the piece of iron in the first place.

An outcry arose and the Normans demanded an act of faith from the terrified priest. When he agreed to prove his honesty, they built two great bonfires very close together and many yards long. As the flames swept fiercely across the path between these bonfires, driven by a strong wind, the priest was kicked forward and forced to run the length of the fire. He reached the other end apparently unharmed, but the Normans would not accept this as a final sign and, turning the wretch about, sent him once more to brave the flames. Emerging for the second time from the roaring furnace, Peter Bartholomew stood bewildered, staring about him as though he could hardly believe his good fortune at being still alive.

Then the Normans, convinced at last that this priest was more than he had seemed to be, rushed forward in a great crowd to obtain holy relics from his person—a lock of hair, a shred of his charred garments, anything to keep as a charm against the power of the infidel. For a time the priest smiled with pleasure at the renewed attention he was receiving; but soon, as crowd massed upon crowd to get at him, pulling him here and there like a puppet, his smile turned to terror and then to shouts of agony. What remained of Peter Bartholomew, who had dreamed up a victory for the Franks, lay torn and bloody, trampled underfoot by those who now praised God for granting them such holy relics, but did not look down to see what they trod upon. After some days of suffering the priest died, having served his pathetic but divine purpose.

14

Jerusalem

The crusaders rested in Antioch for over five months, recovering from a degrading siege which had lasted for almost nine months. Yet for the greater part of the army, and especially the Normans, Jerusalem and not Antioch was the goal; and when Bohemond and the Count of Toulouse settled down to a long quarrel concerning the possession of the city, a group of Normans threatened to burn Antioch to the ground rather than allow it to hold up their march southwards.

If the Moslems had been unified at this point there is no doubt that they could easily have crushed the quarrelling crusaders. However, the twenty-eight emirs who, in theory, rode under the flag of Kerboga, had disbanded and refused to obey him—while the throne of the sultan himself was being haggled over like a bone between ravenous dogs by his four sons. So the crusaders were allowed time partially to settle their differences and at last they began the movement towards Jerusalem.

Against the smaller towns they showed no mercy. Marra, a strong fortress south of Antioch, stood in their way and mocked at all efforts made by Raymond of Toulouse to capture it. At last the famous Bohemond joined in the assault and together the two leaders constructed a tall wooden siege-tower, which the crusaders set against the city walls, hoping to make their entrance over the high battlements. But "the pagan folk, seeing this, built forthwith an engine wherewith they cast huge stones against our castle, so that they nearly slew our knights. Moreover, they cast Greek fire upon it, thinking to burn and destroy it; but God Almighty willed not that it should burn this time."

The immense Christian siege-tower overtopped the city walls, enabling the crusaders to fling down rocks upon the defenders, hurling these men to their deaths at the foot of the fortress. Other crusaders flung out hooks and grappling-irons in an effort to drag down whoever was caught by the barbs. In the meantime, scaling-parties set tall ladders against the walls and did their best, heavy in armour, to scramble up on to the platform. Once the Saracens knew that their main defence might be breached, they retired as usual to the inner citadel, leaving the main gates unmanned.

So was Marra taken. But victory did not come without a bitter after-taste. Bohemond assured the Saracen leaders that, if they retired to a certain palace above the gate, he would see that they and their families and belongings were unharmed, even though he had to defend them with his own life. The Saracens obeyed him, surrendering their weapons. The main body of the crusaders then flowed through the citadel, killing all they saw, including the women and children. As for Bohemond, "he seized upon those whom he had bidden to go into the palace, and took from them all that they had, gold and silver and other ornaments, and some of them he slew, others he sent to be sold at Antioch."

The Franks rested at Marra for a month, during which time the Bishop of Orange, "who had done so much to exhort us to piety," died. The cynical might attribute this prelate's death to sheer despair after Bohemond's lapse, and especially in view of what the indestructible Peter the Hermit is alleged to have told his comrades: "Do you not see these dead Turks? That is excellent food." This is recorded in the *Chanson d'Antioche* of 1130, which adds of the Franks that "they loved Turk flesh better than spiced peacock."

Once more Bohemond laid claim not only to Antioch but also to Marra. When the Count of Toulouse contested him, the common soldiers, wearied by the bickerings of their overlords, began to mutiny. Bohemond, in danger from both sides, now retired in fury with his garrison to Antioch. Raymond, Count of Toulouse, who had assumed that this was his triumphant moment, was brought short by Godfrey de Bouillon, general of the northern French and German contingent, who summoned an immediate council of war, soundly rated Raymond before all the leaders as a man of selfish ambition—and then assumed leadership of the remaining army.

By this coup the crusaders gained the greatest unity they had known in the whole campaign. Under Godfrey they rode down the coastal strip towards the Holy City, supplied from time to time with food and arms by ships from Italy and Constantinople. Sometimes they fed luxuriously, as when they stumbled accidentally into a secret valley full of Arab cattle and sheep, sometimes they starved; but always, as at their capture of Arca, they slew.

Now as word of Godfrey's approach spread, panic-stricken Saracens began to desert their cities and fortessses. The crusaders had marched from Marra in January, 1099—so on to Arca, Tripoli, Beirut, Sidon, Tyre, Acre and Caesarea. Then turning inland they went through Bethlehem and reached Jerusalem. By now their original army of 600,000 had dwindled to 25,000 (of which Raymond's army numbered only 1,000 knights and 5,000 footmen), but all of them, after three years of war and privation, were men capable of facing any opponent.

On June 7, 1099, the Franks began their siege of Jerusalem. Godfrey de Bouillon and his nephew Tancred led the attack from the east; the other commanders drove in on all sides. The movement was conducted with such force that "if ladders had been ready, the city would have fallen into our hands." As it was, the crusaders demolished the outer wall and then, faced with the higher inner wall, scrambled up it as best they might, losing great numbers, but at the same time inflicting heavy losses on the enemy.

For ten days these crusaders were without bread, their convoys from the coast having been intercepted; but thirst, as always in the Holy Land, was their major affliction. "We were so grieved with thirst," says the *Gesta Francorum*, "that we sewed hides of oxen and buffaloes, wherein we brought water from a distance of some six miles. From these vessels we sucked stinking water; and, what with the foul drink and the barley bread, we were daily in utter need and affliction. The Saracens lay in wait for us at every fountain and pool."

The real purpose of the crusading attack is naïvely concealed or explained by the passage which follows:

"Then our leaders took counsel how they could storm the city with engines, that we might enter in, to adore the Sepulchre of our Saviour." The result was two wooden siege-towers which, after five weeks, were still ineffective. By now all men were so weakened with thirst that the leaders realised their situation would be hopeless unless they could effect a sudden and devastating attack without delay.

On Thursday, July 13, the fierce assault began. Godfrey had command of one siege-tower and Raymond of Toulouse the other. The bishops and priests reached a height of exhortation which fell little short of religious hysteria, especially when the Moslems derisively displayed what they alleged to be the True Cross.

At this point the underlying rivalry which motivated much of this crusade, flared out again. When news came to Raymond that Lethold of Tournai was already inside Jerusalem, the Count of Toulouse saw himself as being thwarted at the moment of his ambition and reacted with characteristic extravagance. "Why do ye delay?" he shouted to his straining soldiers. "Behold, *all* the Franks are already within!"

Suddenly he became a blasphemous madman. The emir who guarded the section of the wall which Raymond threatened knew that this man of blood would never rest until he had thrown down the defences. With Oriental resignation he surrendered immediately and flung open the gates. Raymond swept through with his mob of Provençals, drove all before him into Solomon's Temple and butchered them. By now the best of Europe's knights had lost all sensibility. No longer could their behaviour be justified by the early commands of Pope Urban II at Clermont.

On the flat roof of Solomon's Temple congregated

many Saracen women and old men. Tancred, less brutalised than his fellows, sent up his own banners to them to indicate that they were under his personal protection. But what the chronicler tells us seems inevitable: "So our men came rejoicing, and weeping with excess of joy, to adore the Sepulchre of our Saviour Jesus; and they paid their chief debt. Then, when day broke again, they climbed warily to the Temple roof and fell upon these Saracen men and women, beheading them with the edge of the sword; but some cast themselves down headlong from the Temple. When Tancred saw this, he was very wroth." After the massacre Tancred commanded "that all the dead Saracens should be cast forth, for the unendurable stench; because the whole city was full of their corpses. So the living Saracens dragged the dead outside the gates, and heaped them high like houses." There is a revealing sidelight on crusading policy in the fact that Count Raymond of Toulouse, whose mad rage had now subsided, smuggled away the emir who had surrendered to him, and lodged him and all his family safely in Ascalon, so ensuring for himself an ally among the infidel.

On the eighth day after the fall of Jerusalem, as he walked in a clean linen garment barefoot, to pray at the Holy Sepulchre, the crusaders elected Godfrey de Bouillon as prince of that city. Godfrey, with admirable wisdom for those times, wished to avoid antagonising the Christians of Europe and so refused to become king. He said that he had no desire to wear a crown of gold in the city where Christ had worn a crown of thorns. There is some doubt about the parts played by Raymond of Toulouse and Robert of Normandy in this election. Writers of the time allege that both of these leaders refused office: but what we know of the character of one of them, at least, might indicate that the refusal only came when the assured results of the poll were plainly apparent.

Had the papal legate still been alive, he would have taken over Jerusalem, as by the will of the Pope, and the kingdom would have become a religious one. The Patriarch chosen, however, was Arnulf, chaplain to Robert of Normandy. So Robert, the brother of King William of England, still kept some measure of control, however indirectly. Godfrey might sit beside the throne of Jerusalem and dictate military policy thenceforth, but Robert was able to influence the trend of religious opinion, with his old chaplain as his mouthpiece. Ironically, Pope Urban himself never learned that Jerusalem had been recovered. He had died on July 29, before the news could reach him.

The new Patriarch soon had work to do, for the Sultan of Egypt now approached, hoping to regain the Holy City. Arnulf led the confident crusaders against him, to find that the soft-living Egyptians were not to be compared as warriors with the Turks. The outcome of this battle was complete panic among the Egyptians, who, stupid with terror before the berserk crusaders, even climbed orchard trees in a futile effort to escape. Javelins and grappling-hooks dragged them down to their deaths.

Once more, the battlefield was a heap of corpses; once more, the crusaders glutted themselves with captured food, and carried back to Jerusalem more wealth, in precious stones and metals, weapons and herds of cattle, than they had ever known before. The writer of the *Gesta Francorum* ends here: "This battle was fought on August 12, 1099, by the free grace of our Lord Jesus Christ, to whom is honour and glory now and for evermore, world without end. Let every spirit say *Amen.*"

15

The Kingdom of Jerusalem

The new kingdom of Jerusalem was like no other state of its times. Though technically it came under the sway of the Greek Emperor, in fact it denied all allegiance to him despite the oaths which had been sworn when the princes had first entered Constantinople. On the other hand, it acknowledged the Pope as its head, with the consequence that the papal legate held powers, wealth and immunities which set him beside the king in authority.

Further weight was soon given to the power of the Church by the creation of two military orders—the Hospitallers and the Templars, spiritual warriors or fighting-monks; a race set apart from all others, to form the military striking-force of the whole area about Jerusalem. These men, often of noble blood, held their power directly from the Pope and, though they might if they chose aid the King of Jerusalem, were ultimately independent of all secular authority. It is impossible to assess the limits of their influence, for there was much of the secret society about them; but such was their immediate appeal to the upper layers of feudal society that they were endowed handsomely by all who sought their favours and in a short while became immensely wealthy. Their castles, such as the Krak des Chevaliers which belonged to the Hospitallers, were immense and almost impregnable. These knights, moreover, held the astonishing right to make their own treaties with the Moslems, irrespective of any king's wishes or commands.

It is obvious, then, that any future King of Jerusalem would find his own authority decreased by the emergence of this *corps d'élite*. The absence of any efficient system of taxation, together with the lack of co-operation of many of the feudal lords, such as Bohemond and Raymond of Toulouse, increased the king's difficulties. Every nobleman claimed his own individual feudal privileges at the expense of a unified state. The king's anxieties did not end here, for though he held only a small strip of territory himself he was responsible for the well-being and protection of the three minor principalities of Tripoli, Antioch and Edessa, each one of which held the independent right of repudiating the central control of Jerusalem.

The king's hands were further tied by the fact that the High Court of Justice was administered by barons whose decisions were final and against whom he had no appeal. The royal limitations did not end here, for lower down the social scale came the new Court of Burgesses, the merchants who had given their assistance to the crusaders in their long march beside the coast on the way to the Holy City. These merchants were empowered to make all decisions and to settle any differences which had to do with trade, while the king had no authority over their findings or resolutions.

As usual, where there exists a proud military aristocracy, the scapegoat for all mistakes or misfortunes was the subject native population. These were mainly Greek Christians, who had previously supported their Moslem overlords by manual labour, just as they were now compelled to support the warriors of the Latin Church. For them there was little advantage in the change of masters. Their slavery was the only permanent factor in their lives.

To make things worse, after the death of Godfrey de Bouillon there was a constant coming and going of European adventurers, who stayed in the Holy Land only long enough to make their fortune. They returned home only to be replaced by other adventurers, each one brutally anxious to make good and only too eager to exploit this new land and its native inhabitants to the fullest extent.

The chaplain of Kings Baldwin I and II of Jerusalem, Foucher of Chartres, adds another dimension to the picture of Syrian society in 1127. He says: "Consider and reflect how, in our days, God hath changed West into East. . . . He who was a Roman or a Frank, hath in this land become a Galilaean or Palestinian; the man of Reims or Chartres hath become a citizen of Tyre or Antioch. We have already forgotten our birthplaces . . . One man possesses his own house and household in Syria as by hereditary and paternal right; another has married a wife not from his own land, but from Syria or Armenia, or even a Saracen woman baptized into grace."

The picture Foucher gives us is of a new race in process of formation, of landed magnates, speaking French or Arabic easily as the occasion required, and with a wife and family of mixed blood and synthesised traditions. Syria was the El Dorado of the eleventh century. It seems certain that the luxury of life in the Kingdom of Jerusalem at this time both impressed and dismayed later arrivals from the West, where life was still so austere that the average man's woollen clothes were hardly ever washed; where castles were as bare of decoration and furniture as stables; where food was of the simplest and roughest sort, especially in the long dark winter months.

To this European poverty the Frankish East made a striking contrast. Syrian houses often had painted ceilings and mosaic floors. Their open windows looked either westwards towards the sea, or eastwards over green gardens and orchards to the mountains. There were carpets and brocade hangings, carved and inlaid furniture, clean linen, and even gold and silver table-ware. In Antioch, water was piped along aqueducts from the springs of Daphne to keep body and home clean and cool in the Eastern heat. Many houses along the Syrian coast had their own pipe-lines for water. In Palestine the cities had their own water-storage tanks; in Jerusalem, the ancient Roman sewerage system still worked with an efficiency unknown in London or Paris. Such amenities must have amazed the visiting crusaders.

It is an old saying that while the English Saxons ate rich food in poor houses, the Normans who conquered them subsisted on poor food in great castles; but in Syrian Outremer these Normans had both rich food *and* sumptuous fortresses at their disposal. Only the castles of the Templars and Hospitallers, at this early stage when their monkish code was yet alive, were austere. It is likely that in Kerak or Tiberias the average castle-holder enjoyed a life more splendid than any king in Western Europe. A line of such castles defended the eastern frontier from Aleppo or Damascus; another line protected the western seaboard and the approaches from Egypt.

Clothes were just as luxurious. When the knight was not in armour, he often wore silk robes and a burnous. Even on the battlefield, to shield his metal mail from the sun, he rode in a costume which made him almost indistinguishable from a Saracen. Frankish women went veiled like Moslems in the streets, and at home painted their faces and put on a mincing gait—no longer Western, horse-riding hoydens; but now resembling pretty dolls, meant for their lord's delight, much like the girls of Byzantium. But despite their delicate airs and their superficial surrender to Eastern habits, these Frankish women still kept their old inner fire. They were still the great grand-daughters of Vikings and, if their lords were away raiding, knew well enough how to conduct or to beat off a siege.

It is said that even the prostitutes of Outremer—a class previously unknown in Europe—were gorgeously arrayed. Paschia de Reveri of Nablus, whose charms enraptured the Patriarch Heraclius, was so laden with silks and jewels that she was indistinguishable from a noblewoman. In a calling which is essentially mobile, it is better to have one's wealth concentrated upon one's body than locked up in a house that might be sacked or burnt.

Generally, many of the customs which the Franks inherited in Outremer were forced on them by the change in climatic conditions. In the hot Eastern summers, vigorous Northern action was impossible, and the employment of slaves was essential. What is more, Eastern diseases demanded Eastern medicines; and successful shopping required some knowledge of Eastern tongues. And so it was that contact with the Saracen—though not always amicable—was necessary and sustained. Moslem merchants, though required to pay a moderate toll, were allowed to move freely and to ply their trade in Syria.

Moreover, the Templars, who had quickly developed banking houses, set up highly efficient departments which specialised entirely in Moslem financial affairs.

Runciman's summing-up of the situation is invaluable here: ". . . the wiser statesmen among the Franks saw that their kingdom could only last if the Moslem world were kept disunited; and for this purpose diplomatic missions passed to and fro. Frankish and Moslem lords were often received with honour at courts of the rival faith. Captives or hostages often spent years in the enemies' castles or palaces. Though few Moslems troubled to learn French, many Franks, nobles as well as merchants, spoke Arabic. A few, like Reynald of Sidon, even took an interest in Arabic literature. In times of war each side appreciated gestures of gallantry and chivalry. In times of peace lords from either side of the frontier would join together in hunting expeditions. . . . Nor was there complete religious intolerance. The two great Faiths shared a common background. The Moslem chroniclers were as interested as the Christian when relics believed to be of Abraham, Isaac and Jacob were discovered at Hebron. Even in times of hostility Frankish pilgrims could penetrate to the shrine of Our Lady of Sardenay in the hills behind Damascus."

The Moslems themselves generally showed admiration for the Frankish conception of chivalry; and later when Reynald of Châtillon ill-treated Moslem pilgrims, his action shocked his own fellow-Christians as much as it did Saladin. Nevertheless, despite the Moslem faith in Frankish justice, it was still the law of a foreign oppressor and few Arabs, given free choice, would support these foreigners to the detriment of their own emirs. So while life in Outremer was apparently peaceful, just beneath the surface always simmered the possibility of uprising and violent death.

New arrivals from the West immediately sensed the uncertainty, and the precarious nature of life in Outremer, where hardly any man was to be trusted, Jew no less than Arab; and where the trade of assassination had developed to a professional degree unknown in Europe. The man who lounged half-asleep at the street-corner in beggar's rags might well, for all his whining humility, be waiting with a hidden knife for a certain crusader to pass near to him; the smiling, dark-eyed servant, who stood so solicitously by his Frankish master's chair, might be a sworn Assassin, a member of that sect whose blood-oath required him to pour that master poisoned wine, today, tomorrow, or the day after that.

Such was the virulence of Eastern diseases to the Frank that the average expectation of life among Westerners fell rapidly. In this respect, however, women fared better than men, since they not only escaped risks in battle but, because of greater care from well-trained Oriental doctors, found childbirth less hazardous than it had been in Europe. In spite of this, infant mortality was high and most of the male children born to the Franks quickly died. The inevitable result of this particular misfortune was that feudal holdings, or fiefs, tended to pass into the hands of surviving girl children, so that in the hour of military need many of the great manors lacked a lord. Therefore, marriages tended to be made for convenience, with an immediate military end in view, and such alliances were frequently sterile.

Feudalism, as it was known in the West, depended on an unbroken succession through the male line as well as on the retention of a reliable and well-trained standing army. Neither of these requirements was forthcoming after a few decades, and the Frankish lords of Outremer must then have felt as lonely and as isolated as did the last Roman garrisons in Britain. Such sterile loneliness had peculiar effects upon the temperament of the expatriate Europeans in Jerusalem. Their uncertainty about the future increased their tenacity on the present: they tried to hold what they had gained, at all costs. Brutality began to obsess them. As in Byzantium, so in Outremer—an insecure future bred a frenzied and omnivorous zest for the present, a half-crazed fatalism which gave itself vent in lavish tournaments and displays, in luxurious immorality, and then in violent outbursts of cruelty and revenge.

Perhaps Jerusalem fell from Western hands at last because its saviours had allowed Outremer to corrupt them; and perhaps such a loss and such a corruption were inevitable. But it is impossible to imagine how these Westerners, untrained and unadapted to the new world into which they had erupted, might have acted differently or more successfully. At least, for the most part, they put on a good face and went to their deaths with what gaiety their tough natures could summon up, decked out in all the richness the East had given them and for which their unsubtle Nordic minds had once craved.

Nevertheless, the disunity which made itself apparent during the second generation of crusaders, causes us to marvel that the Kingdom of Jerusalem survived for a man's lifetime. A typical case of this disunity is seen about 1132 when Hugh of Jaffa, second cousin of King Baldwin II of Jerusalem, began an illicit association with Queen Melisende. She was married to King Fulk of Anjou, who had succeeded to the throne of Jerusalem on Baldwin II's death a year previously. To defy the king from whom one held a fief was bad enough; but Hugh's crime went further. As a boy of sixteen he had married Emma Garnier, a widow of great possessions and the mother of two sons, Eustace of Sidon and Walter of Caesarea. These sons, little younger than their stepfather, bitterly resented his betrayal of their mother and took their grievances to King Fulk, at the same time making it clear that he too had a score to settle with the promiscuous Hugh.

For a while it seemed that civil war might break out in Jerusalem—with the king's party fighting against that of the seducer. Tension grew through the hot summer and then, during a meeting of the parliament, Walter of Caesarea, anxious to put an end to this humiliating situation, stood up, accused his stepfather of plotting against King Fulk's life, and challenged Hugh to single combat. On the day fixed for this fight, Hugh did not appear at the tournament ground—either because the Queen Melisende had been afraid of losing her lover, or because his aging wife, Emma, fearful of losing her son, Walter, had paid Hugh to stay away. Whatever the reason for his absence, he was judged as a guilty coward by reason of his non-appearance and was deserted by all his former friends.

Hugh's reaction was typically violent even for those days. Though he was in the wrong, he rode to Ascalon and persuaded the Egyptian garrison to support him against King Fulk. For a while, at the head of Moslem troops, he held Jaffa and ravaged the countryside round about. At last King Fulk, finding the situation intolerable, marched against him from Jerusalem with a superior force. Jaffa, where there was little love for Hugh, surrendered without striking a blow. The Egyptians, now aware that their Frankish renegade leader was doomed, deserted him and made their way back to Ascalon. Crest-fallen, Hugh bowed his knee before the king he had deceived and asked for mercy.

Perhaps Queen Melisende begged for his life and certainly the Patriarch, William of Messines, advised King Fulk to be merciful. Possibly Fulk, already accustomed to betrayal, ironically decided that it might be impolitic to destroy a cavalry leader of such merit. At any rate Fulk, who feared civil strife and whose army was suddenly required to face a new Moslem attack, spared his betrayer, merely sentencing him to three years of exile.

But this curious story does not end here. Before he sailed into exile, Hugh returned to Jerusalem to carouse with a few of his old cronies and while he was playing dice one evening in a street of ill-repute a Breton knight came up behind him and stabbed him through the head a number of times before he himself was struck down by Hugh's companions. Hugh was carried away as though dead. Immediately, his friends spread the story that King Fulk had hired an Assassin to perform this murder.

Without hesitation King Fulk handed the wounded Breton knight over to the High Court for trial, during which the wretch confessed that he had attacked Hugh without prompting and as a means of gaining a reward from the outraged king. The poor fellow was treated with typical brutality. The sentence was that his limbs should be hacked off, one by one. This was done and while he still had a head, he was made to repeat his original confession of guilt. Fulk breathed freely once again—especially when news came to him that Hugh, who lingered in Sicily for a while, had at last died from his wounds.

But the faithless Queen Melisende was disconsolate. Suddenly her passions broke out with all the ferocity of a Byzantine empress. Her husband, in constant fear of his life by poison or the knife, surrendered almost all of his political power to her. The lords who had sided with the king against Hugh found themselves being followed by Assassins. At last the queen's attention became occupied in wielding her political power and in seeking a new lover from among the disunified nobles. Such was the manner of those strange times.

Certainly the initial European tradition of the Kingdom of Jerusalem rapidly began to fade when wave after wave of carefree adventurers either used the territory as a temporary site for their fortune-hunting or, perhaps worse still, settled down with a Saracen wife to become more native than the natives. For such men Jerusalem had an irresistible attraction amounting almost to ecstasy.

To the ruddy-faced and simple-minded Franks and Germans, many of them still boys, the towns of the Holy Land must have seemed incomparably beautiful: white houses, decked with laurels and vines, their doors and windows protected by striped awnings, standing along the steep and narrow roads; and where roads met, cool fountains playing, and white doves hovering in the sun-light; turbaned and bearded Armenians speaking with naked black Africans; olive-faced Greeks or Venetians arguing with sallow Arab or yellow-haired men from the far north. One can picture the tiny courtyards, covered with the red cloth from Tyre to protect their dwellers from the midday sun, heavy with the scent of sheep and goats, of cooking-oil, sandalwood, musk, incense and aromatic herbs that smouldered in braziers to keep disease away.

Within the houses would be pillows and divans stuffed with fine down for the travellers to recline upon. Along the walls would hang Persian tapestries. The floors would be of brightly coloured mosaic; the dishes of wrought copper; there would be ivory boxes carved as delicately as lace, containing preserved fruits, almond paste and fragrant spices. And always there would be quietly smiling women dressed in fine muslin, their arms and legs jingling with bracelets of gold, silver and burnished copper.

Even the medicines for the sick had about them the air of magic—potions containing opium and powdered gold, pastes of rose-jelly and spiced cream for delicate stomachs—so different from the crude northern "remedies" the crusaders had known: tinctures drawn from earth-worms; poultices of adder's flesh, pounded together with wood-lice and spiders; broth compounded of human brains, oil, wine and ants' eggs.

The average European adapted himself to the rich and civilised life of Jerusalem without regrets. Quickly he learned to smoke opium, and to make use of the Negro slaves who were so easily procurable from Genoese and Venetian shipmen. Any crusader who had spent more than five years abroad tended to speak Arabic with a fair accuracy and to think of new arrivals from Europe as "foreigners." No longer did one cause, or one leader, excite his interest. Indeed, surrounded by a wealth of luxuries he had never known before, and in a climate which seemed to absolve the average European from violent action, he soon lost all desire to serve any cause or master whose needs were different from his own.

Out of such luxury inevitably grew disunity of purpose. Had there not been an equal disunity among the Moslem warrior-lords, the new Latin kingdom could not have survived for long. Even so, as a reprisal against persistent caravan-raiding by Christian war-lords along the inland borders, the Saracen chief Zenghi, in 1144, easily overthrew the city of Edessa, which had for years been the last outpost of the Western world, situated as it was to the north-east of Antioch on the borders of Armenia.

Such an unexpected and utterly shocking defeat was the first bad news to reach Europe from the East for a lifetime. The Western world had taken this Kingdom of Jerusalem for granted, but now it occurred to kings and princes that the time had come when they must set forth once more, but this time to shatter the power of Islam in such a way that it could never rise again.

16

The Second Crusade

In December, 1145, the year after Zenghi had so mauled Edessa, Louis VII of France vowed that by the following Easter he would assemble a fresh army of crusaders and would retake Edessa in such a way that for ever more the Saracens would respect Christian arms and ideals. Pope Eugenius III gave his approval and on March 31, 1146, St. Bernard, chosen by both Louis and the Pope, began his exhortations of the people in the suburbs of Vézelay.

The effect of this new preaching, which was of a more intellectual order than that of simple Peter the Hermit, was tremendous. This oratorical success was repeated in Germany, which he visited next, though here he had to contend with a new wave of pogroms; the moment it was known that a crusade was in the air, Jews were massacred without mercy in all the Rhineland towns—sometimes even with the approval of the Church.

St. Bernard, a just man who recognised the futile

inhumanity of such brutal behaviour, was largely responsible in calling a halt to this wave of hysteria. His force of personality was apparent also in his persuasion of the German Emperor, Conrad III, to join the Second Crusade, after that proud monarch had at first sneered at the notion of taking the eastward road again. An immense army was gathered, both of knights and commoners, who decided to focus on Constantinople and then cross Asia Minor by the routes which their grandfathers had used.

For a time, it seemed that with such leaders as St. Bernard, King Louis and the Emperor Conrad, men of apparent intelligence and good sense, this crusade might achieve more than the earlier movement had done, since its motives were so civilised, rational and concerned with the practical establishment of the Eastern Christian kingdom. The actuality was quite the reverse. The Second Crusade, for all its stated ideals, was doomed from the start. First, too many non-combatants attached themselves to the army; also criminals, pardoned by the Pope on condition that they "took the cross." Secondly, too many of the war-lords, including King Louis himself, came to regard this crusade as a domestic jaunt and took their women and servants with them. From the start, the army of females which resulted from this noble sanction was a millstone round the neck of any swiftly-moving and arduous military enterprise. To make matters worse, King Louis, who was an inexperienced campaigner, attempted to control the very soldiers to whom his example had given licence by cutting off their ears, noses and feet for any small indiscretion on the march.

Moreover, the initial unity of this crusade rapidly disintegrated: once the German army was assembled, one of their greatest contingents decided that they would "crusade" first against the still-pagan Wendish people beyond the Elbe, and so broke away from Conrad's main force; the English and Flemish armies saw a similar opportunity for crusading nearer at home by attacking the Moors in Southern Portugal and by setting up a Christian centre in Lisbon; Roger of Sicily conceived as his enemy the Greek Emperor in Constantinople, and forthwith declared war on the very man who was to have been his host; this attitude was largely shared by the main force of Conrad's Germans who, savage and illiterate, first drank themselves stupid in friendly Greek taverns and then turned and massacred every Greek they could lay hands on.

Naturally, the Greeks reacted violently to such outrages and attacked the German crusaders. The Germans, when their initial terror had died down, burned down certain districts of Philippopolis, and by this act alienated themselves even from their French comrades. As though these difficulties were not enough to ruin the campaign, the Greek Emperor never trusted Louis and Conrad, and when they would not swear the customary oath of homage to him for all their future conquests, drove these monarchs ignominiously from Constantinople, declaring that their crusade was an act of pillage and a mockery.

Conrad faced the Turks at Dorylaeum, but was soundly beaten there. Louis, chased and harried like a winded stag, reached Antioch; but only at the cost of leaving vast hosts of his men to the small mercies of the now elated Turkish army. When the two disillusioned kings met again, even they realised that their armies had been too mauled and reduced to recapture Edessa from Zenghi. They now turned their thoughts towards

Damascus, which was less strongly defended, and the capture of which would drive a wedge through Moslem territory. The military idea was a good one, but the crusaders had neither the force required nor the friendship between Germans and French which would have made such a move possible.

They marched within sight of Damascus and set up their tents in an orchard there; but after only four days, under desultory Moslem counter-attack, the kings struck their tents and then turned away from their objective. The Emperor Conrad, a proud man whose confidence had been sadly shaken, then embarked for Germany in disgust. Louis, lingering in Jerusalem until Easter, plotting and conniving to rebuild an adequate force, received a message from his minister, Suger, calling him home urgently to attend to the affairs of France. It is ironical that he was still trying to raise an army of crusaders when he died. This Second Crusade had been almost as wasteful and certainly more ignominious than the crusade of ignorant peasants which had first begun the vast movement.

In the meantime, since Zenghi's first blow at Edessa, the Latin kingdom of Jerusalem was tottering. There is little doubt that, with the sudden failure of the Second Crusade, the Latin kingdom would have suffered an immediate full-scale attack and would have fallen—but for one of those trivial accidents which so often seem to change the course of history. Zenghi, though a splendid warrior and administrator, was a tyrant feared as much by the Saracens as by the crusaders; and one night, waking suddenly to find one of his servants in his tent stealing wine, he uttered such threats that the terrified slave stabbed him to the heart. By this providential act, the Latin kingdom was given a slightly longer lease of life: but it had nothing to do with crusades or crusaders!

17

The Third Crusade

Though the First and Second Crusades are best seen from their European angle, we may gain a more balanced view of the Third Crusade by looking from the East towards the West.

The emergence of Salah-ed-din Yusuf ibn Ayyub, better known as Saladin, as sole ruler of Egypt, in 1171, brought a new element into the pattern of the crusades—that of a Moslem sultan of great courage, character and integrity, who hated all things Christian and was determined to put an end to the Latin kingdom.

Saladin, who was born in 1138, a Kurd of Tekrit in Armenia, had been brought up at the court of Damascus. His military and political ideals were Turkish and feudalistic. He learned his soldiership under such generals as Zenghi and was soon widely famous for his high-minded courage both on and off the battlefield.

Of the twenty-four years of his reign as sultan, only

eight were spent in Egypt, though his experience there in suppressing a great revolt of the black troops in Cairo and repelling an attack on Damietta by the combined fleets of the Eastern Emperor and the King of Jerusalem, assured the political stability of that country. His consuming ambition was the consolidation of Syria and Mesopotamia with Egypt for the supreme task of finally driving the Christians out of Palestine. Coinciding with Saladin's rise to kingly power occurred the political chaos within the kingdom of Jerusalem itself, which resulted from the death at the early age of thirty-eight of Amalric, who had succeeded his brother Baldwin III as King of the Holy City. As already pointed out, the Franks in subtropical Palestine suffered physical degeneration. The descendants of royal dynasties tended to die in early youth so that any assured continuity of government became impossible.

In 1174 Saladin seized the moment for which he had prepared for a lifetime, and began his great drive against the Christian kingdom in the East. For three years he gained successes, but in 1177, Baldwin IV, who had succeeded Amalric as King of Jerusalem, halted him at Telljezer. However, Baldwin was a leper and the rapid development of his disease, together with the constant bickering of his barons regarding the regency and succession, wore him out. So Saladin pressed on and took Aleppo in 1183. Baldwin's successor died as a little boy, when the Frankish barons began their quarrelling afresh. The crown of Jerusalem was offered widely—to the kings of France and of England among others—in a pathetic attempt to halt Saladin's onrush.

The treacherous stupidity of the Christians at this point seems hardly believable. In 1180 Saladin had offered the Franks a truce which they might have used to build up their military resources into a strong fighting unit, but in their arrogance they refused it. All that happened was that a previous prince of Antioch, Reynald de Châtillon, built himself a small fleet of galleys, carried them on camels across the desert and, sweeping down the Red Sea, threatened the Moslem holy cities of Mecca and Medina. This force was annihilated with some contempt by Saladin, who then offered the Christians a second truce. Driven by a pride which was little short of insanity, Reynald de Châtillon once more broke the new truce by molesting Saladin's sister as she travelled unarmed along a neutral caravan route.

Now the patient Saladin could control himself no longer, and with 100,000 men marched against Tiberias on the Sea of Galilee. The Franks, able to put only 12,000 horsemen and 20,000 foot soldiers into the field, were caught in the high desert at Hattim, west of Tiberias, and were cut to pieces. Saladin beheaded the faithless Reynald with his own sword and in his own tent on July 4, 1187, though he ransomed King Guy of Jerusalem, the Grand Master of the Templars, and many other noblemen for whom he had respect. That same July Saladin went on to reduce Acre, Jaffa, Caesarea and Sidon. By August he had captured Beirut; by September, Ascalon, Gaza and all towns between these places and the Holy City itself were in his grasp.

On September 17, Saladin's invincible armies surrounded Jerusalem. Only a fortnight later, they were inside that city and celebrating its recapture. Some of the inhabitants secured their freedom and safe-conduct to the coast at the price of a high poll-tax. Even the famous Hospitaller Castle, Krak des Chevaliers, was taken. All that now remained in Christian hands after so many years of bloodshed and financial waste were the fortress of the Hospitallers at Margat, and the cities of Tyre, Antioch and Tripoli. Nothing was to be hoped from Constantinople, where the line of the Comneni had just given place to the Angeli—though Isaac Comnenus, who was in correspondence with Saladin, still ruled Cyprus and called himself "Emperor."

Among those Europeans who really knew him, Saladin was held in high respect and even reverence. They openly declared that if he had not been a Moslem it would have been a great honour to serve him. Some of them said that if he would consent to be christened he would be considered as the noblest prince in the world. Others alleged that his manner was so *royal* that no man dared to laugh or even to look up in his presence. Certainly no previous leader had ever shown himself more generous to his soldiers, or more gentle to the poor of any nation he had control of. It was customary for Saladin to pay half of the ransom exacted by Christians on any of his knights, and, often, to give all the spoils of any city he took to his emirs.

But when the news of his capture of Jerusalem reached Europe, men who had lived a lifetime in the belief that the Holy Land was their own rightful and secure heritage were bewildered to the point of disbelief, and afterwards driven mad with fury. Profiting by the moment, Pope Clement III shocked all Europe by his announcement that the *very existence* of Christianity throughout the world was at stake. After which the papal legate had little difficulty in persuading Kings Philip Augustus of France, Richard Lion-Heart of England and Emperor Frederick Barbarossa of Germany to "take the cross" and to lead a new crusade against Saladin.

Once again the old fever spread across Europe. At Mainz alone 13,000 men offered their swords against Saladin. Twelve thousand Northmen sailed from Scandinavia to save the religion which they themselves had once been so long in accepting. But this crusade was to be different from all others: Richard of England proclaimed a code of almost brutal discipline to all who followed him; Frederick Barbarossa, anxious to dissuade the gaol-birds of earlier campaigns, insisted that each German crusader should possess enough money to keep himself *and a family* abroad for a year. Diplomats rode everywhere in advance of the armies arranging for safe-passage and lodging. *This* crusade was intended to be well organised. Barbarossa was to travel overland; the Kings Philip and Richard by sea.

Nevertheless, hardly anything went right whether by sea or land. Quarrels flared up in Greece and fiery Frederick Barbarossa, the Holy Roman Emperor, pillaged and burned to impress his importance on peasants who had never heard of him and who for generations suffered far more from Christians than they had ever done from Turks. It was only by the narrowest margin that Barbarossa kept himself from sacking Constantinople itself, such was his imperial fury.

However, he achieved this difficult act of restraint, crossed the Hellespont, even took Iconium again; and then tackled that same Taurus range which the *Gesta Francorum* has made so grimly familiar. Of his initial 100,000 men, over half had died or retreated. Barbarossa himself, considered by many to be the greatest warrior of his day, was so oppressed by the summer heat that he bathed in a little river too soon after his evening meal, and died. Thereupon most of his remaining German army turned back towards home. The rest caught bubonic plague in Antioch.

A pitiful handful crawled down to Acre to beg mercy from their fellow-Christians there.

Frederick's body, steeped in vinegar, was carried like some vengeful relic by his warrior-son before what remained of the German army; but Saracen attacks soon proved the inadequacy of this relic to forestall defeat, just as an extremely hot summer soon proved the inadequacy of vinegar as a preservative. The rapidly-decaying remains were hurriedly buried in Antioch Cathedral, though a few bones were carried onward in the forlorn hope that at least a part of Frederick Barbarossa should be present in Jerusalem on the Day of Judgment.

The other branch of this crusade, under Richard Lion-Heart of England and Philip of France, acted differently but fared hardly any better. Quarrelling over loot almost incessantly, they pillaged the Italians and, after a winter in half-Arabic Sicily, sailed towards the Levant. Driven by a storm on to Cyprus, Richard Lion-Heart decided that this island had a market-value and so captured it from its Christian Greek Governor to resell it to exiled King Guy of Jerusalem.

At Acre, which was besieged by Christians, Saracen relief-ships seem to have passed through the Christian blockade fairly regularly, since Saladin's highly-developed spy system gave him advance news of all enemy movements. Moreover, on February 13, 1191, the Saracen leader was able to push overland through the Christian lines to Acre and to relieve its garrison with a new commander and a full force of fighting men with relatively little opposition. The crusaders at this time were so weakened and miserable that had Saladin chosen to make an attack on them he would undoubtedly have been successful. Indeed, towards Easter, it seemed that the army of crusaders which besieged Acre could not hold out much longer.

It is descriptive of the disunity within the Christian cause that while they endured the barbarity of famine, Italian merchants from Pisa lay off-shore with heavily-laden food-ships, refusing to land supplies until the crusaders agreed to their fantastically inflated prices. At last, however, a corn-ship pulled into harbour bringing not only food but also the news that King Richard was approaching with his great English army.

When Richard reached Acre its besiegers had already been two years under a double siege from Saladin. Soon the remnants of the German army joined in under Leopold of Austria and agreed to fight alongside the English and French. The combined forces of the crusaders, English, French, Scandinavian and German, won the Battle of Acre; partly by their unrestrained fury, and partly because Saladin himself was exhausted after his long drive to sweep all Christians from the Holy Land. Nevertheless he made a stately withdrawal.

King Philip of France returned home almost immediately and the leadership of the crusade was now shared by Richard of England and Leopold of Austria, whose drunken habits had earned him the nickname of "The Sponge." It is said that the French monarch's withdrawal was largely due to the fact that Richard had repudiated his betrothal to Alice, Philip's sister. And although King Philip's return to France was openly declared by the English soldiers to be an act of cowardice, the fact was that he suspected Richard of plotting to assassinate him and so to assume complete leadership of this crusade. Philip was, in fact, a sick man, who should never have set out on the crusade. This was known to Richard, who had visited the French king as he lay on his sick-bed to bring him the false news that his only son Louis was dying—an act of barbarity which, though appreciated by the merry English, alienated the sober Frankish barons of the East, who revered Philip and regarded him as the monarch most likely to further the interests of Christianity in Outremer.

This was only one, and a lesser one, of the English king's blunders. Publicly he tore down the banner of his ally, Leopold of Austria, from a tower in Acre, so causing that king to swear eternal vengeance against him. This action of the English king against a notorious sot is not in itself reprehensible, but does serve to illustrate Richard's insensitivity with regard to his associates. It must be admitted that Richard I, a big handsome man with the soul of a poet, was something of an irreverent bully. Reproached in public by the preacher, Foulques de Neuilly, who said that he had three daughters—Pride, Avarice and Lechery, and should give them up, Richard replied: "I bequeath them to those who best deserve them; my pride to the Templars, my avarice to the Cistercians, and my lechery to the prelates."

The English king's acts of brutality after Acre were such that for many years Saracen mothers frightened their children into obedience by saying that Richard would come and take them if they did not obey. For the Saracens he was the ogre, rather than the paragon of his day. When Saladin tried to come to terms with him, offering to redeem the lives of 2,700 Saracen defenders of Acre at the cost of all his own Christian prisoners, the True Cross—which the Saracen had captured in Jerusalem—and a large ransom, Richard agreed; but when this money did not arrive within the stipulated forty days, he coldly butchered the waiting prisoners on August 20, regardless of the sufferings which

Saladin's Christian captives might then endure by retaliation.

It is said that Saladin asked the Templars, whom he trusted, to safeguard the terms of the Acre treaty; but they declined to take on this responsibility since already they suspected that Richard intended to go back on his word. Saladin was faithfully attempting to raise the necessary ransom when the massacre occurred, after which he refused to negotiate for the surrender of Jerusalem, the main object of Richard's journey to the Holy Land, and the True Cross was trailed at a horse's tail. Indeed, apart from agreeing to a truce of three years, Saladin was never again able to come to terms with the English king, whose word he could not bring himself to trust.

Negotiations were constantly attempted and as constantly broken off. Richard, in his confused dream of supremacy, conferred a knighthood on Saladin's nephew, the Sultan al-Kamil, and even discussed, vaguely, a marriage between Saladin's brother, al-Adil, and his own sister, Joanna. But no Saracen of intelligence listened to his promises with any conviction.

Richard's good fame seems largely to rest on the many romances and ballads later woven about his exploits. Undoubtedly his courage, like his stature, was enormous, and he excelled as a skilful commander. Fit only for warfare, he was arrogant, cruel and treacherous. Like all strong men, he has many defenders, but judged dispassionately, it seems that he is notable only for the misery his ever-increasing war taxes caused to his English subjects.

Jerusalem was left in the hands of Saladin, and Christians were only permitted to visit the Holy Sepulchre henceforth in small companies, and unarmed. Since 1187 the Sepulchre had been guarded by Syrian priests and now

Christian pilgrims were allowed to pray there only under the lash, a required penance for the duplicity of their leaders.

After Acre, Richard was constantly, and justifiably, at war with his ally, Leopold the Sponge, of Austria. He also contested the firm opinion of the barons with regard to the crowning of a King of Jerusalem—a title as empty as the air—but was forced by them to grant it to Conrad of Montferrat, who was soon afterwards murdered by the Assassins: partly with Richard's connivance, it has been thought. Richard's favourite, Guy of Lusignan, who had been established as King of Cyprus, eventually renewed his claim on Jerusalem but never reigned in the Holy City. From this Latin state, it seemed that all religious fervour had permanently departed.

On September 2, 1192, exhausted and now uninterested in the Third Crusade, Richard agreed to a treaty with Saladin. "I will return in three years to conquer the Holy Land," Richard wrote to the Sultan. Saladin replied: "If I must lose the Holy Land, there is no one to whom I would rather lose it than the English King." Now Ascalon was to be demolished as a fortress, but all coastal cities as far south as Jaffa were to remain in Christian hands. Pilgrims of whatever persuasion were left free to visit all holy places and both Christians and Moslems were entitled to move without hindrance through each other's territory.

Saladin's tide of conquering fury had been halted by such an army of kings and princes as had never before moved against the East. Tyre, Tripoli, the Island of Cyprus, Acre and the coast down to Jaffa were in tenuous Christian keeping now. The tottering Kingdom of Jerusalem had been saved once more and would struggle on for nearly a hundred years—though the city of Jerusalem itself did not now lie within the boundaries of the kingdom, which consisted of a coastal strip ten miles wide and about ninety miles in length.

Saladin, now fifty-four and a sick man, saw the last of Richard's ships vanish over the horizon and then turned his attention to civil problems in Palestine. For a time he rode about the country he had taken from the crusaders and then, though longing now to make a pilgrimage to Mecca, returned to the mass of adminstrative work which waited for him at Damascus.

That was in November, 1192. He had been constantly in the field with his fighting-men for four years, during which time political problems had developed which might have severely taxed a much younger and fitter man. The pilgrimage to Mecca had to wait. When he was not working, during that severe winter, Saladin hunted a little and listened, though without much interest, to the debates of Arab philosophers.

In February of 1193 he rode out, one bitter day, to greet pilgrims returning from Mecca; but that night he became so feverish and pain-racked that he took to his bed. A fortnight later he fell into a coma and having lingered until Wednesday, March 3, he died with only a few faithful servants at his bedside. So passed a gentle warrior, a man of simple taste and great chivalry. Saladin, in spite of his strict orthodox Moslem education, tried to look beyond a man's beliefs into his heart. Strangely he respected the Christian faith, though he was convinced that the men holding it were doomed to perdition. He never broke his word once it was given, yet when the military need arose he did not draw back at shedding blood for the Moslem cause.

To ignorant Europeans this modest and cultured man typified Anti-Christ; to many of his own noblemen he was often thought of as a Kurdish upstart—yet he had held Islam together during its most trying period of attack and internal dissolution. No other Moslem could have done as much. A small sad-faced man with a charming smile, quiet and cultured in speech, Saladin was respected by most men who really knew him.

18

Assassins, Templars and Hospitallers

During the last decades of the eleventh century, a curious Moslem sect was brought into being by the Persian, Hasan as-Sabah, and was known as the Hashishiyun, or the Assassins. Hasan followed the conservative Ismaili teaching whose patrons were the Fatimid caliphs, but his truly personal beliefs seem to have been of an esoteric, almost trancelike nature. He wished to create a personal fighting force which he might use against the Abbasid caliphs of Bagdad, and which might be employed in any political circumstances requiring swift and violent action. His special hatred was against the Seljuk Turks, whose support of the Abbasids kept them in power. So Hasan founded his order, with himself as Grand Master, whose chief object was political or religious assassination. His followers were prepared to obey his every command, to travel anywhere in the Moslem world with their knives and to risk their own lives without question or doubt.

Hasan set up his first stronghold in 1090, in Khorassan. His impregnable fortress was the citadel called Alamut, or the "Eagle's Nest." Two years later the first assassination took place—that of the Grand Vizier, Nizam al-Mulk, chief supporter of the Seljuks in Iran. Disgust is lent to this murder by the fact that Hasan, his victim Nizam, and also the poet Omar Khayyám, had in their youth sworn lifelong friendship to each other.

This deed caused widespread horror, but all efforts to occupy and destroy the "Eagle's Nest" were unsuccessful. By the end of the century the Assassins had set up strongholds throughout Syria, with Ridwan of Aleppo as their patron and the wealthy goldsmith Abu Tahir as their Grand Master. It was soon apparent that, to the Assassins, the Abbasids were even less desirable than the crusaders. Indeed, before long they were co-operating with Tancred, a Christian.

In 1103 they murdered the Emir of Homs; in 1106 the Emir of Apamea fell to their sudden knife. In both cases the Christians profited more than anyone else, though it was not long before even the most obtuse European saw that in the Assassins the crusading movement might find not only casual helpers, but also its most unreachable enemies. It was one thing to meet an army in the field, openly, with pennants waving and trumpets screaming; another to deal with the smiling servant who poured out a cup of poisoned wine and then withdrew; or the listless beggar at the street-corner who suddenly sprang to life with a dagger in his hand as the confident crusading lord bent to fling down a coin.

In 1100 was founded a Christian military order. Its institution came about in this way: poor pilgrims to Jerusalem needed shelter, so a hostel was provided for them—by permission of the enlightened Egyptian governor of the city—and dedicated to St. John the Almsgiver, an early Patriarch of Alexandria. The staff of this hostel were mainly from Amalfi in Italy. They took monastic vows of a Benedictine sort and worked under the direction of a master. By the time the Christians had taken Jerusalem the Hospitallers had grown in power, since they had a knowledge both of Christian and Moslem customs and, moreover, were well informed as to Moslem military dispositions and strengths. Soon the master of the hostel, or hospital, had persuaded the Frankish conquerors of Jerusalem to make impressive donations to their enterprise. The staff of the hospital was increased by pilgrims, who saw in it the beginnings of a new sort of power. The next step was for the Hospitallers to withdraw from their subservience to the Benedictines and to flower as an order themselves, offering allegiance only to the Pope.

By 1118, such was the wealth and the power of the Hospitallers that they decided to throw aside their simple function as guides and feeders of pilgrims, and to become such a military force as would beat back the Moslem if needs be and so keep open a permanent route to the holy places. The order still contained brothers whose duty it was to tend the hungry and sick, but the main striking force was an army of knights, at first bound by vows of poverty and chastity, whose constant dream was the destruction of Islam. They wore a white cross on their tunics and, to mark their new and independent status, took as their patron St. John the Evangelist.

At the same time, in 1123, another similar order evolved—that of the Knights Templar, probably founded by a knight from Champagne, Hugh of Payens. Hugh persuaded King Baldwin I of Jerusalem to give him a wing in the royal palace, which had once been a mosque and was situated in the area of the Temple. The Templars, though at first under Benedictine control, soon became independent and established themselves as a tight-knit community. With the active support of the king, they recruited far and wide, and formed themselves into three classes: first, the knights, who were often of noble birth and who wore a red cross on a white tunic; then the sergeants, solid middle-class men, who wore a red cross on a black tunic. These sergeants, besides being warriors, also acted as grooms, and bailiffs to the Templars. The third degree of this order consisted of clerics, whose duties were religious, medical and non-military. Though the declared intention of the Templars was to keep open the pilgrim-routes to Jerusalem, it soon became obvious that the knights were men of military ambition who eagerly sought any opportunity of defending the Kingdom of Jerusalem and of gaining favour with its king.

It must be said here, however, that the Templars in their pride did not bow the knee to the king—their only master being the Pope—even though he and his lords endowed them lavishly with money and vast estates. Baldwin I was shrewd enough to see that in the Templars he had a permanent standing army, on whom he could call with confidence at any time: which was more than could be said of the great mass of crusaders, whose desire only too often was simply to get rich without delay and then to sail back to their castles in France or Germany.

Soon the glamour and fighting-fame of the Templars rapidly spread through Europe; and it became the ambition of many a young lord to leave his impoverished estate and to enlist in an order whose temporal power and wealth were increasing yearly. One day, it was thought—and rightly—these arrogant horsemen in the white tunics would become the most powerful Christians in the Arab world. One day they might even challenge the Christian King of Jerusalem himself.

In the meantime an unforeseen pattern presented itself. The Assassins, who, after certain underground activities in Northern Syria had obtained the frontier fortress of Banyas, had begun so to terrorise their Moslem neighbours that all efforts to wipe them out were made both by the Arab tribes and by the city-rulers of the Moslem world. Riots in Damascus and other places were carefully organised and all Assassins found on the streets were savagely mutilated by the terrorised crowds.

In 1129 Ismail, leader of the Assassins, became so alarmed that he opened negotiations with the Franks, and especially with the Templars, in whose military ideals he found some reflection of his own. Here a curious situation evolved: King Baldwin, anxious both to control and to absorb the Assassins, marched north with the biggest army he could muster to take the Banyas fortress and so to settle the useful Assassins within his own new boundaries. But Ismail fell sick and died of dysentery, and Baldwin's vast army, having taken Banyas, was brought to a halt six miles from Damascus by an equal host of Moslems. The Franks would not keep together. Their interest was in foraging, in gaining what loot they could from the surrounding territory. The result was that many Frankish detachments were cut off and butchered, far from their main camp, by Turcoman cavalry.

And when Baldwin, accepting this bad news but hoping to crush the Moslems in their relaxed moment of apparent victory, started to move his heavy and more experienced detachments forward on Damascus, the

November rain began to fall in torrents. Through a plain which rapidly became a sea of mud, the heavy Frankish cavalry found it impossible to make the charge they had planned. So the floundering men and horses at last gave up the struggle and made their slow way back to Palestine where the army dispersed, disappointed and baffled.

Nevertheless, this failure did not prevent Baldwin from settling the Templars, Hospitallers and even the Assassins, in various other fortresses along the borders of his territory, as fierce and, as he thought, incorruptible watch-dogs. As the years went on, the Christian military orders, composed as they were of so many European peoples, assumed the status of a permanent standing army. The average crusading lords, and even kings, were in a sense mere migrants, sometimes idealistic and often predatory *visitors*, who would come and go as soon as their immediate purpose was fulfilled: but the Templars and the Hospitallers were dedicated and disciplined *residents*. Furthermore, the Grand Masters of both orders were no longer the mere heads of military contingents but became more and more elevated until they sat at the treaty table even with kings, patriarchs and great barons. In the field, as at Hattin, the two orders generally provided half the Christian striking-force.

Of the "sergeants," or armed troopers of Frankish origin, there were perhaps 5,000, supplemented by half-caste mercenaries and "Turcopoles" of native origin. While the nobility tended to marry into other European, Greek or Armenian families, the sergeants and mercenaries were less discriminating, and found wives where they could, many of them Turks or Arabs. Nevertheless, the dominant language used for common intercourse was probably northern French, though of course Greek, Italian and German would be heard here and there. Little Hebrew was used since the Jews, perennially fearful of massacre, had, like the more inflexible Moslems, largely withdrawn from the coastal strip of the Holy Land once the Franks had established themselves.

The political system in the Kingdom of Jerusalem was basically a feudal one, each community tied to the land and paying a proportion of its produce to the overlord so as to feed his standing army of "sergeants" and "Turcopoles." Of the great landholders the Templars and Hospitallers were among the most powerful, and, long before the twelfth century had ended, they overshadowed most aspects of life in the Middle East, largely because there was about them the air of a permanent institution in what otherwise was a seasonally-changing world.

Wealthy enough to build and maintain great fortresses at strategic points, and now constantly supplied from Europe by idealistic young recruits of good family, they made themselves increasingly necessary in the social system of Palestine and elsewhere. No king, however misguided, would care to offend them for fear of losing his own kingdom to the watchful Saracens who surrounded the crusading states.

As "policemen" of the routes leading to holy places, they were undoubtedly superb. The rich Hospitallers, always more concerned with charitable acts than the military Templars, housed and tended upwards of a thousand sick and needy pilgrims in Jerusalem alone. The Templars, though giving alms on a less generous scale, were esteemed both as an offensive striking-force and as bankers. No doubt the rate of interest on all loans would be very high, although usury was forbidden by the Church, but the bankers of the Temple had their secret methods of collecting payment.

In all the feudal world there can have been nothing quite like these two military orders, who could disregard the word of the king, who held their lands for ever, whose tenants were not required to pay church-tithes and who fought only when they chose to do so. Their Grand Masters, or their representatives, sat in judgement in the High Courts of Jerusalem, Antioch and Tripoli, and often gave their verdicts as it suited them and not as it suited justice or kings and princes. They made their own diplomatic advances and treaties with the Saracen rulers, irrespective of the official policy of any feudal monarchs in Outremer. Both to Hospitallers and Templars, the military order came first, the Kingdom of Jerusalem a poor second. The Templars' treaty of alliance in 1172 with the Assassins demonstrates only too clearly the degree of independence which they had reached, even by that date.

Yet, though these orders might at first seem disruptive elements in the Holy Land, it is possible that seen against the corruption of the Venetian and Genoese merchant princes and the weak indecisions of the barons and lordlings freshly out from Europe, they were points of stability—headstrong, spiritually arrogant and unscrupulous—but solid. This unscrupulousness was mainly seen among the Templars, who as bankers were as willing to oblige Moslem as Christian clients, and who retained a large staff of Saracens intimate with all Islamic affairs and requirements. The spy-system of the Templars seems to have been the most efficient in Outremer and after a while most of the Knights of the Temple spoke Arabic as well as they did their own native language. In many ways they seem to have anticipated both the political princes of the Renaissance and the fighting Jesuits of the Catholic Church.

By the middle of the twelfth century the European

noblemen of Outremer were at the edge of that sort of madness which comes when a man, though surrounded by all kinds of material wealth, fears that he may not be allowed another day in which to enjoy it. Such a state of mind, or of society, cannot last for long, and the enemy knew well enough into what straits their "conquerors" had fallen. The Moslems only awaited a leader forceful enough to unify them and to ride before them.

In 1147 their chance came: Nur ed-Din, Emir of Aleppo, and later a king, an old campaigner against the West and the holder of territories which encircled the Christian kingdoms, began to loosen the sword once more in the scabbard. His chief enemy was proud Raymond of Antioch who, like so many Christian overlords, was afraid to move with the main Christian host in the Second Crusade lest the Moslems attack his kingdom in his absence. Raymond, torn between rival expedients, made an alliance with the Assassins under their Kurdish chief, Ali ibn Wafa. At first Christian and Assassin swept Nur ed-Din aside, though the Saracens had 6,000 cavalrymen in contrast to the 4,000 which Raymond put into the field.

It was not long, however, before Nur ed-Din, now possessed of accurate information regarding his opponents' strength, turned and surrounded them by stealth. In the June of 1149, between a marsh and a desert plain, Nur ed-Din attacked. A high wind swept dust into the eyes of the Christians. In that battle the chief of the Assassins was butchered by his own old enemy, Nur ed-Din's lieutenant; proud, frightened Raymond of Antioch was beheaded and, with typically sophisticated savagery, his skull was mounted in silver and sent as a trophy by Nur ed-Din to the Caliph of Bagdad. Only the appearance of the Templars riding with King Baldwin of Jerusalem persuaded the victorious Nur ed-Din to suspend his forward sweep at that time.

In effect, this incident was typical of the spasmodic alliances, victories, defeats, reprieves and brutalities of the period; and, as always, it was the Templars who were given the task of clearing up the mess left by the lords and monarchs who had been so short a time in that intricate maze of political treachery, the Holy Land. As for the Assassins, so secret was their policy, so uncertain their motives, that they could seldom be entirely trusted. Just when all seemed to be going well for the crusaders, a single Assassin fanatic would strike his blow. Then all would be confusion: Christian knights would butcher every Moslem in sight—but more often than not the assailant would have vanished.

Yet almost equally uncertain were the arrogant Templars. In 1153, when the Christians were making a unified attack on Ascalon with some success, the Templars, anxious that they alone should have credit for victory, actually drove back their fellow-Christians with the sword while forty Knights of the Temple rushed through a breach in the city walls to subdue the Moslem garrison. Once inside the citadel, the Templars were hacked down to a man and their corpses suspended from the hastily repaired walls as a gesture of Islamic derision to the crusaders without.

Only the capture of this fortress, after further furious bombardment, justified the rashness of these fantastically proud warriors. Yet their irrational ferocity made them marked men. Their reckless behaviour often created a war within a war, and though the average crusader might be spared after a Moslem victory, the Knights of the Temple were allowed no mercy. They were well aware of the reputation they had created and held it as a point of honour neither to ask nor to accord mercy in their dealings with the Saracen.

Their cynical outlook, in which money rather than human life often seemed to them the more important, may be deduced from their treatment of the young Moslem renegade, Nasr, who during a midnight orgy had assassinated the Caliph al-Zafir, with whom he had previously conducted a liaison thought to be homosexual. When Nasr was captured, with the treasure he had stolen after the murder, he was handed over to the Templars for imprisonment. Either because the young man was genuinely impressed by his captors, or because he wished to safeguard his own life, Nasr suddenly declared that he wished more than anything else to become a Christian. The amazed and amused Templars began to instruct him, treating him much like any other convert from Islam.

However, after a short while, the Moslem court of Cairo heard of this and, without any reasons being given or asked, offered 60,000 dinars for his person. The Templars immediately stripped Nasr of his novice's robe, bound him with chains, and escorted him to Cairo, where they collected the ransom money, and where the now half-insane youth was mutilated by the four widows of the dead Caliph. After he had lingered for a while, Nasr was hanged and his body left suspended as a warning to other regicides.

This type of cynical intervention in Moslem politics was not confined to the Templars alone. In 1163 Shawar, the homicidal Governor of upper Egypt was ejected from his position by court pressure. He appealed to Nur ed-Din for reinstatement and, after some typically Oriental dalliance, was given back his position by that monarch, whose forces were led by Nur ed-Din's great captain, Shirkah, and his young nephew Saladin. However, once Shawar was safely installed once more, he sent his deliverers packing, having enticed King Amalric of Jerusalem and his crusaders to defend him for a bribe of 27,000 dinars, with a special gift for all Hospitallers who rode for him, and full fodder for their horses.

It was at this time that the two military orders were granted the greater part of their enormous territories, with castles to go with them, as an inducement for them to preserve Amalric's Kingdom of Jerusalem. Amalric himself was occupied otherwise, in forming a marriage alliance with Maria Comnena, the beautiful young grand-niece of the Emperor of Constantinople. This took place with immense pomp on August 29, 1167, in the Cathedral of Tyre, while the hard-faced Templars and Hospitallers stood with drawn swords in every street of the city to see that the ceremony was undisturbed. On the other hand, at this period, it was not unknown for the Templars to refuse to fight beside their brother order if, by doing so, they endangered their own trading ventures either with the Moslems or with the extremely prosperous Italian merchants, whose revenues from trading with Egypt had now become enormous.

In 1169 Shawar was deposed and killed during a palace rebellion in Cairo. Immediately Saladin's uncle, Shirkah, was made Governor, and, within a few weeks, Vizier and King of all Egypt. When he died from over-eating, after a reign of two months (having nevertheless demonstrated the importance of Egypt to the Moslem world), his titles passed to his nephew, Saladin, who had long been apprentice to his virile uncle. This sudden occupation of Egypt by the associates of Nur ed-Din was regarded by many

Franks as the fault of the Hospitallers, who had not kept a strict enough watch on Egyptian affairs. Their master was relieved of his post and sent ignominiously back to Europe. He was fortunate to have escaped so lightly.

How it was possible for law and order to subsist at any level is difficult to understand. It was common for such borderline peoples as the Armenians to take vows as Templars, to attempt private acts of assassination to further their own ends, and then, as an escape from rough and ready Christian "justice," to cross over to the Saracen side and there become Moslems. But this disunity in the Christian world was equally well reflected in Islam. For instance, the Assassins, who had been quiet for some years, in 1173 made fresh overtures to the Franks. From their new headquarters at Alamut in Persia came an old warrior whose heart flamed in anger both against Nur ed-Din and Saladin: it was the Sheikh Rashid ed-Din Sinan of Basra, a violent leader of Assassins, who set himself up in a fortress among the mountains of the Nosairi province. To the Frankish crusaders, this Sinan soon took on almost supernatural qualities, and they spoke of him with a certain backward-looking apprehension as the Old Man of the Mountains.

Nur ed-Din, although a redoubtable warrior against the Christians, had long sought to suppress the Assassins. One night he went to bed in his closely-guarded tent but found that he could not sleep because his pillow was uncomfortable. He took it up to rearrange it, and then discovered beneath it an unsheathed dagger such as only the Assassins carried. The Moslem leader at this time had little force to spare against this wide-spread and doubly secret fellowship; he was being kept too busy both by the Franks, who now once more had an alliance with Constantinople to the north, and by his growing discord with Saladin in Egypt to the south. Saladin himself, no lover of the Assassins, found the business of ruling Egypt exhausting and frightening. At this stage of his life nothing seemed secure: indeed, he had already made preparations for flight and self-exile, either into the Sudan or Southern Arabia, where his brother had prepared a hiding-place for him. His final destiny as the shaper of Moslem greatness was as yet concealed from him.

The Old Man of the Mountains, the Sheikh Sinan, growing rapidly in power, dared to send envoys to King Amalric of Jerusalem asking for a strong alliance between Assassins and crusaders, with the object of crushing both Nur ed-Din and Saladin. Sinan made it quite clear that in consideration of such a pact he would arrange for every Assassin to become Christian forthwith. All he asked in return was that the tribute which the Templars had imposed on many Assassin villages should now be cancelled and that both orders, Assassin and Templar, should live and fight as brothers and as equals.

King Amalric, anxious for a settlement to his own problems and weakened by recurring attacks of dysentery, welcomed Sheikh Sinan's proposals and promised to seal the bargain. The Assassin party set off homeward to Nosairi in good spirits and feeling safe within Frankish territory. Just outside Tripoli they were ambushed by a squadron of Templars and butchered to a man. It had been too much to hope that the Templars would accept any alliance which decreased their own financial profits in the Holy Land. When King Amalric received news of the treacherous affair, he was furious that his own name should have been stained by the murder of his new allies. He commanded the Grand Master of the Temple, Odo of

Saint-Amand, to hand over the leader of this ambush, a knight named Walter of Mesnil, for execution. Typically, the Grand Master replied to the king with some contempt that if Walter had to be sentenced it should be by the Pope himself and not by any mere temporal monarch.

With a strong body of men Amalric burst suddenly into the room where the Templars were holding their Chapter at Sidon, captured the offending Walter of Mesnil, and flung him into a dungeon at Tyre. He followed this act of violence by appealing directly to Rome that the Order of the Temple should be abolished without delay: a request which was naturally ignored. Only then did the king feel able to apologise to the Old Man of the Mountains and to assure him that justice had been done. Careless of the life of his followers as he was of any other life, the Sheikh Sinan accepted these apologies and assured King Amalric that his offers of an alliance with the crusaders still held good.

But fate saved Nur ed-Din from defeat by a Franco-Assassin force: in the spring of 1174 the Saracen was suddenly taken ill, and died a few days later. There was an immediate scramble among Saracen claimants to take Nur ed-Din's place: Saladin, writing from Egypt, the wealthiest province of the Moslem world, stated his own rights to become regent, though at that time he had not the armies to back up his desires.

For King Amalric the sudden death of Nur ed-Din seemed to provide the almost divine opportunity he had awaited, to seize Moslem territories. He was bought off temporarily by the new regent in Damascus, but even as he returned home to Jerusalem was already contemplating a campaign which would finally crush Islam in the Holy Land. Yet once more fate struck without warning or pity.

In July, 1174, only two months after Nur ed-Din fell from his horse in his orchard, Amalric took to his bed, gravely ill. As already mentioned, he was only thirty-eight when he died, having held in his hands the power to become the greatest Christian monarch of the East. Indeed, with the death of King Amalric, the Kingdom of Jerusalem was already moribund.

For Saladin the reverse held good. The disappearance of the two monarchs, one Moslem, one Christian, left a place for him in a world which otherwise might not have accepted him. Saladin's was now the duty, it seemed, to sweep the Franks out of the East. A man with a renewed mission, Saladin set himself up as King of Egypt and Syria and at his coronation in Hama wore the royal robes which the Caliph of Bagdad had so graciously sent him.

But Saladin's rise to kingship had not been without its obstacles. The Hospitallers and Templars were joined in one respect only—to destroy him and his dream of a united Moslem state. The Assassins also, ever-restless and seeking blood, decided to eliminate him in their search for power: twice they nearly murdered him in his tent. The second attempt decided the sultan to wipe out the Assassins for ever, and he rode without delay into the Nosairi mountains to ambush and kill the Old Man of the Mountains. But as this formidable sheikh came into view Saladin's party felt all the strength drain from them. The sheikh passed on his way, unharmed.

Saladin records that he returned to his tent to sleep fitfully, his dreams obsessed by some smothering and evil presence. When he woke at dawn, he found upon his bed three things which struck terror into him: a hot flat cake, such as only the Assassins made; a poem on the subject of death, and an ornate dagger whose blade was smeared with a resinous poison. With a certainty which he could not explain, but which now was nevertheless a reality to his sensitive mind, Saladin *knew* that Sinan, the Old Man of the Mountains, had been in his tent that night. His nerve now gave way. It is probable that he suffered some sort of nervous breakdown, for, although he had had years of hard fighting in the field, he was by nature better fitted for the life of scholarship or of pleasures, such as hunting and polo-playing. Moreover, he was that type of introvert, like Nur ed-Din, Ousama and even Mohammed himself, who seems to be thrown up almost naturally from the desert and mountain peoples of the Middle East; people strong in their ambitious drive, intelligent and sensitive to a high degree, but in times of emotional stress, liable to act unexpectedly.

On this occasion he sent a messenger to Sheikh Sinan, imploring his forgiveness for riding against him, and promising to leave the Assassins undisturbed in the future. He asked in return the Old Man's assurance that he and his company should be allowed to return unmolested towards the south. Sheikh Sinan sent back a polite note, in which he pardoned Saladin—as though he were a caliph or a patriarch—and expressed a laconic hope that this "treaty" between them would always be kept. Saladin, who at this time was weakened with malaria, was only too glad to withdraw alive from the fear-laden mountains and to summon up his strength to attack once more his less sinister Frankish and Moslem enemies.

Singularly, Saladin's next great reverse took place at the hands of the Templars. In 1177, relying on his spy-system, which was normally excellent, he launched an attack against Jerusalem, having learned that the Frankish alliance had broken down and that many military leaders were absent in other places. Moreover, he knew that both King Baldwin of Jerusalem and his aging constable were ill and bed-ridden. However, the military orders were still on their feet and alert: nothing, it seemed, could ever damp their ambitious ardour except death.

Saladin, unaware that the Templars were waiting, marched against Gaza and was surprised to find it fully defended by the orders. He turned his attention to Ascalon, which he knew was manned with hardly more than 500 knights. Leaving a token force to contain this city, Saladin pressed onwards towards Jerusalem, now confident that he could meet no opposition from Christian levies. His sense of caution seemed to leave him. He even gave orders that his troops might break their battle-formation and gather what loot they could from the surrounding villages. While this was happening, sick King Baldwin rose from his bed and broke out of Ascalon, backed by the Templars. Riding furiously, they came on the relaxed and disorganised Saracen forces carousing in a ravine at Montgisard. The result was almost complete annihilation for the Moslems. Those who still lived abandoned both loot and weapons, and made their demoralised way back towards Egypt.

Saladin was saved only by his tightly-packed Mameluk guard, who led him from the blood-bath in the ravine into the almost equal nightmare of the Sinai desert, where, racked with thirst, he somehow beat off the following Templars who had now vowed to take his head. He also had to contend with frequent ambushes by Bedouins, who waited for his straggling column behind the sand-dunes. Egypt had already received the news of their monarch's defeat and Cairo was in a state of rebellious chaos. Saladin, regaining his shattered morale, sent messages by fast camel-riders and carrier-pigeons to Egypt, saying that he was alive and that all would be well, if only his people would keep faith with him.

If King Baldwin had pressed home his advantage, the Kingdom of Jerusalem would have survived indefinitely, and Saladin would have disappeared from history as a great military leader. But Baldwin was a sick man whose soldiers were widely dispersed and too few in number to tackle the furious Egyptian levies. Nevertheless, he was still able to humiliate Saladin even further by fortifying the southern boundaries, and penning in those Moslems who lived on the Christian side of the frontier.

Saladin himself offered the king 100,000 gold pieces not to proceed with this fortification, and it is probable that Baldwin would have ceased work on the walls and castles, if only in deference to the treaty which had earlier required this frontier to be left open, but once more the immense power of the Templars showed itself. They forbade the king to abandon his work, although this fortification was soon to become the scene of bitter and resentful conflict which led to the capture of Odo of Saint-Amand, Grand Master of the Temple. A little later Saladin was successful in mining and destroying the castle and walls at Jacob's Ford—though by then such reinforcements had arrived in Palestine from France that the Saracen leader, having put to death all the garrison, let prudence lead him away from trying to enter the Kingdom of Jerusalem. In May of 1180 he signed a two-year truce with King Baldwin since it was obvious to both of them that after a prolonged drought, famine would soon follow in Syria.

Saladin consolidated his forces while the crusaders tended to lose touch with Constantinople, and to fall into quarrelsome and weakening disputes among themselves. It was then that the leprous King Baldwin handed over the regency of the kingdom to his brother-in-law, Guy of Lusignan, a weak and cowardly man who at last so offended the dying Baldwin that he banished him, together with the Grand Masters both of the Temple and the Hospital.

It was at this point that the perfidious Reynald de Châtillon, Prince of Antioch, entered the story. He had followed King Louis from France in the Second Crusade and had stayed behind in Palestine when the other crusaders returned home, first ingratiating himself with the widowed Princess of Antioch and then marrying her against the will of her people and of the Emperor Manuel of Constantinople. Handsome, resourceful and undoubtedly brave, Reynald had soon commended himself to King Baldwin of Jerusalem as a good ally to have in the north. What is more, Reynald possessed those qualities of ruthlessness and ambition which appealed to the Templars, with whom he struck up a lasting if selfish friendship.

It is impossible to follow the intricacies of his turbulent life as Prince of Antioch, but it is true to say that he was such a character as enters late in a play and thereafter dictates the course of the plot, the movements of the players and even the falling of the final curtain. In this instance, the play concerned was called *The Kingdom of Jerusalem*: and it was Reynald de Châtillon who put an end to this Christian venture, if any single man did.

Keeping the support of the Templars by giving them certain territorial gains, Reynald began to blackmail the Emperor in Constantinople. When the Patriarch of Antioch expressed disapproval of his actions, Reynald had him thrown into prison, where he was cruelly cut about the head and his wounds smeared with honey. For the length of a burning summer's day, this churchman was chained on the roof of a high tower until the attentions of flies and other insects sent him almost insane.

Such acts shocked both Christians and Moslems alike, as did Reynald's sudden and vicious attack on Cyprus, which had by this time become prosperous under the rule of the Greek Emperor. Though King Baldwin did his best to warn the island of Reynald's intentions, the message arrived too late. Soon his soldiers were streaming over the island, burning churches and crops, butchering cattle, raping women, cutting the throats of old men and children, in a three weeks' nightmare. The island of Cyprus never quite recovered from this brutish holocaust. This, too, was the man who, in 1182, raided the pilgrim route to Mecca and planned to destroy the Holy City of Islam itself. Sailing down the Red Sea, he burnt the shipping in the ports of Medina and sank a ship laden with pilgrims for Mecca, standing by, speechless with laughter as the Moslems, many of them old and infirm, cried for help in the bitter waters.

This savage deed shocked the Moslem world as much as Reynald's rape of Cyprus had the Christian world. Saladin, now strong enough to see himself as the protector of Islam, swore the most solemn oath that Reynald of Châtillon should suffer for his godless cruelty. Again and again he tried to trap this man; but the Prince of Antioch seemed to possess an almost diabolical foresight, and withdrew to his great fortress of Kerak, almost as fearful a figure now as the Old Man of the Mountains himself.

But fate had a pattern already woven for Reynald, and one of the threads of that pattern was Guy of Lusignan who had so offended King Baldwin, and who, in 1184, showed how closely he resembled Reynald in cruelty by attacking a peaceful tribe of Bedouin, who paid a tribute to the Christians for the privilege of grazing. With his well-armed knights he fell without warning on the tribesmen, massacred every one they could catch, and then drove away their flocks.

Two years later King Baldwin died, unable any longer to control the intriguers who surrounded him. By the support of the Templars, who thought they had much to gain from him, Guy of Lusignan was crowned King of Jerusalem behind locked doors so that the incensed barons should not prevent the unholy ceremony. Though the Templars, worldly and cynical, packed themselves round the new king, it is to the eternal credit of the Hospitallers that they would have no part whatever in the ceremony. Disgusted, Roger, the Grand Master of the Hospital, flung his key of office from the window and led his knights away from the scene of the mockery.

It was inevitable that the dissension between the two military orders should flare up into open conflict after this. It was equally inevitable that Reynald de Châtillon and King Guy of Jerusalem, carrion birds of the same dark feather, should feel drawn towards each other. In the summer of 1187, the climax of this drama was played out, in the valley wherein lies the Sea of Galilee, at a spot called the Horns of Hattin because of two strange rocky peaks which raise their points above the scrub-covered slopes.

Saladin, whose armies and allies had by now encircled Christendom, had mobilised the full forces of Islam and on Easter Day had declared on the Franks that Jehad, or Holy War of extermination, which was the true object of his life's work. Reynald of Châtillon had sworn openly to ride into Arabia to dig up the sacred bones of Mohammed and scatter them abroad; a threat which had struck horror into every Moslem heart, and which marked him in the Islamic mind as the symbol of all Christian diabolism and brutishness. The soldiers of Saladin were convinced that Reynald must be destroyed if their Faith was to survive at all.

The punitive force of Islam was the greatest men had seen for a lifetime; 100,000 strong, in all, it was led by 12,000 Saracen knights, as well mounted and armed as anything the efficient Templars or Hospitallers could put into the field. The crusaders, however, could muster no more than 20,000 infantrymen and a little over a thousand knights; and this they could only do by sadly depleting the garrisons of most walled cities in Palestine. Saladin's first objective was Reynald's great fortress, the Kerak of Moab, but though he set his finest siege-engines against it, the thick walls showed themselves impregnable. The Moslem leader, at his best a calm strategist, was undismayed by such a small reverse and, withdrawing his army, rode along the valley of Jordan to capture rich Tiberias on the Sea of Galilee.

This seemed to be the chance King Guy needed to establish himself in the eyes of the Christian world as a champion of the cross. He set out after Saladin with all his tenants-in-chief and their footmen, and backed by the strongest armies the military orders could give him. These orders had a special reason for revenge: earlier that year, in spring, they had been ambushed in the valley of Cresson, near Nazareth. It had been more a massacre than a true battle, and the squadrons of Templars, who had suffered most, since they lacked the caution of their brother-order, lost eighty-seven out of their ninety horsemen. They had set King Guy on the throne as their puppet and now financed his expedition against Saladin, handing over to him the last penny of the conscience-money which Henry II of England had recently sent them, in his hope to expiate the sin of assassinating Thomas Becket, the Archbishop of Canterbury.

Indeed, it seems that King Guy of Jerusalem was completely in the hands of the Templars: he owed them money, men, and his crown itself. A coward at heart, Guy was said to be more afraid of Gerard, the Templar's Grand Master, than of Saladin himself. And when Reynald of Châtillon, Prince of Antioch, added his loud voice to that of Gerard—there was no turning back. Once, in the past, he had been warned by the Count of Tripoli (who had had private dealings with the enemy) that to fight Saladin would be to lose his painfully-acquired Kingdom of Jerusalem. But the Grand Master of the Templars rose in a flaring rage and said, "Sire, will you trust a known traitor?" He added that his Templars would rather disband their order than lose any chance to crush Saladin.

So, dominated by the Templars and Reynald of Châtillon, King Guy gave the order to ride at dawn, leaving their green and well-watered encampment to take the parched and dusty road towards Tiberias. It was the most fateful decision he ever took, for on it depended the future not only of the Kingdom of Jerusalem but, in the long run, the future of Christendom in the East. It is ironical that such immense issues should fall to the decision of cowards or megalomaniacs.

The rest of the story has the grimness of an Icelandic saga. The Christian army set out on the morning of July 3, 1187. It was a Friday. To emphasise the holiness of their cause they carried with them the True Cross—a fragment of wood encased in gold and studded with precious stones. The day was airless and as hot as an oven. There was no water whatever to be found among the baked hills; no verdure to be seen anywhere. Above them in the hot and pitiless sky, kites hovered and soared, as though they knew what was to come.

By evening they reached the plateau, above which the two Horns of Hattin reared themselves a hundred feet into the hot air. The well was dry when they reached it. Only one brackish trickle of a stream still flowed, and that was blocked by the rotting carcass of a sheep. The Count of Tripoli, already nerve-racked because his wife was being besieged many miles away, flung himself from his exhausted horse and croaked, "Lord God, our war is over! We are nothing but dead men—and the Kingdom has come to an end!" His feeling was shared by many, who suddenly realised that they had walked into a trap.

That sultry night the sleepless crusaders heard the chants and prayers of Saladin's Moslems in the irrigated green valley below. A few crusaders, already insane with thirst, made their way down towards the water only to be captured and decapitated without mercy. Then in the darkness the Moslems fired the dry grass which covered the hill; the flames swept over the plateau, causing frightful suffering to men who had already marched twenty miles in full equipment through the desert. At dawn the Saracens had so encircled them that, according to the chronicler, "not a cat could have slipped through the net." And for each exhausted crusader, there waited ten fresh Moslems.

Soon after dawn the Moslems began their attack, with the blowing of horns and the beating of gongs. The Christians, now maddened beyond endurance, begged to die so that an end would be put to their sufferings. The same Count of Tripoli who had foretold the fall of Jerusalem, now gathered a squadron about him and charged down the hill, willing to die rather than to suffer any further. A Saracen chronicler records: "The Franks came on as though driven to certain death. Before them lay disaster and ruin, and they were convinced that the next day would find them in the tomb . . ." The Moslems, seeing the count's headlong charge, did not try to meet it, but, opening their ranks, let the horsemen through, then closed the circle again so that the squadron could not return.

After that they began to come up the hill in charge after charge. The Christians, their lips cracked and their tongues swollen, fought back silently, their numbers always growing fewer and fewer. As the hideous day wore on only a few hundred knights still clustered about King Guy's red tent on the hill-top between the stark Horns of Hattin. These crusaders formed a tight-packed ring and stood, leaning on their hacked and bloody swords for support, watching the red sun begin to sink on the horizon. For many of them that dying sun was an omen of their own death and of the death of the Kingdom of Jerusalem.

Years later Saladin's young son al-Afdal, who was beside his gallant father at this battle, recalled that he had said, "We have routed them!" But Saladin had turned on him, pale-faced, and replied, "Be quiet! As long as that red tent stands there, we have not routed them." Inside the tent lay King Guy, clutching the True Cross, for now the Bishop of Acre had been killed, like any other warrior. Suddenly there was another terrifying Moslem charge—then the tent was down and being trampled on in triumph. Guy's bodyguard fell to the ground, exhausted, unable even to hand over their great swords in surrender.

So the Christian leaders were dragged to their feet and escorted down the hill to a tent which Saladin had had erected for such an occasion. The common soldiers were handed over to the Moslems as slaves. One Saracen had as many as thirty crusaders, whom he led, tied by tent cords, like a string of cattle. Another had so many that he was willing to trade one Christian for a pair of shoes. However, in a manner which had now become typical on such occasions, Saladin would not allow the military orders to leave that dreadful place as prisoners or slaves. Sparing only the Grand Master of the Temple, he forced the remaining Knights Templar and Hospitallers to kneel while a band of Moslem fanatics beheaded every one of them. As was their custom, they died silently and uncomplaining.

Before the sword fell, one Hospitaller called out to a Templar, "This night we shall have a word or two to say to each other in Heaven!" The Templar made the motion with his cracked lips of spitting on the dry ground. "I doubt it," he said. "Our tents will surely be pitched on the opposite side of that place from yours."

In his tent, Saladin sat in judgement. He spared the lives of all the barons, though he set a high ransom-price on each of them, largely to pay for their entertainment while they were with him, he explained. It was on this occasion that the Moslem sultan showed one of his rare moments of cruelty. Like so many of his race and religion, although he could go for months on a level of philosophic calm and even gentleness, he was also the victim of sudden and almost irrational reverses of temperament. A strict Moslem, he prayed five times a day whatever the circumstances and however sick he might be with the malaria which hardly ever left him; he was a devoted father and a lover of books. Yet when the moment came, his religious resignation, kindliness and tolerance deserted him.

King Guy of Jerusalem, who was lying on the ground too exhausted even to feel fear any longer, was offered a bowl of rose-water, iced with the snows of Hermon. For a while he drank deeply, being half-dead with thirst. Then, seeing the eyes of Reynald of Châtillon turned towards him, he held out the bowl to this man who had once watched the Moslem pilgrims drown and had molested the sister of Saladin himself. Immediately the sultan sprang from his chair, his normally pale and composed face contorted in fury at Guy's action, since by Moslem rules of hospitality the life of any man to whom food or drink were given was safe. Saladin kicked the bowl from Reynald's hands and shouted to his interpreter, "Tell King Guy that he, and not I, gave drink to this man!"

As Guy shrank back at this sudden blaze of anger, Reynald, his cracked lips scarcely damp, looked up at Saladin and spoke to him as though he were some common Arab street-sweeper. "What does your Prophet command?" he sneered. For a moment Saladin tried to regain his composure; then with a rising voice he cried out, "You have always scorned the Prophet. So I will support Mahomet against your treachery!"

In a horrible movement Saladin dragged out his long Damascus sword; then in the deathly stillness of the tent he strode towards the kneeling Reynald and slashed off his arm at a single stroke. Almost before the doomed wretch realised what had happened to him, a soldier ran in and decapitated him. Reynald's spouting head rolled to the feet of King Guy, who by this time was almost out of his mind with terror. But Saladin's moment of hysteria was over. Shaking with spent passion, he turned to the King of Jerusalem and said quietly, "Have no fear. It is not the custom of kings to kill kings." In the following year, after imprisonment at Nablus and Lattakieh, Guy was released, though now a broken man.

After the Horns of Hattin, Saladin was master of the Moslem world, and rode through the streets of Damascus with the captured True Cross tied to his horse's tail and dragging in the dust. On yet another fateful Friday, only three months later, he entered starving Jerusalem in triumph—but, in contrast to the Frankish capture of the city in 1099, with such humane restraint that not a citizen was harmed or a building looted.

The Templars and Hospitallers were allowed to escort safely from the fallen city those refugees who could scrape up their ransom. The Emperor of Constantinople, Isaac Angelus, even sent a congratulatory message to Saladin, asking that the Holy Places of Jerusalem now revert to the Orthodox Church, since the Latins had so dismally failed to administer them properly. Saladin courteously agreed to this though, with his customary desire for justice, he ordered that Frankish pilgrims should be permitted to visit the Church of the Holy Sepulchre, on payment of a fee.

So he passed on to other conquests up and down the Holy Land, while the Christian state in the East decayed. From time to time, forlorn efforts were made to re-establish a Frankish kingdom but, in effect, that hideous day on the Horns of Hattin had sealed the fate of Latin power, despite what Richard Lion-Heart tried to achieve four years later. As for the Templars, the Hospitallers and the Assassins, they seemed to stand outside this collapse for a while; but, though it seemed a long time approaching, their end was assured, if only because no man, Christian or Moslem, could trust them any longer.

19

The Saracen Ideal

The Sultan, Saladin, is generally regarded as being among the first men of his age for tolerance, chivalry, culture and military skill, but he was not alone among Saracens in possessing such virtues. North of Antioch lay the little Moslem principality of Schaizar, with a fighting population of 5,000 men. Its prince was Mourschid, who fought for almost forty years against the European crusaders and who, appalled by court-intrigues among his own people, at last renounced his title of prince and from that time onward rode as an ordinary knight in the Moslem armies. This Mourschid, as reported by his son Ousama, was typical of the highest-minded ranks of Moslem society. Trained as a philosopher, he set quality before quantity in all things, and especially in his judgement of men: "A hundred bad men cannot be weighed against a single man of truth and honour."

But Mourschid was no study-bound philosopher. Like

Richard or Godfrey de Bouillon, he was noted for pushing into the forward ranks when the swords began to flash and the arrows to whine. His body was a mass of scars and one of his wrists was slashed through. Yet Mourschid survived these wounds and died peacefully in his bed in 1137.

About him there was a serene atmosphere of quiet courage. Once when his son Ousama, riding beside him, sighted a Frankish ambush and begged his father to ride hard, Mourschid replied gently, "Son, it is written in the stars which rule my life that fear shall never touch me." Ousama adds, perhaps a little ironically, "My father was a passionate student of astrology, in spite of his faith, his continual fasts and his recitation of the Koran."

However, this astrologer had his relapses like any other feudal lord when his commands were disobeyed. Once when a groom was slow to bring forward his warhorse, Mourschid took a sheathed sword to the fellow, with rather more force than he intended, and whipped him along so furiously that the man's hand was severely damaged. The repentant Mourschid, coming to his senses later, realised his obligations to his retainers and gave the wounded man a pension, which extended to his family after their father's death.

Harsh though this incident is, at the core at least it illustrates the Moslem overlord's sense of responsibility to his servants, a feeling which few Christian feudal barons possessed at this time when human life was held so cheaply. Richard Lion-Heart, like most of his fellows and underlings, was prone to outbursts of uncontrolled rage when servants or soldiers were slow to obey. In losing their hands, they gained no compensatory pension. It was not unknown for a Christian leader to cut off the feet of those soldiers who misconducted themselves on a campaign. So Mourschid's one indiscretion should not, perhaps, weigh too heavily against him.

Even during wartime he forced himself to sit long hours at his desk, copying out the Koran in his beautiful handwriting. Such an act of devotion would have taxed the patience, skill and energy of the most sedentary Western monk or scribe; and it must not be forgotten that Mourschid was constantly in the saddle, if not riding against Christians, then out after the birds and beasts of Schaizar, since he was passionately devoted to hunting. At the age of seventy, Mourschid could still out-ride his four lusty sons, who often fell back exhausted while their old father galloped on.

Ousama quotes an incident which deals as much with old Mourschid's love of his family as with his enthusiasm in the hunt. They had followed a lion as far as a river, where the trapped and furious beast realised that it must turn and face them. Mourschid, long-experienced in such affairs, tried to hold back the impetuous Ousama, who was anxious to show his father something of his own prowess. "Madman," cried Mourschid, "advance not against him, lest he seize thee!" But Ousama went on and, aiming an arrow carefully at the waiting beast, transfixed the lion where it stood.

Another section of Ousama's autobiography emphasises the differentiations within Saracen society and that stoic attitude which distinguished the lordly classes. The Bedouin tribes, whether in Arabia or North Africa, were inveterate wanderers, keen-eyed snappers-up of anything which lay within reach, and owing allegiance to no one beyond their immediate tribal leaders. They lacked education, could not see the broader issues in any war, and lived only for the moment of plunder, often savagely conducted despite any commands which might come from their leaders. Ousama records how his father's fortress of Schaizar was attacked by Bedouin. Ousama and his fierce brothers rode down and drove off the tribesmen; but on returning, Ousama could not find his sister anywhere in the house. He asked his mother where the girl was, whereupon the lady, by her reply, gives us at one time a striking picture of aristocratic Saracen pride and fatalism. "Dear son," she said, "I seated her on the balcony, and sat down behind her. As soon as those Ishmaelites [Bedouin] reached us, I would have hurled her down into the valley, that I might see her dead rather than led into slavery by wanton peasant boors."

This episode is only equalled, in its description of high-caste Moslem self-discipline and piety, by Ousama's other comment that he and his brothers knew the Koran by heart and, even when out hunting with their father, were required to recite parts of it before they enjoyed the excitement of the chase, and to inform Mourschid accurately how much they had chanted before he would allow them to ride any further.

At ninety, the cultured and pious Ousama continued with his autobiography, and even at that great age still left his bed in the middle of the night to say his prayers. And always, whether he writes of peace or of war, he stresses his faith in fate or predestination—a vital element in the Moslem code. "Praise be to Allah, who can perform the thing that He wishes, even as He wishes it. A man no more prolongs the appointed term by shirking, than he advances it by rashness." It is obvious that this belief, held firmly by most men of Ousama's class, would produce warriors of such dash and singleness of mind that they would compare favourably with the Europeans they met on the battlefield.

It is a safe assumption that the knightly class of Saracen (that is, the warrior aristocracy of the Middle East, an amalgam of generations of fighters—Greek, Roman, Persian and Tartar—a turbulent and virile brew) was in no way inferior physically or culturally to its Christian opponents from Europe, themselves the product of centuries of racial admixture—Celtic, Roman, Saxon, Scandinavian and French.

Ousama reports another incident which shows the sensitive compassion of the best type of Saracen. One of his teachers, Abou Tourab, was out hawking and in a period of inactivity sat down to read the Koran. Suddenly a partridge alighted on a nearby rock and slipped into a crevice. The pursuing falcon swooped, missed its prey and then hovered above Abou Tourab who immediately prayed, "O Allah! Hide this partridge!" When the falconer rode up, found the cowering bird and flung it to his falcon, Abou Tourab exclaimed, "Her fate broke my heart!"

This natural gentleness and concern for the things of the mind and spirit is again shown in the words of the elderly warrior, Ousama, when he writes of his situation after the ravages of war: "My children, my brother's children, and our wives were saved; that made it easy to endure the loss of my goods. All that I deeply felt was the loss of my books; I had 4,000 of them, every one a precious volume. Their loss has been a lifelong heartsore to me." A hundred years after these words were written, a sensitive and literate king like Edward II of England possessed nine books, which was considered by the barons a number worth commenting on for its indication of learning, especially at a time when the Mother Church seemed anxious that not too many men, even kings, should possess books.

The Saracen ideal was that a man should be noble, valiant and learned, both in reading and writing. It is understandable then that Ousama, while praising the fighting qualities of the Franks, was contemptuous of them in other respects: "In them we have seen beasts who excel in valour and in love of war, but in nothing else. . . . The Franks have no human superiority but courage, and the only folk distinguished by any pre-eminence among them are the knights; in truth, the knights are the only real men they have."

On the other hand, Ousama, while admiring the courage and determination of the Frankish knights in contesting even their kings in matters of law, was disgusted by the way in which this law was sometimes arrived at—especially by the celebrated Norman ordeal by battle, in which the contestants attacked each other brutally. He records one such combat, at which he was present, when an old man was matched with a blacksmith, against whom the aged warrior at first had some success because of his skill and intelligence, until finally by superior brute strength alone the blacksmith knocked him off his feet and then killed him, to be rewarded by his lord with a horse and a holding of land.

He watched with disgust on a feast-day while Frankish knights compelled two decrepit old women to race against each other the length of the tournament-field with a pig for the prizewinner. These old women tottered forward, fell and rose again, always "escorted and embarrassed by a detachment of cavalry," until one of them reached the prize. What seems to have appalled the Saracen lord on this occasion was the Christian lack of reverence for age and the indignities shown to the human person by the shouting Franks. It is the contempt of the subtle and cultured Easterner for the blunt and barbarian West.

Yet for the best of the Franks Ousama had only praise: "There was in the army of King Fulk of Jerusalem a distinguished French knight who had come to accomplish his pilgrimage and return forthwith. We became acquainted and he attached himself so strongly to me that he was wont to call me *Brother*. We loved each other and were much together. When he prepared for his return, he said to me, 'O my brother, I am now about to depart, and, if you wish, I will gladly take your son home with me. . . . There he will see our knights, and learn wisdom and the science of chivalry.'"

Ousama's private comment, however, pulls one up with a jerk: "My ears were hurt by words *which seemed scarce those of a man in his senses*; for even though my son had been taken prisoner, he could have had no worse lot than to be carried off to France!" His reply to the well-meaning Frank, however, serves to show the vast gulf which separated the two peoples when it came to a matter of plausibility and subtlety: "By thy life, such was my intention, but I am prevented by the love which my mother bears to my son. She would not let him go [even] with me, until I had sworn to bring him back." At this, the Frank seems to have been satisfied and to have returned home alone, well content with the good impression he had made on the smiling infidel.

In other places, Ousama reports that there was a considerable amount of social intercourse between the leaders of the opposing armies, and that many Franks, attracted by the Saracen way of life, settled down and married Eastern women. These Franks, Ousama considers, "are far superior to the others" who came to Syria later.

Although, in matters relating to religion, Ousama feels that the Franks (apart from "my friends the Templars") are unreasonable—an opinion due largely to an incident which happened in a little mosque, al-Aksa, when a Frank knocked him down for praying to Allah and was soon kicked out for his pains by Ousama's friendly Templars!—he was most interested in Frankish surgery and records that the axe was used for a leg amputation, while, for a woman in a state of fever, the head was shaven and a priest made on the bare head two razor-cuts in the sign of the cross, to let Satan out of her brain. Regarding women still, he is horrified at the liberties allowed among the Franks to their wives. This comment is hardly to be wondered at, since the type of woman who frequented the camps of the crusaders is not likely to have been of the most moral.

Why then, in view of the superiority of such men as Ousama, did the Christians achieve for a while their military successes? The answer is a simple one: because there was so much dissension among the Saracenic strata of society. While even the most plunder-drunk Franks made some effort to fight together, under their feudal lords, the devout Moslem acted always individually, as prompted by Allah. "Master," said Ousama to his uncle, before a battle, "tell me what dispositions [of troops] to make when I meet the enemy." His uncle, the general, replied, "Dear son, war directs itself."

20

The Fourth Crusade

Innocent III, who became Pope in 1198, was the very symbol of militant Christianity. A man of sensibility and strength, he purged the Church of its immorality, humbled the over-proud nobility and set up such a body of canon law that no monarch until the time of Henry VIII of England felt secure enough to contest it. From the moment of his papal election, Innocent struck hard at all visible inadequacies of church or state. To him the Church was in a state of decadence which *must* be corrected. And a situation in which Christians might only pray at Christ's tomb in Jerusalem by the permission of the infidel Saladin was unthinkable to his proud, overbearing mind.

All around him Innocent heard so-called Christians bewailing the fact that Mahomet had defeated Christ, and to this Pope it seemed that the Church itself was in danger of dissolution. It was little consolation to him that the Moslem world was also suffering from a desperate stage of disunity. The Assassins, whose secret societies had now insinuated themselves throughout Islam, were a sharp thorn in the flesh to both sides, but specially to the Saracens themselves. When the Old Man of the Mountains died, in 1194, his successor swung over to the side of the Franks and arranged a treaty with Henry of Champagne. The new sheikh loaded Henry with priceless gifts and vowed to destroy anyone he named. As proof of the seriousness of their vows, scores of al-Kahf's fanatical warriors flung themselves into the ravine below, until even Henry of Champagne, a hard-bitten Norman warrior, pleaded with the sheikh to stop such a distressing and embarrassing spectacle.

This widespread Assassin force, so dedicated to their own esoteric policy and at the same time so little concerned for their own lives, would always constitute a rebellious danger, an irrational source of explosive energy, as long as it was allowed to exist in the Near East, whether among Saracens or crusaders. But orthodox Moslems put a good face on it and tried not to let their internal problems destroy the fierce image which European Christians had had of them since the time of Saladin.

In 1198 Innocent III preached publicly: "While Christian kings wallow in adultery and in warfare against Christians, the Pagans [Saracens] are crying, 'Where is now your God? Presently, while weakling fights against weakling in Europe, no longer daring to measure himself against our manly forces, we in our turn shall cross the seas and sweep you all away.' Words cannot answer these taunts, for they are only too true; there can be no answer but in deed; it is a matter of life and death for Christendom that Jerusalem should be recovered."

Certainly the Latin Church, under whose command the

crusades had begun, was now being stigmatised by the decay of the ham-strung Christian forces in the Holy Land. Moreover, the popes had always expressed by their legates that it was a papal duty to organise and control all princes and barons who rode to the East, even in other than spiritual matters.

This close connection, this surveillance, had the ultimate result of making each individual crusader a servant of the Church, and so by implication absolved him of civic responsibilities and even of obedience to civil law in many cases. In taking the cross, a man set himself above earthly contracts or the necessity to pay his debts. By joining a crusade, he became free of oppressive and unwanted obligations. It was the Pope who set him free, he argued; therefore the Pope was the man to believe in, not the lords and their officers.

Obviously, such popular adulation of the father figure gave Innocent an immense control over European man-power and hence a political force sufficient to rock the throne of any king who dissented. Suddenly impatient, Innocent III addressed the archbishops in Europe, commanding them to provide and subsidise *their own* contingents of crusading soldiers. When these clerics were slow to follow this command, the Pope instituted a compulsory tax, on a *per capita* basis, on all churchmen from himself down to the humblest monk. Even those monks who had deserted from the disciplines of the Church were tracked down and forced to pay their contributions to the formation of this new holy army.

All seemed on the verge of readiness for a fresh attempt to strike once more at the Saracen; yet for a while the spark that would fire the powder-train did not flash out. In Germany, however, a new military attitude of mind became apparent in 1198 with the institution of the Teutonic Knights, an order based largely on that of the Hospitallers and dedicated to the Virgin. In preparation for the struggle which they felt was coming to a head, these German warrior-monks bought themselves a castle at Montfort in the Holy Land and characteristically rechristened it Starkenberg.

Outside Europe, in Outremer, Christians were interested neither in Innocent nor the Teutonic Knights. Their lazy acceptance of the Eastern situation as they knew it is seen when ex-crusaders married Moslem wives, settled down to forget their past lives in Europe, even took Moslem names and minted a coinage bearing the name of Mahomet. Such communities had no interest in co-operating with a new force from Europe, any more than did the merchants of the Mediterranean seaboard who, by now, were building up a trade with Saracen buyers which included weapons of war and the like, which had not previously been known. As for the Saracens, they rested reasonably secure, for though they realised their own basic lack of military unity, they knew well enough that its counterpart among the Christians was equally widespread.

So there was a stalemate in Europe and the Middle East; and in the meantime men waited to see whether the Greek Empire would totter or whether the ambitious rulers of Germany or Sicily would destroy the limiting papacy. Or whether, by some explosive miracle, the lounging armies of Europe could be inspired or terrified into action.

At this point occurred one of these treacherous episodes which characterise all medieval "politics," ecclesiastical and otherwise. Usurping Alexius III had seized the Greek throne by force, blinding his imperial brother and imprisoning his nephew, Alexius "The Younger"; for all of which, he curiously asked the blessing of Pope Innocent. The Pope replied that he must first be assured that the Greek Church would submit to that of Rome, and that the two should collaborate in a crusade. Here the Greek Patriarch disagreed, pleading that the Church of Rome was in a state of disruption and that he could not pledge the Greek Church to such a collaboration.

Suddenly, while face-saving and time-serving messengers were passing between Rome and Constantinople, Alexius "The Younger" escaped from prison in a barrel, flung himself on the mercy of his relative, Philip of Suabia, and put in a claim for the Greek Empire, as Alexius IV. Philip, son of Frederick Barbarossa, was at that time putting in his own claim to the crown of Germany against a claimant supported by Pope Innocent.

The effect on the dilatory Greek usurper, Alexius III, was immediate. He asked without delay for the Pope's support against "Alexius IV," on the grounds that if that young man were not prevented, he would persuade Philip of Suabia to support him in his claim to the Greek throne; after which, the grateful young Alexius would undoubtedly back Philip in gaining the German crown. So, alleged Alexius III, both he and the Pope would suffer a loss of prestige.

The cunning Pope replied that if German Philip did indeed become Western Emperor, then his first imperial act would be to attack Constantinople. He ended his letter with these words: "Nevertheless, many men assert that we [Rome] ought to take this young man's side, *in order to punish the Greek Church for its disobedience to the Roman See.*"

By this implied threat, Innocent III ensured himself of support from Alexius III, and, to a large degree, the submission both of the Eastern Empire and the Orthodox Greek Church.

On November 20, 1199, a group of young nobles took the cross during a tournament at Eri, having suddenly "seen the light"; whereupon the excitement of war began once more to spread even among laymen. Medieval tournaments were in reality bloody affairs which often resulted in sudden deaths and secret feuds. The Church, believing that a knight who died before he could receive the sacrament would go to hell, forbade them as a matter of Christian principle. Innocent III had suspended all tournaments for five years, for another reason: so as not to interfere with his expected crusade.

Once more, as after Clermont the papal legate proclaimed "that all who shall take the Cross and *serve in the host for one year* shall be delivered from all the sins they have committed, provided that these have been duly confessed." Geoffroi de Villehardouin, both a great nobleman and a chronicler, adds, "And because this indulgence was so great, men's hearts were greatly stirred, and many took the Cross by reason of the greatness of this pardon." The most powerful princes and lords began once more to mass, the majority of them discounting the purely spiritual side of the proposed crusade and privately estimating what they were likely to gain from it in terms of treasure or territory.

By 1200 they had decided that their forces were not yet big enough to effect an *immediate* defeat on the Saracens. They wanted no long-drawn-out campaign which would place them in physical danger and would let their estates at home run down. Quick and profitable returns were uppermost in their minds. In 1202, they sent envoys to mercantile Venice, asking for assistance, men and sea-transport for their venture. The extremely old Doge of Venice, Henry Dandolo, blind but in all other ways most acute, kept the envoys waiting for a week and then informed them that *in a year's time* he would be prepared to furnish ships and food-supplies for 4,500 knights and 20,000 foot soldiers. For this service, which he would guarantee over a period of nine months, he required payment at so lowly a level that the envoys thought he was joking. To make the bargain even more puzzling, Dandolo vowed solemnly that he would add fifty armed Venetian galleys as protection to this convoy—free of charge. The snag came in the second clause of Dandolo's agreement: "On condition that, so long as we act together, we shall take the half of all that is conquered, whether in territory or in money, by land or by sea."

Villehardouin reports that 10,000 citizens of Venice assembled in St. Mark's Cathedral to hear these terms and he even addressed them himself, begging that they should agree to their Doge's offer. The response was enormous; men out-shouted each other in their excited anticipation of great fortunes, until the Frankish envoys were stunned with the noise. The blind Doge knelt, and wept as he handed over the contract (as well he might) with joy for the hard bargain he had made but which, at that moment, had not been realised by the anxious envoys, who had already been kept waiting so long that they had come to fear a direct refusal of transport.

In the meantime and after the usual delays, Boniface, Marquis de Montferrat, was chosen by the new crusaders as their military leader. He had experience of Eastern warfare and also had family connections both in Constantinople and Jerusalem. Like the Saracen Ousama, he was not only a fine warrior, but also a scholar and a practising poet himself. This was a man whose wealth, influence and courage fitted him to be regarded almost worshipfully by the rough-and-ready soldiers and the simple country knights who rode behind him.

In June, 1202, the Fourth Crusade began, the armies marching through Lombardy to Venice, where the blind Doge, Henry Dandolo, had promised to await them tearfully upon his knees. They expected that his old hands would be shaking with anxiety to serve such a noble cause. At this time Dandolo was over ninety years old and was much given to emotional outbursts, which only served to disguise the keenness of his thought.

The meeting did not work out as the Franks had expected. The vast number of fortune-hungry crusaders were behind time in reaching Venice, thereby putting the Italians to great expense in waiting for them. In consequence, they were not welcomed with the warmth their dreams had invented. Dissensions began immediately, even among the separate contingents of crusaders themselves. At the last minute some decided not to pledge themselves to Dandolo's contract, but sailed instead from Marseilles at their own expense. Others swore to join the main force in Venice, but afterwards failed to present themselves. Some voted to sail direct to Syria and others to approach Jerusalem via Egypt.

The fact was that too many Europeans were by now becoming cynics in crusading matters. They knew that however they reached the Holy Land they would be welcomed by their fellow-Christians, who had settled there, no more warmly than by these mercantile Venetians. Moreover, since Saladin, they had a healthy respect for the Saracen fighting force. No crusade could be an easy war.

It was apparent by this time that however strong a

hold Pope Innocent III may have had at the inception of this crusade he had now lost it completely. The great landowners and merchants were acting as they wished; the solemnly-sealed contract with Venice was being openly flouted, and with each day previously-sealed arrangements were getting more and more out of hand.

Henry Dandolo, the old business-man who had wept as he delivered the contract in St. Mark's Cathedral, was not easily outbargained. The main body of ordinary crusading soldiers, those who were serious in their spiritual intentions, had been lodged on the small island of St. Nicholas which lay off the city. At the outset their food and entertainment was of the best. But now the crusaders on St. Nicholas were informed by the Doge that unfortunately they would have to be left there to starve.

The frightened crusaders then agreed to pay whatever was asked for their food and lodging, but the inflated expenses of these wretches mounted so fast that it began to appear they would never be free men again, even if they could escape from the over-crowded sandbank on which they were virtually imprisoned. Judging the appropriate moment with an assurance which came from long experience in all the markets of the world, Henry Dandolo offered to overlook their debts until such time as they could repay them out of captured spoils, provided that they besieged and captured for Venice the rival Hungarian merchant-city of Zara.

The lords who were on St. Nicholas accepted this compromise, though in fact few of the common soldiers knew about it. These men only sensed that Henry Dandolo had relented and as a celebration they held great festivities. The papal legate, who knew the conditions of their release well enough, agreed to these terms, but insisted only that once Zara was taken, the crusaders would then waste no more time but would proceed immediately to overrun Egypt, where the Moslem forces were centred.

So on October 8, the crusaders set out from Venice in such splendour as may never have been seen in the Mediterranean before. Apart from the 300 mangonels, or stone-throwing artillery, the hosts of war-stallions, the enamelled shields and the numberless banners, the ships themselves were of the greatest magnificence. It was a gay, tapestry-like embarkation—all colour and the gallant blaring of trumpets; but we must not forget that the surface glamour of this occasion belied its true underlying nature. Only the ordinary men were sailing for the glory of God and the relief of the Holy Sepulchre; most of the lords and knights were sailing, in commercial agreement with the Doge, to grasp what they could, under the full but uninformed indulgence of the Pope.

Henry Dandolo himself, sheltered from the sun by vermilion samite and smiling as the silver trumpets snarled across the water, sailed to make certain that Zara was captured for him from the King of Hungary—and to be sure that the contract with the Franks was not broken a second time. He was prepared to face even the everlasting fires of excommunication rather than let go the bargain he had cleverly engineered.

On November 10, a month after their embarkation, the crusaders broke the harbour-chains of Zara and sailed in to set up their siege-equipment; all the same, many gazed up at the ancient towers and wondered if they were doing right in attacking so fine a city. A monk who was there before the walls actually read out a letter from the Pope threatening excommunication for any who pillaged Christian property; and certain of the higher-minded nobles declared their complete lack of wish to sack such a place. But Henry Dandolo countered this by saying, "Not even for the Pope's sake will I give up!"

The knights and common soldiers, bound by contract, agreed to continue with the attack. In five days the undermined walls fell and the citizens threw down their weapons on being told that their lives would be spared. Dandolo, now anxious to involve his companions more deeply in the affair, agreed to share Zara equally with them and suggested that the whole army should winter in the comfortable city. But after only three days the arrogant Venetians quarrelled with the worried Franks and from a small beginning a great tension developed. Common soldiers from either side fought each other in every street and alley, although the mounted and armoured knights rode among them, trying to restore order. It was a week before this first insurrection was put down, by which time a great deal of blood had been shed; undoubtedly to the delight of the citizens of Zara.

The Pope quickly received news of this outburst from a Cistercian spy who made his way to Rome with a report, and sent a letter reminding the Franks that "We have expressly forbidden you to attack your brother Christians, *under the severest penalties*." He went on once more to threaten excommunication of all present unless Zara was restored to its rightful citizens without delay. This so appalled the Franks that they sent back immediate word of their intention to give up their captured holdings in Zara. They begged Innocent III to absolve them. Like an over-indulgent father he replied that he would since he was not anxious to see his conception of the Fourth Crusade dissolve into nothing.

Then followed a secret papal declaration to the

Franks, which can have no parallel outside the writings of the later Machiavelli—himself no man of God: "If it befall that these Venetians care neither to give satisfaction nor to be absolved (and indeed they are said not to grieve but rather to boast of what they have done), then we permit you to sail with them to the land of the Saracens or the province of Jerusalem, according to what you have contracted *or shall lawfully contract with them*; but deal as little with them as possible, and with grief and bitterness of heart, and in hope of pardon. For, seeing that they have already received from you the greater part of the passage-money, nor can they be persuaded or even forced to disgorge this, therefore, if you acted otherwise, you would seem to suffer for your penitence and they to profit by their contumacy. . . . Now though the Doge be excommunicated, yet you . . . so long as you are on board his ships, will not be touched by his excommunication, but will be excused in God's sight."

Blind Henry Dandolo was not concerned by these threats once he had his hands on Zara and its trade. The Venetians and the Lombards could have given a lesson in usury and deceit to any Jew living at the time. Shakespeare's merchant Antonio, in tricking Shylock, was not simply performing a dramatic function; he was doing simply what all Venetians had done for centuries—and breaking *his* contract into the bargain.

The Pope's next words to the Franks show a subtlety of thought which is anything but Churchly: "Deal ye prudently and cautiously, in order that if it befall that the Venetians seek occasion to break the expedition up, *ye may be careful to dissemble and suffer many things for a season*, until ye be come to your destination; and then, *when opportunity presents itself, ye may take proper means to repress their malice.*"

There can be little doubt about the meaning of these words: the Pope was positively recommending his crusaders to deceive the Venetians and to murder them on arrival at the Holy Land, their purpose having been served. Boniface, the chivalrous leader of the Frankish Christians, knelt humbly to receive this letter from the papal nuncio and was naturally careful to keep its contents from Venetian eyes.

The duplicity of this stage of the crusade is bewildering. It is difficult to see where any honour rested among the armies at this time, for the two leaders were planning another attack on fellow-Christians, this time on the Greeks, even while professing penitence for what they had already done to the Hungarians. Secretly they were negotiating with Alexius IV and Philip of Suabia, and while they were still at Zara, Alexius made them an offer—heavy contributions in men and money for the crusade, *and a solemn promise that the Greek Empire would henceforth subject itself to Rome* in all religious matters. In return, Alexius required that the army should immediately sail on to Constantinople and protect his usurped throne for him.

Boniface of Montferrat completely agreed to these terms, thinking only that he was doing a service to Pope Innocent, and commanded his followers to do likewise. The great majority of the common soldiers, puzzled by politics, disgusted at the delay in getting to the Holy War they had been promised, and unable to see what profit they might obtain from these aristocratic arrangements, came very close to mutiny; while many honest barons left the official army and made their own way to Syria, anxious not to be connected with such an act of open villainy.

Thus Montferrat, by title the leader of this crusade, together with other powerful magnates, accepted the

Greek offer as a rare bargain: but some thousands of the "lesser folk" sailed away in merchant ships, ashamed of their leaders. One ship sank with a loss of the 500 crusaders on board. Another contingent marched away through Sclavonia, to be ambushed and cut to pieces by the now justifiably suspicious peasants. Even among the greatest lords, suspicions now arose, and some sailed away, easily promising to join the main army at various rendezvous—never to be seen again. As one examines the Fourth Crusade more closely it becomes apparent that only two men connected with it showed any consistent desire to see the journey to a conclusion—Pope Innocent III and Henry Dandolo: one for what he conceived as the good of the Church; the other for the benefit of Venice—and each entirely ruthless in the expression of his will.

At Corfu, young Alexius IV joined the main force of the crusaders. Whereupon at least fourteen suspicious barons decided not to proceed to the Holy Land, but to stay in Corfu, and to proceed no further in the miserable affair. Montferrat, who was by contract sponsoring young Alexius at the Pope's orders, tackled these Frankish rebels by long arguments, trying to prove that they were really acting against the Holy Church. In this he had the support of many bishops and abbots, who added their pleas to his own. A temporary agreement ensued and the dissatisfied barons contracted to stay with Montferrat but only until the following Michaelmas.

The attitude of Pope Innocent III to all this is not surprising, in view of his earlier letters to Boniface of Montferrat. Though he had forbidden "his" crusaders to attack Christian territory under threat of excommunication, his only fear now was that a direct attack on Constantinople might fail, owing to the fact that the fishing-fleet alone of that city was more numerous than the war-flotilla of the crusaders. However, the offer of young Alexius IV to submit the Greek Empire to papal rule was a dream come true for Innocent III. For the sake of the Roman Church he could not desert that plausible young Greek now.

On May 24, after a theological tussle between the Greek Orthodox and Roman Catholic priests, the great fleet neared the city, fabulous Constantinople, the gateway to the Orient, the ancient mother-city of the West. No wonder the simple men-at-arms from their thatched villages in Normandy or their draughty halls in Aquitaine were impressed by the grace, colour and design, the deathless classical majesty that lay before them, rising tier upon tier above the blue sea; red and white buildings, high towers, gilded domes against the deeper blue of the sky. On May 25 the crusaders' fleet hoisted all banners and moving as in a street procession before the city walls, shot at the fishing vessels which were anchored along the harbourside. The Greek citizens swarmed upon the high parapets of the city to gaze down at this show.

At Scutari the crusaders dropped anchor and then sent a peremptory message to the usurping Emperor, Alexius III, to relinquish his throne to his nephew. The resident Emperor answered this command with defiance and even threatened to attack the crusaders, since they had now only 20,000 men to put against his rapidly enlisted 400,000. This was just the sort of reply that Boniface needed to give him an excuse to begin the battle, and the sort best calculated to rouse the tempers of the fierce and unpolitical Franks.

In any case, no one took Greek threats seriously. In European eyes the men of Constantinople were a decadent race, rotten with centuries of luxury and dependence on a mercenary army. The Greeks had not known what it was to defend themselves entirely since the Hunnish tribal invasions, and for over two centuries they had relied on the barbaric warriors from surrounding states—Bulgars, Patzinaks, Turks and even Northmen, who came south along the Dnieper to join the Varangian guard and incidentally to gain a fortune by looting Christians and pagans alike. The Greeks had long satisfied their own private instincts of violence, not by action, but by watching such wild beasts as lions, leopards and bears fighting each other in the immense Hippodrome of Constantinople.

Geoffroi Villehardouin's description of the Frankish attack carries all the conviction one would expect from an actual eye-witness: "A little after sunrise, the morning was fair; and on the other side the Emperor Alexius awaited them with a great army in fair array. Then the trumpets sounded, and every galley took a transport in tow, that we might come more quickly to the other side. None asked who should go first, but each made for the land with all speed. Then the knights went forth from the transports, and leapt into the sea to their waists, fully armed, their helms laced and their lances in hand; and, as soon as they touched ground, the good archers came and the good soldiers and the good crossbowmen, each in his own company. The Greeks made a fair show of resistance; but, when we lowered our lances, they turned tail and fled away and left the shore to us." The following day the Venetians stormed the harbour while the Franks attacked the towers. But on the shore the food situation gradually became desperate and men were forced to eat the flesh of their slaughtered horses.

"Never," says the chronicler, "did so few men

besiege so great a city." And during that ten-day siege, the Franks had occasion to meet and to respect the Emperor's Varangian guard. A scaling-ladder had been set up against one of the main towers. Almost a score of Frankish knights and their followers gained a footing on this ladder just when a party of the Emperor's Northmen appeared and, beating down their swords, knocked them down with axes from the tower on to the rocks below. In the meantime, the Venetian galleys pressed in relentlessly, scattering all who came at them in boats on the water.

This was perhaps Henry Dandolo's greatest moment. Although old and blind, the Doge made his way, fully armoured, to the prow of his galley which carried the standard of St. Mark, his own cathedral in Venice. Roaring threats to his men if they did not obey him, he had his personal galley run aground and scrambling ashore set an example which the younger men were compelled to follow. Galleys came ashore wherever there was space for them and soon the shouting Venetians forced the Greeks to retreat inside the city, abandoning twenty-five towers. These were promptly manned by Italian mercenaries, despite a later attempt by the Greeks to turn them out. The Emperor, Alexius III, made one more effort to intimidate the approaching Franks, but Dandolo joined in with his confident Venetians, and the imperial forces withdrew.

Then followed one of the strangest ironies of history. Blind Henry Dandolo went down to the dungeons and set free blind Isaac, father of young Alexius IV. In an episode laden with fierce pathos, the two blind men set the youth on the imperial throne. He was then formally crowned as the Emperor Alexius IV, with common consent of Franks and Greeks, on August 1, and with the blessing of

Innocent III. As a token of gratitude for their help this new Emperor persuaded the crusaders to winter in Constantinople, free of all charges, until the following March, when they were to proceed to the Holy Land. Then, feeling secure, he went on a triumphal progress through his Greek provinces, to visit his newly acquired subjects.

21

The Tragedy of Constantinople

As so often happened during the crusades, a promising situation suddenly deteriorated, owing to an act of sudden and violent irresponsibility. While the young Emperor Alexius was away among his people, a quarrel prompted by religious differences flared up between the Greeks and the Latins who had lived together in Constantinople for years. Someone, whose identity is unknown, set the city on fire and the blaze continued for eight days, with a frontage of three miles. The Latins, or Catholic Christians, knowing that they would be blamed for this disaster, left the city with their families and all they could salvage from the fire, and crossed the harbour in ships and barges, to seek protection from the kindred Franks.

Villehardouin comments slyly, "And they were in no small number, for there were a good 15,000, great and small; *and afterwards it was very profitable to the pilgrims that these had come over to them.*" The inevitable result, nevertheless, was that blame for the fire should now be transferred to the Frankish foreigners who had given the Latins refuge, though no one knew who had started the blaze. The young Emperor, returning to a blackened city, shared the suspicions of his Greek citizens and from that moment withdrew from the crusaders the supplies of food and money he had promised them. At last, conditions became so bad that Boniface of Montferrat, the leader of the Franks, even challenged Alexius to single combat. The Greek answer was to let loose seven fire-ships one night among the Venetian fleet.

The chronicler describes with high praise how the Venetians went forward with boat-hooks and dragged these blazing hulks out beyond the straits, where they drifted harmlessly away. He also tells how the Greeks took this opportunity to set out in barges and boats and to shoot flight after flight of arrows at the Venetian shipmen, as they struggled with indisputable courage to avert disaster. From that moment, there was no hope of reconciliation between the young Emperor Alexius and the crusaders who had put him on his throne.

In theory, it might still have been possible for the crusaders to have proceeded on their journey, with the object of retaking Jerusalem, without further waste of time at Constantinople. But it seems that the crowning of Alexius, the firing of the city and the antagonism of the Greeks towards the Venetians and Franks all contributed to turn the minds of the crusading leaders from their true purpose. The great mass of pilgrims, many of them inflamed to anger by the stories of Latin refugees, waited like a pack of wolves about the charred city which had seemed so beautiful when they first sighted it, as they brooded on vengeance.

The tension was suddenly and violently released into action. Certain Greek nationalists, who felt belittled that their Emperor owed his throne to the barbarous Franks, rose without warning under the leadership of Marzufle, strangled young Alexius and renounced all homage to the Pope of Rome. This situation could not have suited the politic crusaders more: here, at one time, was the perfect opportunity to avenge themselves on the Greeks, and to acquire what riches still remained in the city. Furthermore, by bringing Constantinople once again under papal rule, the Franks could pacify Innocent III, whose mind still revolved round the excommunication of all who had had dealings with the rebellious Venetians under Dandolo.

The crusaders held a great council during which they decided formally, and a little too piously, that Marzufle had no right to hold lands and that all Greeks who followed this rebel must assume an equal responsibility for the murder of Alexius, whom they now took as a Christian symbol. Suddenly and officially, the Franks announced the Greeks and not the Saracens as their true enemies, and Constantinople as yet another Jerusalem—but one to be sacked for its sins and not saved.

On April 12 the crusaders fought their way into the city and set fire to one of its suburbs. "This was the third fire in Constantinople since our arrival," writes the chronicler, "and more houses had been burned in the city than could be found in any three of the greatest cities in France."

The nationalist Marzufle escaped in the confusion, gave himself up to blind Isaac's brother, the ex-Emperor Alexius, who thereupon blinded him. When at last the useless wretch came into the hands of the Franks, they showed to what extent they also had become influenced by

Oriental custom: in formal council they decided "that he should be taken to the top [of one of the tallest towers in Constantinople], and compelled to leap down, in the sight of all the people, because it was fit that so notable an act of justice should be seen by all men." The looting which followed the terrified surrender of the city was on a scale previously unknown in the Western world. Henry Dandolo and the Frankish leader, Montferrat, cleverly attempted to control this pillage and ordered that all objects must be taken to three churches, where they would be shared out to the crusaders in proportion to their rank or military status. There were naturally many who tried to avoid this order, but all who were caught by the patrolling officers were hanged; knights with their shields about their necks to make public their dishonour, the common soldiers quickly and quietly on any tree along the broad avenues.

Then, even when the Franks had repaid their agreed financial debt to the Venetian shipmen, they found that they had never before been so wealthy. Ordinary foot soldiers suddenly found themselves rich gentlemen. Gibbon stresses the extent of the pillaging by saying that the spoil taken during one week in Constantinople equalled seven times the whole revenue of England at that time.

Perhaps the Orthodox Greek churches suffered most, for the crusaders brought horses into them and loaded them with plate, vases, reading-desks and even doors. Careless of their beauty the Frankish soldiers melted down priceless bronzes to use as coinage and tore precious stones from chalices to sell by the handful to merchants in the taverns. Dandolo and his followers, however, long used to works of art, were more moderate.

It is probable that in this sack of 1204 the knowledgeable world lost more of its artistic treasures than at any other time—even in 1453, when the triumphant Turks repeated the outrage on Constantinople. It is a moving thought that for many years after this grim April, shaggy-haired children in draughty Norman castles may have played with pretty toys, little knowing that these had once been holy relics; while russet-faced countrymen drank rough ale and cider from dented vessels that had once held Christ's holy blood.

When Pope Innocent heard news of this pillaging of churches, his reply to the legate was stern in the extreme: "The Latins have given an example only of iniquity and of works of darkness," he wrote. "The Greeks may well detest us as dogs. These defenders of Christ [the Franks], who should have turned their swords only against the infidel, have waded through Christian blood. . . . They have presumed to lay hands on the Church's wealth. . . . They have been seen tearing away the silver plating of the altars, breaking them into fragments which they have disputed with each other, violating sanctuaries, and plundering icons, crosses, and relics."

Perhaps the real reason that Pope Innocent was so furious was that now he realised completely his own lack of power over the crusaders. He must submit to this hideous act if his cherished crusade was still to proceed. Indeed, he was in the hands of the very men he had first incited to shed the blood of the infidel. He was their puppet; and Henry Dandolo, the excommunicated Doge of Venice, was the first man to realise this. Without delay and at the height of the confusion which reigned in the city, Dandolo now demanded a letter of absolution from the papal legate. This official, surrounded by threatening and plunder-mad Venetians, hastened to pacify the Doge, who immediately wrote to the Pope saying, "Your Legate has absolved us." Short of dismissing his legate and so losing touch with events in Constantinople, Innocent was forced to confirm this act of extortion.

After that, affairs moved so swiftly that the Pope lost all control. The crusaders appointed a new Emperor for themselves, in Constantinople—Baldwin of Flanders; as a counter to which, Dandolo elected his own Patriarch, a Venetian named Morosini, who was not at that time in holy orders at all.

Insult after insult was flung at the Pope, who compromised again and again: Emperor Baldwin wrote to Innocent, claiming to have acted at God's behest and almost demanding indulgences. Trapped Innocent replied with lamb-like mildness, regretting that the crusaders had not taken Constantinople even earlier, and giving his permission (as though he could withhold it!) for them to stay for a year in Greece so as to consolidate "all their good work" there. Whereupon the legate who had absolved Dandolo, went a stage further and absolved each man present *from his crusading vows* for a year! The Pope bowed his head in acquiescence once again, though he "was in the sorest straits, not knowing what course to take." He could see the Greek Church falling into the power of the nobles, who had elected their own puppet Patriarch and who had pillaged the very churches themselves.

The Emperor Baldwin, almost in contempt, then sent the Pope certain relics and jewels—but these were captured by Genoese pirates as they passed through the Mediterranean. To get back his gifts Innocent went to the length of threatening to excommunicate the whole city of Genoa.

The new Venetian Patriarch, Morosini, "a short, stout man, like a fatted hog," was the cat's-paw of his feudal masters: he appointed or expelled such bishops as these masters chose, only retaining those Greeks who humbly submitted to the Roman Church. He agreed to a barbarous and self-seeking rule that only Venetians should become canons of Santa Sophia, that all archbishops should be Venetians—and that they should always elect, as Patriarch, a Venetian! Soon it was seen that blind Henry Dandolo had been more far-sighted than anyone else in the Western world when he had so humbly presented his crusading contract, on his knees and with the tears coursing down his wrinkled cheeks, that day in the Cathedral of St. Mark.

Now, like any other puppet, Morosini was twitched by strings, and his puppet-masters were many and irresponsible. In a city without standards or honest faith he was involved in intrigue and counter-intrigue, was defied alike by the papal legate and the humblest clergy. At last, unable to serve so many derisive masters, he appealed to the Pope himself for aid and died a madman, exhausted by his impossibly arduous tasks.

No Patriarch dared follow him for four years. And in the meantime, Innocent allowed all Greek clergy who paid lip-service to Rome to act according to their lights, provided they were not openly rebellious to his edicts. But the new papal legate, Pelagius, who replaced the one who had given absolution to any who applied for it, was a man of strong fibre. He rode into Constantinople dressed in scarlet from head to foot, like a Greek emperor himself, and soon asserted that the easy days were over. Thenceforth the Greek clergy must adapt themselves in all religious rites and beliefs to those of the Church in Rome. He was prepared to wade through blood, he quickly showed, should the Orthodox Greeks deny any part of his assertion.

In the Roman background feeble Innocent nodded his grey head and smiled on his new chaplain, hoping that at last all problems would be solved and that his great crusade would move onwards to free Jerusalem from the Saracen. But nothing was as simple as that in Constantinople, the city of beauty and intrigue, of art and treachery, of religion and sudden death by violence. When Baldwin of Flanders was offered the imperial crown, he was allowed only one-quarter of the territory Alexius IV had held. The remainder was divided among the Venetian merchants and the Frankish crusaders. The power of the excommunicated Doge of Venice at this time was greater than that of Baldwin; he had control of the Greek Church itself.

If ever the Fourth Crusade was a holy action, it had become by 1204 the merest excuse for gaining territorial and spiritual power in Europe. The men of the Fourth Crusade did not even enter the Holy Land, and did not cross swords with the Saracen at all. They fell an easy prey to a scheming Venetian and thenceforward burned and hacked themselves out a new holding on the doorstep of the East, in a vainglorious and always treacherous pretence of furthering the interests of Christianity.

Nor were the crusaders even successful in that. Emperor Baldwin I was within a year left dead on the field of Hadrianople in a fight against the always rebellious Bulgarians, having gained little profit by his crown. Gradually, because of luxurious living and the ensuing degeneration of all moral standards, the Franks lost their power in Constantinople. Emperor followed emperor, powerless figureheads in a world of treachery which at last engulfed them.

Constantinople ate up the unprepared Franks like

some insidious disease. The simple-minded, bluff European stood no more chance of survival there than he had done earlier in the wind-blown wastes of Syria. By 1261 the crusaders had become so decadent that the ever-surging primitives about them, the Bulgarians and Serbs, the Wallachians and Greeks, beat them out of Constantinople like figures of mockery in an old play. Henry Dandolo and his Venetian merchants had been the only ones to profit by this strange crusade.

22

The Children's Crusade

While the world of grown men was so split by religious differences and the rivalries of ambition, the world of the European child was strangely unified and honest. In 1212 an event took place which has no resemblance to any other in world history: the children of France and Germany went on a crusade, ill-prepared, unarmed and with nothing but their innocent integrity to aid them.

King Philip of France was at St. Denis when a twelve-year-old shepherd boy, Stephen of Cloyes, near Orleans, came to him with a letter which the peasant lad said had come from Christ himself, bidding him organise a crusade to march on Jerusalem. It is suspected that this idea, and perhaps even the "letter of Christ" itself, had been given to the lad by the Albigenses; an heretical sect which had sprung up about 1209, in the southern Toulouse area of France and conducted a furious civil war against the French king and the Pope in the name of their own religion.

These Albigenses based their beliefs on the doctrines of the Persian reformer, Mani, who was crucified in the year 277, and whose liberal mind accepted *all* the great and ancient religious founders—Moses, Zoroaster, Buddha and Jesus Christ. He accepted both God and Satan and, superficially, his ideas were so close to those expressed by Jesus that many of Mani's later adherents, distinguished by their virtue and discipline in those violent and vicious medieval times, thought of themselves as *devout* Christians. His ideas were so appealing that they lasted a thousand years in Europe and even took root in places as far away as India and China. His gentle and frugal sectaries in thirteenth-century France, however, offended Pope Innocent III by denouncing the riches and immorality of the clergy, with the result that the Pope preached a "crusade" *against them*, so giving complete licence to any wandering scoundrel to rob, rape and kill these unfortunates.

When Stephen of Cloyes presented himself to Philip at St. Denis, the French king ordered the boy to return to his father's house; but Stephen was under the spell of religious, perhaps Albigensian, mania. He even dared to disobey his king, announcing that, in a vision, Christ had promised that the sea would dry up and allow Stephen, and whoever followed him, to walk dry-shod to Jerusalem, just as the Red Sea had opened for that other shepherd, Moses.

Certain clerics were appalled by the simple lad's blasphemy—but Innocent III, curiously, announced that "the very children put us to shame," and, undoubtedly, Stephen had a most bewildering power of persuasion for one so young and unlettered. Children from many parts of France flocked round him, carrying banners bearing the sign of the Oriflamme. By June, 1212, at the meeting-place,

Vendôme, it is estimated that 30,000 young people had assembled for this pathetic march to the Holy Land, without maps and even without food supplies. They were about to participate in what can only be called a pathetic act of faith.

How so many children evaded the prohibitions of their parents cannot be known: perhaps the parents, hearing of the Pope's admiration, were afraid to contest papal approval; perhaps there was little parental authority exertable in those areas where the fathers themselves were away with Boniface and Dandolo; and perhaps the hypnotic power of Stephen's words had transported these boys and girls in such a way that they were invincibly deaf to any remonstrance. At any rate, they set off that summer, joined by many adult hangers-on, including priests who found themselves caught up by this infectious ecstasy, and marched through Tours and Lyons down to Marseilles, finding food and shelter where they could.

But the summer of 1212 had been unusually hot, grain-crops had not thrived, and food and water were scarce because of the drought. Many of the children died by the wayside, while others turned back and tried to find their way home once more. When the remainder at last reached Marseilles they found to their great disappointment that the sea did not dry up as the shepherd-lad Stephen had promised, to let them walk to the Holy Land.

After a few days of misery in the port, they were approached by two unscrupulous merchants, later to be hanged for attempting the kidnap of the Emperor Frederick on behalf of the Saracens. These men, called Hugh the Iron and William the Pig, offered to transport the horde of children to Palestine in seven ships, free of all charge.

Stephen of Cloyes saw in this offer the hand of God,

who works in a mysterious way, and accepted gladly. Some days out, however, this strange, doomed fleet ran into a great storm. Two of the transport-ships were wrecked on the island of San Pietro, off Sardinia, with an almost total loss of life. When the storm abated the remaining five ships sailed on, but now southwards and not towards the Holy Land. Their destination was the Saracen port of Bougie, in Algeria, where all the French children were sold into slavery.

After another period of utter misery, some of the little "crusaders" were sent on to Egypt, where Frankish slaves then fetched a good price. Here about 700 of them were bought by the Governor, al-Kamil, a liberal man interested in European languages, who used the children as interpreters and secretaries. It is likely that those children who stayed in Egypt led a relatively comfortable life, since al-Kamil was a civilised and enlightened monarch who made no attempt to convert any of his slaves to Islam. Nevertheless, not all of Stephen's followers were so fortunate. A company of children were taken as far away as Bagdad, where eighteen of them were beheaded for refusing to become Moslems. It is alleged that of the 30,000 children who set forth from Vendôme but one, a young priest, ever returned to France—and that only after eighteen years of slavery.

This crusading fever spread among the German children, who were excited by the preaching of a boy named Nicholas. Nicholas told the same story of the seas opening to let the faithful walk dry-shod to Jerusalem. His estimated "army" was of 20,000 children and hangers-on, good and bad. This ragged horde struggled over the Alps and, sadly depleted by death and desertions, at last got as far as Genoa. Here they were turned away from the city walls by a governor who would not tolerate such a hungry and sickly rabble. Then, like creatures in a dream of death, they shuffled on southwards, their visions of relieving the Holy City forgotten in their hunger and agony. They found little pity among the Italians, whose language they did not even speak, and who, in all conscience, had little enough food for their own scarcely-nourished families. Some of the children were halted by the Bishop of Brindisi, who did what he could to feed them before ordering them to return to their homes across the snow-covered Alps. A pathetic few reached Rome, and these begged leave to abandon their "crusade" until they were older.

"The very children put us to shame," had said Pope Innocent III. He spoke truly, though perhaps in a different sense from his intention. The shame was on the Pope himself for not forbidding this cruel wastage; on the parents for letting their children go; and on the peasants who denied them food and shelter all along the route, or who took them in only to profit by their slave labour. It is estimated that of the 20,000 German children who set out to save Christendom not more than 2,000 ever reached their homes again. In this they were more fortunate than their French counterparts.

23

Frederick the "Stupor Mundi," and the Fifth, Sixth, Seventh and Eighth Crusades

From this point the crusades dragged on for more than eighty years, always doomed by their greed to failure. The total loss of European life cannot be estimated. All the same, when we consider the obviously immense losses of life in Bulgaria, Constantinople and the Holy Land, and the secondary losses by Oriental plague throughout Europe, we can only wonder that the Western world survived with sufficient man-power to conduct its own personal and almost incessant wars—the Hundred Years' War in France, or the Wars of the Roses in England—well into recognisably modern times. For the population of medieval Europe was only about a fifth of what it is today.

The thirteenth-century picture is inevitably muddled by internecine confusion. For example, in 1213, at the command of the Hospitallers to whom they now paid regular tribute, a group of Assassins made their way into the Cathedral of Tortosa and there murdered Raymond, son of Bohemond the Prince of Antioch. The distracted father's reaction was to call in a company of Templars hoping that, by paying off old scores against their rival order, they would gain revenge for him. The attempt failed but it was symptomatic of the piecemeal disintegration of the times throughout the East.

In 1217, inspired by the words of Pope Innocent before his death in the previous year, Andrew of Hungary sailed for Acre, was joined by 300 ships from North Germany and Friesland, and eventually captured Damietta at one of the mouths of the Nile. This time the intention was simply to capture Egypt. The crusaders temporarily seemed to be in a strong position, now led by John of Brienne; but once again the papal legate, that same scarlet-clad dictator Pelagius who had interfered already in Constantinople, forbade this crusade to accept the Egyptian sultan's peace terms, which would have given the crusaders the Holy City they desired. In 1221 they were driven from their stronghold by a flooding of the Nile, whose nature the Egyptian Moslems knew well and could use to their own advantage. So ended the Fifth Crusade; an utter failure.

Pope Innocent was succeeded by Honorius, whose own death in 1227 placed Pope Gregory in a position of righteous power. Gregory immediately threatened the German Emperor with excommunication unless he conducted yet a new crusade. There was perhaps some justice in this threat since Frederick was so lukewarm in religious matters that he was considered to be an atheist by the Germans, the Latins and even the Turks themselves! He is worth close consideration as being one of the most fascinating men brought to light by the crusades. Indeed, it is probable that much of the glory and many of the adventures attributed to the earlier Frederick Barbarossa were really his, for Frederick II—though beset by European criticism on all sides because of certain apparent faults in his character—was that most interesting of types, a man born before his time; he belonged more properly to the fifteenth century—a man of the Renaissance.

In appearance he was not heroic, being middle-aged and fat. His sandy hair was falling out rapidly and his green eyes, for all their piercing appearance, were in reality short-sighted. Yet what he lacked in physical glamour was compensated for by his brilliance in other directions. He spoke fluently in German, French, Italian and Arabic, and read both Latin and Greek as though they were his native languages. Apart from this, he had absorbed the ancient philosophers of all Europe and the East; knew what there was to know of medicine, the sciences and the geography of every country abutting on the Mediterranean and the northern seas. There was not a scholar living who could stand up to him in the cut-and-thrust of intellectual argument on any topic. It was said that when Frederick spoke the room was silent, as though a sorcerer had cast a spell on the assembled folk. It was not for nothing that he was generally known as the "Stupor Mundi"—the Wonder of the World!

In spite of these excellences—or perhaps because of them, for he must have found the limitations of medieval life inhibiting—Frederick was not popular. He was cruel, arrogant, untrustworthy to the simpler folk about him who desired his friendship, and was undoubtedly licentious in an age whose common standards of morality were shocking themselves. Frederick often delighted in outrageous comments on religion—not that he could have believed half of what he said, but he took pleasure in baiting the narrow-minded priests about him. In education and outlook, he resembled an old Greek Emperor rather than a more modern European one: he had learned liberality from his extensive studies and early understood that no one system of religious belief was infallible. And in this no bishop, or even Pope, could produce arguments which would convince him. He was as much at home in the Orthodox ideals of Byzantium and in the concepts of the Koran as he was in those of his own Roman Church; and quite as sympathetic towards them, by reason of his breadth of learning.

Runciman's assessment of him in *The Kingdom of Acre* is very much to the point: "Though he was by blood half-German, half-Norman, he was essentially a Sicilian by upbringing, the child of an island that was half-Greek and half-Arab. As a ruler in Constantinople or in Cairo, he would have been eminent but not eccentric. As King of Germany and Western Emperor he was a terrifying marvel."

He kept a harem at Palermo, to which he sent his seventeen-year-old Empress, Yolanda, and where she bore his son, Conrad, before dying a week later. He persisted in tormenting his old teacher, Pope Honorius, on all points of doctrine and morality, until in despair that worthy man died in 1227. The following Pope, Gregory IX, was of altogether different metal. A hard-thinking lawyer and philosopher, a proud defender of papal divine rights, Gregory almost immediately began to attack Frederick, whose indifference to Jerusalem was so marked, although he had been elected to the imperial throne only on condition of his leading the Sixth Crusade, that Pope Gregory formally declared a crusade against *him* and commanded both Templars and Hospitallers to attack Frederick in Palestine.

However, by choosing his moment, Frederick II concluded a bloodless treaty with the Saracens and in 1229 was granted Jerusalem, Bethlehem and Nazareth by that same liberal Egyptian Sultan, al-Kamil, who had employed Stephen's boy-crusaders as translators. He was forced to place the crown of Jerusalem upon his own head—there being no cleric present who dared to defy the Pope. So the Holy City was regained, cynically and unobtrusively.

But never had a crusading "victory" been received with such general abuse. Despite the fact that Frederick had arranged for all prisoners to be set free, and had engineered a ten-years' truce between Christian and Saracen, both sides conspired to insult the Emperor. The more ferocious Latin Christians openly deplored that Jerusalem had been retaken without the sword being drawn, and that the Sepulchre by the treaty with al-Kamil still remained under the guardianship of Saracens. At Damascus, an-Ṇasir, just as furious with al-Kamiḷ, "ordered public mourning for the betrayal of Islam."

This was a typical reaction to peaceful negotiation in those times; but Frederick, the most educated of monarchs, did not wish for popularity and laughed in the faces of the Christian barbarians who despised him. When both Templars and Hospitallers refused to give him armed support during his stay in Jerusalem, he shrugged his shoulders—and then handed over complete military command in the East to his own countrymen, the Teutonic Order. These tough warriors were more than equal to the task suddenly imposed upon them and, in their way, resembled the Viking Varangian guard of the Greek Emperor more than anything else.

Frederick's later reaction to his abusive Christian colleagues in Jerusalem was equally cynical. He begged that the Moslem "priests" should not change their customs out of deference to him, but should make their religious appeal from the minarets as usual. He even alleged that he had only come to Jerusalem to hear the muezzin's call to the Faithful, and not for any reasons of conquest.

At the mosque of Haram-al-Sharif, Frederick issued an edict that no Christian priest should ever enter a Moslem shrine without first gaining Saracen permission, and at least on one occasion a disapproving churchman who followed him into a mosque was roughly thrown out into the street with the Emperor's smiling approval. Addressing an Arab audience in that mosque, Frederick used the Moslem term for Christians, calling *them* infidels and mentioning them as "the pigs." Nevertheless, this did not entirely please the Moslems present, who had a strong sense of propriety and who felt that this unheroic-looking emperor should not have spoken so against his own folk. Nor did Frederick gain any ground with them when he sneeringly described Moses, Christ and Mahomet as three impostors: they, like the Pope, felt that this emperor *must* be a godless man to use such words.

Yet Frederick was not abashed and when the Templars, who preferred their own sort of anarchy, threatened him, he threw a surprise cordon round their great fortress at Athlit and then hinted he would imprison their own Grand Master, John of Ibelin, unless they concerned themselves entirely with their own affairs in future. He said that, since he owed them nothing, they must not treat him like one of their banking clients. It is likely that if Frederick had been able to call on a bigger army than his Teutonic Order, he might have given all Christians in the Holy Land a salutary and even a bloody lesson.

His departure from Jerusalem when he heard that his own treacherous father-in-law, John of Brienne, led a papal army against his Italian states, was typical. On May 1, 1229, Frederick made his way quietly down to the docks; but the news of his departure had spread fast and all along the Street of Butchers Christian and Moslem crowds pelted him with entrails and dung. When his faithful deputies Balian and Garnier came forward to bid him goodbye, the emperor turned round and cursed them. So he went aboard.

He had been less than a month in his new Kingdom of Jerusalem but now was more concerned with returning to Europe so as to be able to carry on his quarrels with the Pope at closer range. Undoubtedly Frederick was a man of extreme brilliance, who knew the Moslem mind intimately and, with a bigger army at his disposal, might have established a different type of Eastern kingdom, which could have survived the centuries: but he was in orthodox eyes a non-conformist rogue and a menace to established, if ineffective, ritual. Moreover, it is likely that had Frederick entrenched himself firmly in the East all skirmishing wars between isolated bands of crusaders and Saracens would have ceased, which would have taken the bread out of the mouths of the war-lords, most of whom were frankly more concerned with the results of their own pillaging than with political stability. So for the next fifteen years the second Kingdom of Jerusalem, neglected now by any formidable European army, fell into decay.

In 1244 the Sultan of Egypt, seeing once more dissension in Christendom, put in the field a force of 10,000 Turks who easily retook the Holy City. The Frankish governor was killed; 6,000 Christians, who attempted to make their escape to Jaffa, were ambushed, and 2,000 of them were massacred. When the sorry remainder reached the sea, they numbered 300. In Jerusalem a new wave of fanatical Turks sacked the Church of the Holy Sepulchre, and even murdered the priests celebrating mass. Then, having disinterred the bones of the Kings of Jerusalem from their tombs, they set the church on fire before riding on to join the main Egyptian army at Gaza. In the blood-bath which followed at Gaza, the two orders of Templars and Hospitallers—who had left Jerusalem to its fate—were decimated.

In Acre at this time, the Templars and Hospitallers each put 300 knights in the field under the command of their Grand Masters in an attempt to give a core to the Frankish army. But their defeat also was complete: both Grand Masters were killed, and of the separate companies only thirty-three Templars and twenty-six Hospitallers survived. At this battle alone, the number of dead Christians exceeded 5,000, while more than 800 were taken back to Egypt as slaves. Even these appalling losses were intensified six years later when at Mansourah near the Nile, only five Templars out of a contingent of 290 survived a hideous day of street-fighting. Long before this, the Teutonic Order, seeing no financial future for itself in Syria (now that Frederick had gone), had turned its main attention to the Baltic, where it was given castles and wide territories in exchange for help in taming the Prussians and other kindred tribes.

So what remained of the Templars and the Hospitallers were left to hold what places they could in Syria, to feud among themselves and to die against superior Moslem odds if their proud spirits chose. Now they had neither help nor interference from the West.

Yet for still another fifty years devout Christians

dreamed that the impossible could be achieved. Louis IX, King of France, known as "Louis the Pious" and later to be canonised as a saint, was a great revivalist and was himself largely responsible for the Seventh and Eighth Crusades. A religious but unworldly man, he put on armour in 1248 and rode into Syria, with trumpets blowing and cymbals clashing as though crusading was at its beginning. He might equally well have fought against Frederick, the German Emperor—who was nearer at hand and was considered by all loyal Christians to be just as unholy as the Saracen. Instead of which, Louis entered into an armed treaty with the Assassins themselves; partly out of the sheer necessity of having some allies in Syria, and partly because his learned emissary, in looking through the library of this sect, had discovered what he thought to be an apocryphal sermon by Christ, addressed to St. Peter. His intention was to attack Egypt.

King Louis, who did not lack courage by any means, was the first of all the leaders to jump into the sea in the attack on Damietta; later, tortured by scurvy and dysentery, he held out when all about him had surrendered. A blunderer despite his honest righteousness, and still blinded by the myth of the Holy City, he plunged on to attack Alexandria, accompanied by his rash brother, Robert of Artois. In the excited fighting, men of both sides, especially the constantly luckless Templars, were unnecessarily butchered. The main force of the crusaders, blind to the exact pattern of the battle, were easily surrounded by the Saracens, who as usual used the Nile waterways with precise military cunning.

The Egyptian Battle of Mansourah in 1249 was the real and final death-blow to any Christian hopes of controlling the Holy Land. Not again until 1917, when

Lawrence of Arabia and General Allenby occupied Jerusalem, was this hope to be in any sense realised. In fact, 1249 was the year when, for all effective purposes, we might date the end of the crusades.

Then disease struck even where the Moslem scimitar had missed: "The flesh of our legs," writes Joinville, "dried all up, and the skin of our legs became mottled with black and clay-colour, like an old pair of boots. . . ." During the retreat back to Damietta, the crusaders were followed and killed without mercy by the Turks. King Louis, fighting a useless rearguard action, was captured; though he ransomed himself for 800,000 gold pieces, his army was utterly destroyed.

Then for three agonising years Louis waited like a royal beggar in the ports of Syria for someone to help him make a fresh attempt on the Holy City; but no sympathy came from the indifferent noblemen of France, or of any other kingdom in Europe, where social changes kept kings occupied. Certainly there was an abortive attempt by some of the common folk of Northern France to save their king. They called themselves "The Crusade of the Shepherds," but this unprepared rabble, already excommunicated because of their openly-stated denial of the Pope, was met and destroyed by their own French army at Villeneuve-sur-Cher, and Louis, now weakened by the news of his queen's death, returned to France in 1254 with little achieved but a prolonged and painful act of penitence. As late as 1270, more than twenty years after he had first taken the cross, King Louis led yet another crusade, this time with Tunis as his goal. But he was no more successful than before, and died in this last and pathetic attempt to conquer Islam.

24

The Mongolian Adventure

All this time a situation had been developing which completely upset [and afterwards revived] the tired Moslem world. It resulted in the wiping-out of the Assassins; the creation of a pattern which was later to destroy the Templars; the abortive Crusade of King Louis in 1270; the rise of a new dynasty in Moslem Egypt.

In 1254, the same year in which the disheartened King Louis returned from his first crusade to France, there occurred one of the most violent and explosive invasions that the East had ever known: the Mongols entered Syria, their vast hordes rolling relentlessly forward, killing almost hypnotically all who stood in their path. Emerging from an almost complete obscurity at the end of the twelfth century, these Mongols had made their appearance in the lands north of China, and under Jenghis Khan grew rapidly to an amazing unity and power. Tent-dwelling nomads, they lived largely on mare's milk and horseflesh, drifting northwards for summer pasture as the snows melted and then moving south across the steppes when winter came again. Their entire lives were given up to pasturage, hunting, and savage warfare.

It was the self-imposed task of Jenghis Khan to organise the many Mongol tribes into one great organised army with which in 1214 he captured Peking and soon became master of China. In this campaign he was aided by the almost complete lack of interest of the Chinese people, who carried on with their subsistence tasks as though quite unaware of their change of overlords.

Within four years, seeking new kingdoms, the great host of Mongol horsemen swept westwards against Russian forces on the Caspian, and southwards into India as far as Lahore. When Jenghis Khan died in 1227 at the peak of his triumph, his empire stretched from the Dnieper to the Pacific, and was still rapidly growing. Constantinople, made hysterical by this new threat, began the task of refortification, this time not against the Moslem Turk but against an opponent even less understandable. That under Jenghis there had been an almost total religious toleration, and even great consideration for the arts and sciences, did not impress Constantinople. Since the time of Henry Dandolo this city had mistrusted *all* men.

By 1240 the Mongols had destroyed Kiev, had made all Russia into a tributary province, and had even ravaged Poland. The German Emperor, Frederick II, made no move to halt them as they rode into Hungary, either because of his natural lethargy or of some ingrained cynicism. The most curious fact is that the Mongols suddenly stopped of their own accord in this westward drive—and very probably because they felt unsure of themselves in the strange wooded and hilly territory which now confronted them. Soon they were streaming back across Hungary, to settle private dynastic bickerings among their noblemen.

Nevertheless, their sudden emergence, the speed of their movement and the apparent invincibility of their armies whenever they encountered an enemy, struck weary Europe and the East with a horror that was mingled with a sort of fearful admiration. All eyes were now turned upon the new Great Khan Mongka, and his brothers Kublai and Hulagu. Karakorum suddenly and fantastically became the political centre of the world; Rome, Constantinople, Bagdad, Alexandria, Paris fell under the awful shadow of the Khan, in whose skin-draped palace now waited anxiously embassies from the Greek Emperor, the Caliph, the King of Delhi, the Seljuk Sultan, the emirs of Kurdistan, the princes of Russia, the order of Assassins and even the court of France.

Hulagu was an epileptic. His so-called "tolerance" of Christians, Moslems and Buddhists was probably no more than the sheer inability to distinguish between them which ultimately produced a lack of concern in what his clouded mind could not comprehend. If Hulagu was religious at all it was in the direction of Shamanism, or the "inspired" rantings of any man who felt he had the momentary "gift of tongues." In 1256, as though to implement his threats to all the envoys who had visited Karakorum, Hulagu moved at the head of an immense Mongol army across the river Oxus in Persia, with his siege-engines, gun-powder and Chinese archers. Every tribe of the Mongol Confederacy was with him.

At first the nature of his enemy was obscure since the Caliph of Bagdad had never done anything to enrage him; but soon Hulagu's intentions were made clear. Years before, in pursuance of their hidden policy, the Persian Assassins had once made the great mistake of killing one Jagatai, a son of Jenghis Khan; and now epileptic Hulagu remembered the occasion. So the vengeful Mongols had decided to wipe out the Assassins in Persia for all time and, having torn down many of their fortresses, went on to destroy the infamous "Eagle's Nest," Alamut itself.

The Assassin Grand Master, Rukn ad-Din, suddenly realising that in his position he could expect no help from any side, surrendered to Hulagu, who surprisingly spared his life but confiscated all his possessions. The proud Grand Master felt that such treatment was unjust and, driven by his immense arrogance, he set off secretly to Karakorum, intending to demand better terms from the Supreme Khan Mongka. But after the incredibly long and arduous journey, Mongka refused to see this Assassin. Instead he sent a verbal message to Rukn ad-Din to say that he was a fool to exhaust good horses on such a fruitless errand, and commanding him to ride back to Persia immediately so as to arrange for the instant surrender of all Assassins. Rukn ad-Din, who had never before experienced such treatment, bowed his head in defeat and set forth on his homeward journey. Only a few miles from Karakorum the Assassin party was ambushed as Mongka had already arranged with Hulagu. Rukn ad-Din's head was chopped off without delay and all his relatives who rode with him were handed over to Jagatai's daughter so that she could amuse herself by torturing them as she wished in revenge for her dead father.

Back in Persia the slaughter was continuous. Under the pretext of conducting a census of the population, Hulagu collected almost all the Assassins together and then massacred them in thousands. Their Assassin brothers in Syria saw their own end approaching now and began to disperse, some even into Europe. It was a typical act of Mongol behaviour that the fine Assassin library at Alamut, which contained many important works of philosophy and science, should be wantonly burned to the ground. The only documents to be saved by the superstitious nomads were copies of the Koran. By some strange balance of fate, it is curious to note that almost on the same day the famous Moslem library at Medina was struck by lightning and utterly destroyed.

Encouraged by his success against the Assassins, Hulagu now decided to destroy Bagdad, the greatest stronghold of Islam. Almost as though hypnotised by the victorious Mongol epileptic, the Caliph of Bagdad, who could have put 120,000 cavalrymen into the field against the enemy, chose to disperse his forces and to rely on his own personal dignity in refusing to surrender to Hulagu. Perhaps, by this act, the caliph intended to show the whole Moslem world how great was the protective power of Allah. If so, the demonstration failed completely, for the Mongol hordes came on without hesitation, or divine intervention. In February, 1258, Hulagu sat on his horse before the caliph's palace with Bagdad lying waste about him. Only then did the caliph and his officials come out and bow the knee before a terrible silent enemy, who listened impassively while they told him where the city's treasures lay hidden and then turned his back when the guard ran in and butchered all who had given themselves up.

This unchivalrous act struck terror into the whole city. Now both those who surrendered and those who fought were killed without partiality or exception. In the forty days that Hulagu's tribesmen spent in Bagdad, 80,000 citizens were butchered. It seems that the invading army made no attempt at all to tidy up the shambles which their swords and lances had created; consequently by the end of March, the smell of the decaying bodies in Bagdad became so sickening that Hulagu withdrew his force for fear that plague might spread among them.

The Mongol victory, hideous as it was, is undeniable. Hulagu now found himself the possessor of the vast treasures which it had taken the Abbasid caliphs five hundred years to accumulate and protect. So he moved out of Bagdad, leaving it under Mongol control but allowing it a Moslem vizier. It was forty years before Bagdad rebuilt itself—by which time even it had only the status of a small provincial town. Runciman makes the comment that the fall of Bagdad half a century after that of Constantinople in 1204, *permanently destroyed* the old humanitarian balance in the Near East, which was "never again to dominate civilisation."

But this was no concern of Hulagu, who now turned his brooding attention to Syria as he moved on westwards. Christians and Moslems alike made haste to bow the knee before him. The one exception was the Moslem prince, al-Kamil, who, in a stupendous misjudgement of the situation, saw fit to crucify his envoy. Because of this, al-Kamil's fate is one of the most horrible to be recorded in history. When at last Hulagu captured the prince's fortress, the unfortunate Moslem was compelled to eat his own flesh until death relieved him of this horror. This was the Mongol leader whom innocent, trusting King Louis of France had seen as a fellow-crusader, a brotherly Christian king.

Yet, for a while, it must be admitted, the false glow of Hulagu's possible turn to Christianity blinded many of the Franks. The Mongols easily took Aleppo, Antioch and

Damascus, and the King of Armenia together with Prince Bohemond of Antioch were elated to ride with the triumphant army. For the first time Christians formed the majority in Syria, since during this Mongolian avalanche they had been spared and the Moslems slaughtered. But such a slavish condition was unacceptable to any sincere Christian, for the Franks in Syria soon saw that they were the pawns of the Mongol chief, who was concerned only with their utter obedience to him and not with their particular religious views.

What might have happened at this point is beyond speculation, for the situation has the peculiar quality of nightmare rather than of rational human behaviour. What did happen was that the distant Khan Mongka died and dissension about the successor flared up in Karakorum; moreover, the impulse which had first prompted Mongol aggression had somehow expended itself; also, at the same time, it seems that the Sultan of Egypt for the first time in decades was confronted by such a menace as would rouse the dissentient elements of Islam to unite and to strike a great blow of deliverance for their faith.

In September, 1260, four years after the destruction of the Assassins and two years after the butchery in Bagdad, the unbeaten Mongols under their general, Kitbuga, were drawn into battle at Ain Julud, or the Pools of Goliath, in Eastern Galilee, a place where the Franks had once defeated Saladin in 1183. Kitbuga's opponent this time was an army under Sultan Qutuz of Egypt, which comprised all of the best warriors still remaining in the Moslem world.

The confident Mongols attacked with their customary ferocity and skill: but the surprisingly vast army, which outnumbered them, was fighting for more than mere territory, treasure or political power. It was stating its ultimate and almost despairing belief in Allah, the One God, the Only Faith. Against this unity of belief and fierceness of endeavour, the careless Mongols broke. Suddenly they found that they had little which could be set against the fighting fervour which repeatedly charged towards them.

The Mongol general, Kitbuga, was captured during the battle, and when the battleground near the Pools of Goliath was silent once more he was taunted by the now laughing sheikhs and emirs, and finally beheaded. In their triumph, for some days the half-delirious sheikhs played with Kitbuga's head, using it as a ball in their games of polo. It had become nothing but a bauble, the symbol of Mongolian stupidity and of the abiding strength of Islam.

Now the Mongol's myth of invincibility had been destroyed at one blow. Islam was saved, and for the next 200 years the Mameluk Sultans of Egypt became the dominant power in the Near East. Of course, this also meant the end of Christian power, and the dissolution of the crusade states.

A year later in 1261, as though to restore the balance of powers as they had been before Clermont, the Christian Greeks recaptured Constantinople from the Christian Latins. Now the tide had turned. Both the papacy and the Mongols were in retreat while the Greeks and the Saracens came into their own once more. The only Europeans to be pleased with this change were the Genoese, whose mercantile princes had, since 1204, supported Greece against Rome. Now that their rivals, the Venetians, had been turned out of Constantinople, Genoese trade would flourish once again!

25

The Triumph of Islam

At this point it is important to see how the Christian hold on the East came to decline, and to know who was largely responsible for its end. This man was far more important than even the great Saladin—but far less likely to gain our admiration for his good qualities. He was an ambitious upstart, a liar and a murderer: but, nevertheless, he was a great man.

On October 23, 1260, only a month after the Mongol defeat, the victorious Sultan of Egypt, Qutuz, set off for a day's hunting with a party of his friends, including a Kipchak Turk named Baibars—a lieutenant of huge physique, a deep brown skin and unusually blue eyes. Baibars, a man of loud voice and crude manners, had first come to Syria as a slave and, having impressed all by his quick though coarse wit, was purchased by the sultan who had put him in the Mameluk Guard. Used to fending for himself, Baibars showed abilities as a fighting man and was soon considered to be among the ablest of the Mameluk soldiers. Having spent most of his life fighting against Franks and Mongols, he rose until he held a position roughly equivalent to that of a modern general. Yet always he remembered his slavish origins: and he grew up without any feelings of gratitude or mercy.

After the Mongol defeat at Ain Jalud, a month before, Baibars asked his master, the Sultan of Egypt, to grant him the governorship of Aleppo—but had been abruptly refused. So this day in October as the sultan's party rode out of sight of their camp, Baibars nodded to one of his friends, who came forward and took the hands of Sultan Qutuz reverently as though to kiss them in homage. As the sultan waited, Baibars moved behind him and carefully drove his sword through his master's back. The sultan fell dead immediately. Baibars then rode back into camp surrounded by his fellow-generals and quietly announced to the sultan's chief-of-staff what had happened. Seeing that this deed had the support of the military leaders, the chief-of-staff bowed before the ex-slave and motioned respectfully towards the sultan's chair. Baibars sat down in it and so became the new Sultan of Egypt.

All Egypt, by now conditioned to military revolts, accepted him without question; and elsewhere Baibars established himself either by force or diplomacy. Such Christians as had helped the Mongols—especially the Armenians and Prince Bohemond of Antioch—were reserved for his later revenge. Moreover, among the defeated Mongols there were many who now elected to embrace the Islamic faith and side with Baibars rather than make the long journey home across the steppes.

In 1263 the former slave Baibars marched into Frankish territory, pillaged Nazareth and almost sacked

Acre. This was little more than a reconnaissance mission. Two years later with an immense army at his disposal he began his offensive in earnest, turning his fierce attention especially upon the Templars and Hospitallers. At Athlit the Templars successfully defied him: but moving on, he took the Hospitaller fortress of Arsuf by treachery. Two hundred and seventy knights had held it with immense courage but after a third of their number had been killed they surrendered it when Baibars gave his solemn word that they should go free.

Instead, Baibars flung every survivor into his dungeons to rot. Even the Templars were horrified by this lack of honour. With a typical irony, one of their troubadours composed a wry ballad which proclaimed that now God loved everyone—save Christians.

The same year saw the death of the Mongol Hulagu, who had held the title Ilkhan and had governed all South-western Asia. His loss weakened the Mongols, who now lacked a leader. Baibars saw his opportunity and in 1266 moved against the Franks once more. Characteristically, his first assault was on the Templar castle of Safed which dominated Galilee. The Templars, fearless as ever, beat him back time after time and now sneered openly when Baibars' herald offered them freedom if they would surrender.

But once more grim tragedy overtook these arrogant Christian warriors. Their Syrian infantrymen, terrified by stories which had grown up round Baibars, deserted in droves at night. After almost a month of siege, the Templars became only too aware that they, the knights, alone held the fortress of Safed. It was a hot summer and the month was July. Battling with sword and axe day after burning day, the Templars soon became exhausted, having no one to prepare meals for them or to aid them in any domestic way. So, when Baibars at last promised to allow them to retire in peace to Acre if they opened their gates, they were so weary that they reluctantly accepted what now seemed to be a genuine offer. Naturally, he beheaded them all; after which all Galilee was his.

Moving up the coast, he then burned all villages and butchered all Christians, regardless of age or sex. The Armenians and Prince Bohemond were next on the list of death. Baibars soon defeated the Armenians and would have destroyed Antioch, had not Bohemond bribed the tired Moslem enemy into withdrawal for the time being. In any case winter was coming on, and fighting must be postponed.

When war-time started again in the spring of 1267, Baibars stood once more outside Acre. With typical cunning he was able to march up to the walls unharmed because he displayed banners which he had captured from Hospitallers and Templars. When at last his ruse was discovered and he was beaten back, he ravaged the countryside about Acre and left all the fields and orchards full of headless bodies. Though Baibars moved temporarily from Acre, he gained many compensating victories against the Templars and by 1268 gained his revenge on Prince Bohemond of Antioch by breaching the wall of the city after a brief four-day siege.

In general, the crusades reek with the stench of brutality and death but the fall of Bohemond's Antioch was laden with such horrors that even the Mameluks themselves were sickened by the carnage which they caused or witnessed there. The vast treasures of Antioch were piled high—a mountain of gold and silver—for each Moslem to help himself as he wished. Now even the fiery Templars were dismayed and began voluntarily to leave their fortresses: Prince Bohemond gladly accepted a truce and was fortunate to escape with his life.

The fire of Christian fervour in the Near East was at last dying down for ever. King Louis of France, Saint Louis the Pious, might have stirred up the embers again, but instead of attacking Baibars in Palestine, when the Bagdad Mongols would have helped him, he chose to strike at Tunis on the North African coast, where no one could reach his holy but ineffectual side.

As early as 1266, Pope Clement IV, appalled by the barbarian Sultan Baibars, had exhorted all French Catholics to destroy this Moslem brute. So Louis, now a sick old man, rather like Don Quixote in his self-tormenting romanticism, felt compelled to ride out once again and tilt against the Mameluk windmill. It took him four years to raise an army, but in 1270, a great array of princes and noblemen rode behind him on a despairing crusade. However, despite the theatrical pomp, the pikemen and archers who marched behind the horses were almost all paid mercenaries and not religious soldiers. They were the sort who would break and run if the battle became too intense; for them this particular crusade was a business matter and nothing more.

The whole tone of this holy war is expressed by the nobleman Joinville, who went with his king out of loyalty, but with no real desire to save Christendom: "And never . . . would I turn my eyes towards Joinville, for fear lest my heart should melt within me for the fair castle that I was leaving, and for my two children . . . These things I write, that you may see how foolhardy is that man who dares to put himself in such peril; for as you go to sleep at night you know not whether you will find yourself at the bottom of the sea."

In these dour words, we read the passing of crusading glory, as we do also in Joinville's later regretful comment on sick King Louis: "The King was so feeble that he suffered me to bear him in my arms from the Count of Auxerre's mansion to the Franciscan friary. And yet, ailing as he was, *if he had stayed in France he might have lived long enough, and done many good works.*"

Misled by a false report that the Bey of Tunis wished to be baptised as a Christian, the deluded Louis landed in North Africa and was immediately blockaded inside Carthage. The crusaders were tormented by heat and especially by thirst, for the city's wells had been carefully defiled before Louis walked into the trap.

A refinement of Eastern torture came when the Tunisians arranged for loads of hot sand to be blown on the prevailing wind into the suffering citadel. This was followed by an attack in which the rotting bodies of dead men were pitched over the city walls by the Moslem siege-engines. Soon the Christians were choking with the stench and within a short time plague had begun to spread through Carthage. The princes suffered every bit as much as their mercenaries now, and many of them fell sick in the North African heat. King Louis died, still praying, and having first seen his beloved son Tristam lowered into a shallow grave.

Charles of Anjou, landing a short time afterwards, rapidly conducted a peace treaty with Baibars which left his own island kingdom of Sicily well provided for—a kingdom which, however, he was to lose before long. To his credit, Edward I of England, who had joined this abortive crusade at the last moment, was so disgusted by Charles's treaty with the godless Baibars that he straightway set course towards Acre on a private mission of revenge. Something of the old spirit flared up again for a moment when Baibars engaged a party of the few remaining Syrian Assassins to murder a Frankish baron, Philip of Montfort—a task which the killers undertook gladly to gain a little revenge on those Franks who had allowed the Mongols to destroy their Persian stronghold of Alamut. This murder took place, characteristically, in a chapel at Tyre where Philip was kneeling to pray.

But when King Louis died at Tunis in 1270, Sultan Baibars knew that he had no more to fear from the Frankish West in general. Now he took on the particular task of destroying finally the Templars and Hospitallers. In this, he was ironically aided by Assassin contingents who had now lost all their political loyalties. After a fortnight they broke into Krak des Chevaliers, the last symbol of Hospitaller strength, and slaughtered all its defenders. Many Templar fortresses then surrendered without even a token struggle. Even the Teutonic castle of Montfort fell after only a week's siege. Bohemond, once Prince of Antioch, was spared again only because Baibars, who needed a noble hostage, had heard that Edward I of England was sailing on a crusade of his own in revenge for King Louis' betrayal.

Edward landed at Acre in 1271 and was horrified to find that throughout this period Venice had been conducting a flourishing trade with Baibars, while the Genoese were in complete control of Egyptian slave traffic But a year later Edward found himself so outnumbered that he was only too ready to accept a truce with Baibars. Yet it must be said in his favour that his intention was really to return home for a long enough period to assemble a suitable force with which later to overcome the Moslems. On June 16, 1272, Baibars hired an Assassin to hide in

Edward's room and to stab him with a poisoned dagger. Characteristically, he survived, to receive Baibars' warm congratulations on his stamina. After which he returned to England since his father, King Henry III, was gravely ill. Arriving there, he found that Henry had died and that he himself was already king—and so he had no further opportunity of visiting the Holy Land. Affairs in his own fermenting kingdom kept him too occupied.

Indeed, at this latter end of the thirteenth century there were few men of any social group whatever who saw much point in protracting these desultory crusading wars of attrition and revenge. Runciman on this topic, however, makes an astounding though wonderfully evocative comment. He says that the new Pope Gregory X sent out messages "as far as Finland and Iceland" in an attempt to whip up renewed crusading fervour among Christians. But, as he says, there was no response.

Nevertheless, even such a slight lifting of the veil reveals to us the fact that the world was rapidly growing smaller: men from its farthest-known points were meeting or were in communication with each other. They were already standing on the doorstep of modern times without knowing it. And when, once more, the yeast of enquiry had started working, then Columbus would come at last, he or someone else who was weary of the Mediterranean and anxious to find new and far-distant places.

After the loss of Krak des Chevaliers, the Order of the Hospital declined in importance. Now it possessed only one castle, at Marqab, and could maintain no more than 300 knights, in comparison with the 10,000 of its great days. The Temple was more subtly fortunate, since it held a number of castles and was supported by its diminished but still substantial banking speculations throughout the Islamic world.

However, these crusaders had now largely become policemen, keepers of some sort of law and order. While the Templars protected Moslem merchants, the Hospitallers looked after the interests of Nestorian Christians; and when the Venetian and Genoese traders came to blows, the orders took one side or the other, as best suited them.

This decline suited Sultan Baibars very well. He was only too willing to permit the old type of crusaders to die of their own accord, while he turned his attentions on a new ilkhan, Abaga, of the Mongols. This ilkhan asked for crusading help from the West and to prove his sincerity even sent representatives to Lyons to be baptised as Catholics. But the promise of Heaven was all they got: the West could send no military reinforcements. The great days were over and the Mongols who had once bowed to no man were compelled to return empty-handed and do the best they could against resurgent Islam.

In the spring of 1277, Sultan Baibars moved north into Anatolia to be met and surprisingly repulsed by the new ilkhan. Baibars himself died in the summer of the same year, having drunk by mistake from a poisoned cup which he had prepared for someone else, to be succeeded by Sultan Qalawun. Brutish and coarse, of the lowest origins, Baibars had done more to destroy Christianity than any man since Saladin. True, he had not cleared the Franks entirely from the East, but by limiting them to the narrowest coastal area, he had made their decline as landowners—though not as traders—inevitable. In less than fifteen years all the fighting in Syria would be over—but not before Christians had turned on each other, as in Tripoli in 1282. Again and again, Moslem or Mongol moved forwards or backwards, as policy or strength demanded: again and again the depleted military orders—

and especially the Templars—were alternately used by one side or the other as allies or scapegoats.

In 1281 the Mongols were pushed back by Islamic forces beyond the Euphrates after a defeat at Homs. A year later, the mixed inhabitants of Sicily rose and massacred their own overlords, Frenchmen who had supported Charles of Anjou. This was a signal for all subject-peoples of the Mediterranean to rise and bring his "empire" toppling down. The Emperor of Constantinople was well contented by this new phase of disintegration. While Constantinople smiled, the newly elected Sultan of Egypt began to root out the military orders.

By 1287 the despairing Mongols had again sent their ambassadors to France, where they were shown the sights of medieval Paris but were offered no promise of a crusade. At his French capital of Bordeaux, the old crusader, Edward I of England, received them pleasantly and with every apparent sympathy: but now Jerusalem seemed far away to him and his domestic troubles in Scotland seemed very near.

And all the time the Sultan of Egypt was coming closer to the point when he would finally destroy the last traces of the Christian states in Syria. By some strange irony, it seemed that only the once-brutish Mongols were concerned with this peril. As for the kings of the West, they were too preoccupied to give any attention at all to the danger. The Pope sent gifts to the ilkhan and the Mongols—but he, too, was overwhelmed with European politics. This farce of request and refusal went on for four years.

In 1291 the Mongol ilkhan again sent westwards to the French and to the English kings, imploring them to make a crusade, promising them all the food-supplies they needed and an allied army of 30,000 cavalrymen. The French king did not bother to reply. King Edward of England, a little more politely, referred the ilkhan back to the Pope—who answered that he was incapable of organising a crusade without the active assistance of all the European kings themselves.

Then for the last time the ilkhan sent ambassadors to call on the various kings of Europe, more urgently than ever before; and for the last time his messengers returned without achieving anything. But now they had a double cause for grief: for they arrived back to the court to find that the ilkhan himself had died and that now they could never regain their dominance by another great crusade.

Perhaps if Edward of England and Philip IV of France had moved in alliance with the Mongols at the first invitation, Moslem power might have been limited and Christendom in the East might have survived, at one level or another. But while this momentous issue was being considered and discarded in Europe, the Franks of Outremer seemed bent on destroying themselves in prolonged bouts of reckless abandon, while Pisans, Venetians and Genoese pirate-traders used the Syrian coastal waters as private battlegrounds. Cynically, the Hospitallers and Templars stood back and watched. Indeed in 1289 it was the Grand Master of the Temple who, nauseated by the stupidity of his fellow-Christians, sent to the Sultan of Egypt and warned him that out of this shambles the Venetians might well rise supreme and even come to dominate the entire trade of Alexandria.

No second warning was needed. The Sultan Qalawun accepted the invitation to intervene without delay. In February of 1289 he marched the entire Egyptian army into Syria and attacked Tripoli. The Grand Master of the

Templars who had caused this and who himself was warned of the sultan's every move by one of his emirs, now saw that Qalawun wanted nothing less than the complete destruction of Outremer, Templars included! Though many non-combatants fled to Cyprus, the Christian army and the military orders made ready for war while Venetian and Genoese galleys patrolled the waters round the peninsula on which Tripoli was built.

When the Moslem bombardment began, however, it was so thunderously crippling that the old walls instantly crumbled. The Venetian and Genoese galleys made off without delay while the defenders vainly tried to beat back immense hordes of Moslems. Typically, the Templars were in the forefront of the battle and suffered great losses. Also as typically, when Christian refugees rowed out to a little island off the coast, the victorious Mameluk cavalry swam after them on horseback and killed them in the sea. Sultan Qalawun had the port of Tripoli demolished entirely before moving on towards Acre, which was his main goal.

Even at this time, had Edward of England, the only crusading king of repute still alive, left his Scottish forays and moved East he would have been followed by masses of revengeful Europeans; but what he was not prepared to do for the friendly Mongol ilkhan, he would not do for the decadent and contemptuous lords of Outremer. Certainly a rabble of peasantry from North Italy, anxious rather for personal salvation and loot than to save Christendom, made its way to Acre. Here for a time they found such food, drink and excitement as they had not known before in their impoverished and brutish lives; but their behaviour was much the same as that of Peter the Hermit's barbaric crusaders. Debauched and befuddled by unaccustomed luxury, these Italian peasants refused to obey their noble

Christian commanders, broke out, and in a terrible spate of incoherent bloodlust hacked down everyone who seemed to them an infidel. Peaceful Moslem peasants, visiting Acre to sell their grain, as well as Christians who had adopted Eastern dress, were slaughtered without mercy.

And though the military orders rescued as many Moslem traders as they could, and ruthlessly battered the Italian rustics into submission, the damage had been done. This was the final excuse the Egyptian Sultan needed to flush all Franks from the Near East. Sultan Qalawun vowed to leave no Christian alive in Acre, at which the Grand Master of the Templars gave up all hope. His name was William of Beaujeu and he was undoubtedly one of the bravest as well as the craftiest men of his time; but there was nothing he could do against the implacable hatred of the sultan on the one hand, and against the suspicions of his fellow-Christians on the other. William's last frantic offer of Christian lives to the sultan embittered all against him; though not one among all his detractors had an alternative to offer for the salvation of Acre.

Suddenly, after all the tension, came a curious release. Just as he was about to begin his attack, in November of 1290, Sultan Qalawun fell sick and died near Cairo. All the same, this relief was short-lived. Qalawun left a son to succeed him, who had vowed by the most sacred of relics to carry on his father's project. Representatives of the military orders who went under a flag of truce to intercede with him were brutally mutilated, and at last it became clear to every man in Acre that the place was doomed. Suddenly it seemed that the whole Moslem world had converged on Acre, the last symbol of Christian rule in the East.

The battle began on April 6, 1291 and ended on the night of May 18. This was the final death agony of the crusades, during which Templar and Hospitaller at last stood side by side, holding gate after gate, tower after tower, while arrows fell upon them in an almost solid volley. Cymbals clashed and trumpets screamed as the enemy came on, and on, and on. And at last the walls of Acre were down and the inevitable massacre began. No mercy was shown to age or sex: the young sultan commanded that all Christians must die.

Those Christians who could get away from the corpse-clogged city made for the shore, where Venetian ships lay waiting for a cargo—a terrified cargo that would more than pay its way to safety. On that horrifying night any man with even the most leaky vessel could make the fortune of a lifetime from his ferry-fees. A certain Spanish Templar named Roger Flor was such a man. Through the nightmare siege he had fought with the courage of ten men but now that it was all over, now that Outremer, the Christian world in the East was finished, he was not foolish enough to miss the last chance. Commanding a Templar galley, Roger Flor rode in to shore as far as he dared and bargained with the assembled noblewomen of Acre who were sobbing on the wharfside. Distracted with the horror of the rape, mutilation and torment which would happen to them if they were caught, they offered him all they possessed for a safe passage in his stolen ship. That night Flor sailed away with a full load. Before dawn he was a fantastically rich man; and a true Templar to the end.

While Acre was being systematically destroyed by the sultan all remains of the orders were wiped out. Not all Templars were as lucky as Roger Flor. Many of them became slaves; others disguised themselves, forgot their native tongue, and lived among the Arabs in the beggars' quarters of Cairo; while others settled near the Dead Sea as peasant wood-cutters for the rest of their lives. The few Templars who had stayed on in Acre defending their treasury were at last offered freedom by the sultan; but as usual they were beheaded as soon as they had sheathed their swords and given themselves up. Forty years later, Acre was still a wilderness of rubble in which only the poorest peasants and outcasts carried on a squalid life among the flies and dust.

The Templars who had escaped before the city fell, still guarding what remained of their treasure, by some miracle made a stand at Sidon until they also were forced to retreat. They gave up castle after castle along the coast, in a constant withdrawal, until finally they held only the little island fortress of Ruad off the coast from Tortosa. There they stayed until 1303, while the sultan methodically obliterated all remains of Christian dominance on the mainland. Now all was desolation. Those Christians who could not escape, hurriedly merged with the natives and forgot their origins.

The few Templars of Ruad sourly watched the power of their order end—brave, bitter, arrogant men, who would in a few years find themselves regarded by the whole Christian world as devils incarnate and no longer the soldiers of Christ. Outremer had gone—and they had gone with it, like the Assassins before the Mongol onslaught, in all their pride and cynical courage.

26

The End of the Templars and of the Crusades

After the fall of Acre the Christians who still lived in the Near East—as in Armenia, for example—could do nothing but accept the end of their old way of life. As for the common people of Europe, they had now lost interest in the promised comforts of nebulous Hereafter, since their social condition had changed for the better and they had developed such political awareness as showed them that the profits they were to gain in life might better be obtained by staying at home than by trailing towards treachery and death among the alien people of the East.

Their newly-awakened sense of criticism and education taught them to see the promise of papal indulgences as false, and directed solely towards territorial gain for the Church. They had seen through the apparent glamour of Holy Wars: they had watched even the proudest feudal lords being tumbled in the dust and had sensed the emptiness of that formal chivalry which professed to aid the weak, but only too often acted towards it with an outrageous barbarism. Now it was becoming increasingly possible for men of the humblest origins to gain knowledge and intellectual status in the schools and even the universities; men who would often pass back some of their learning, and with it their cynicism, to their brothers in the villages.

True, there was much empty talk of possible new crusades for still another hundred years: even Shakespeare, in *Richard II*, makes his Bolingbroke vow to visit the Holy Land as an act of expiation: but such outbursts were little more than figures of rhetoric. The common men now had work to do and pockets to be filled in the various wars being conducted up and down Europe. Certainly Pope Nicholas IV tried to whip up Christian fervour: but no one listened to him with more than polite scepticism. Nor could the Byzantine Emperor offer any rewards: he was too impoverished by beating off the Turks to the East and the Bulgars and Serbs to the West. There were no pickings to be had there for mercenaries. No longer did the decadent Mongols send their ambassadors to Europe: the ilkhan himself had become a Moslem, and the Great Khan had lost all interest in the Holy Land.

As for the famous military orders, their purpose had disappeared. The Teutonic Order had long ago moved back home to the Baltic: the Hospitallers and Templars had set up their base in the island of Cyprus, there to occupy themselves in local administrative affairs. Their stormy career as professional soldiers had exhausted them and many of them were now content simply to enjoy the fruits of their widespread endowments and financial speculations in Europe. True enough the Spaniard, Raymond Lull, preacher, Arabic scholar and traveller in the Near East, had a plan for their further use which he made public in 1305 in his book, *Liber de Fine.* In this he suggested a great intellectual and spiritual movement for converting Islam to Christianity, supported by an army led by a king and composed entirely of the military orders.

King Philip IV of France volunteered to act as its leader and to become the *Rex Bellator* as described by Lull. But in secret fact, inspired by the French lawyer Dubois, Philip intended to use the occasion only as a means of gaining control of the Church and its revenues, and perhaps of establishing an empire in the East under one of his sons—but certainly of suppressing the Templars completely in Europe and confiscating for his own use their property and investments. This last point became the first one to be mentioned on the programme which King Philip presented to the Pope: *the Templars must go.* In the past they had so overreached themselves in pride and power, in their self-sufficiency and assumption of almost sovereign rights, that Philip had not felt safe in his own kingdom while they existed. Moreover, their still great wealth was the obvious means by which to replenish his own exchequer at a time when the French government urgently needed money. There was much gossip of negotiation between Philip, the Pope, the Armenians, the Genoese and even the Mongols; but the whole affair was a charade conducted by insincere and self-advancing potentates.

At last the grand masters of the Hospital and Temple were slyly asked for their opinions, and encouraged to submit their own military plans for such a campaign. No doubt it was with confidence that the Grand Master, James of Molay, went to France in 1306 to discuss his plans with the Pope at Avignon; but what he, surprisingly, did not seem to suspect was that he was walking into a trap which would mean death both to his order and himself.

For years Philip of France had been building up an extensive dossier against the order, based on the secret reports of spies, renegades, and to some extent on the arrogant and extravagant public claims of certain Templars themselves. It is understandable that the limited European mind of the times should suspect *any* tight-knit body of men who spoke Arabic as fluently as they did French or Italian or German, and who were often more at ease following Moslem customs than Christian ones. It is equally understandable that French bankers should envy the Templars' still widespread business with parts of Islam, or that Latin Churchmen should abhor the understanding of and tolerance towards the teachings of the Koran shown by the order. To most ordinary men of Europe, the Templars were regarded with the same mixture of fear, suspicion and admiration which were accorded to the Assassins, whom they so closely resembled.

Envy and curiosity are always directed against any secret society by those who are excluded from its carefully-guarded meetings; and what detractors may not know of the truth, they often invent in their effort to support their own envy. So the Templars were variously accused of black magic, of denying Christ and of spitting upon the cross as a daily routine. They were also charged with bestial initiation ceremonies and of homosexual orgies behind their locked doors. In fact, there was nothing bad that could be said against all mankind which was not said against the members of this first and most powerful of the military orders.

In 1307 King Philip stopped talking of a crusade and suddenly arrested all the Templars in France. Then he accused them of heresy on the evidence of two ex-Templars who had been expelled from the order, and began a long-drawn-out process of torture which resulted in absurd confessions, followed in moments of recuperation by denials. Early in the following year the French Pope, influenced by Philip, commanded *all the Kings of Europe* to carry out a similar extinction of the order. Everywhere except in Portugal Templar estates were seized and the knights themselves put to the torture. In Cyprus, their headquarters, the Templars resisted for a short while but at last surrendered, having first safely and typically hidden the greater part of their treasure. The Cypriot scapegoats were not brought to trial until May, 1310, when seventy-six of them were accused on false evidence—and acquitted. This was indeed amazing since all over Europe their brother-knights had been burned at the stake or flung into prison for life.

So furious was the Pope made by this acquittal that he ordered a retrial of the Cypriot Templars in the following year, with the instruction to the Dominican and Franciscan orders that, should a second acquittal appear likely, extreme torture was to be applied to gain conclusive confessions. As a result, all of these Templars were eventually gaoled for life and their Grand Master, after six years of torture, was burned to death in Paris during the spring of 1314.

In this way the order came to its squalid and blood-stained end. Its wealth and possessions were in theory to be handed over to the Hospitallers, but so costly were these "trials" alleged to have been that the rival order received very little from the downfall of the Templars.

So the Templars who had enjoyed 200 years of triumph were now wiped out.

In his survey of Edith Simon's book on the Templars, *The Piebald Standard,* Valentine Heywood says of the order: "Its real weakness . . . was in its very success and strength. It had become a Church within the Church, a State within the State, not only in Palestine but throughout Western Europe, and particularly in France. There was no future in that kind of structure in a Europe in which the national and centralised State was evolving from the warring medley of duchies and principalities."

Whether these latterly-maligned Templars were good or evil is of little importance now. Certainly, they were dedicated men, impatient of all other authority; and just as certainly they always stood where the swords flailed most fiercely and the arrows fell most thickly on the battlefield. They had immense courage, and at a time when courage perhaps meant more to Christian survival in Syria than did the ritual mouthing of prayers.

When the Templars were destroyed, all hope of a durable Christian kingdom anywhere in the East went with them. True, remote monarchs in obscure feast-halls in Europe waved their wine-cups and threatened "the Infidel" for another 150 years; but such utterances had become a commonplace formula. New kings at a loss for revenue founded new orders, solicited the aid of the merchants of Venice and Genoa, and even went through a formality in which they "took the cross." Galleys were fitted out and painted to sail only a few pointless miles. Busy warrior-magnates, like the English Black Prince, were approached about crusades and gave smiling assurances—but nothing else. In 1365 Alexandria was sacked by a mercantile rabble from Europe and everyone within the citadel massacred, Moslems, Christians and Jews. Here mosques, churches and tombs were despoiled by crusaders whose only desire was to gain what loot they could; but when the strong Egyptian army approached, the "crusaders" withdrew in panic. The only results of this shocking and abortive escapade was that Islam began once more to persecute Christians and that in 1426 the old crusading kingdom of Cyprus was obliterated by Moslems in an act of revenge.

In the meantime, yet another wave of Turks, the Osmanlis or Ottomans, had become powerful in Asia Minor and had begun to threaten Constantinople once more, moving gradually closer in their thousands and knowing well enough that the Greeks would get no help from the West unless they bowed the knee to Rome, and perhaps not even then. In 1396, to save themselves and not Christianity, Hungarian King Sigismund and princes from most of Europe did march against the new race of Turks at the head of 100,000 men. After certain minor victories, in which the Christians behaved with the utmost brutality to their prisoners, they eventually came face to face with the pick of Turkish chivalry under the Ottoman Sultan Bayezit himself at Nicopolis on the Danube. Though many of the Christians fought furiously they were no match for Bayezit's 100,000 splendidly-disciplined array.

Sigismund barely escaped with his life, in a *Venetian* ship which carried him to *Constantinople*! The European army was utterly shattered. Sultan Bayezit, in revenge for the Christians' treatment of his own subjects, caused 3,000 Christians to be beheaded when the battle was over. He spared only a few noblemen whose ransoms were set at so high a price that contributions had to be levied throughout Christendom to meet them.

This was the last engagement that could by any stretch of imagination be called a crusade, and ironically it came to grief in *Europe* and not in the East. It was now obvious even to the most stupidly reactionary of Europeans that the Holy War against Islam was over for ever. Certainly the Byzantine Emperor Manuel II came asking for help as far west as misty London, appalling all the solid citizens who saw him by the threadbare poverty of his clothes and the beggarly hopelessness of his manner. No one was prepared to assist him, any more than they had assisted the Mongol supplicants 100 years earlier.

Meantime, in the Near East, conqueror jostled with conqueror for the privilege of dragging down beggared Byzantium. In 1439 the new Greek Emperor, John VIII, gave up the long religious fight against the Roman Church and submitted to the Pope, simply in order that his city might be saved from the Ottoman Turk. But Constantinople was not to be ransomed for long, in spite of this ridiculous bargain. The new breed of Turks had vigour, ambition, vast numbers; whereas the forces of the West were sapped by intrigue, by generations of wasteful bloodshed, by a cynical materialism which vitiated all their efforts. The time was near when Turks would come to replace Byzantines at the edge of Europe, and when the crafty merchant-states of Venice and Genoa must look for their markets elsewhere.

In 1464 the half-crazed old Pope Pius II, against all wise advice, set out to lead what he considered to be the last crusade of them all. His fleet waited at Ancona, the shipmen nudging each other and smiling at the old fellow's stupidity. The Pope, travelling almost like a prisoner in a covered litter, was never told that no princes and no armies followed him. He did not even know that most of his sailors had deserted. Death mercifully overtook him at the port of embarkation on August 14, 1464; and with him faded the crusading concept, quietly, hopelessly, and finally. Moslems now ruled the whole of what had been for over 1,000 years called Eastern Christendom.

PART
THREE

27

Some Results of the Crusades

The crusades were not merely answers to a cry from Constantinople, not merely an impassioned invocation from Clermont, or a fighting-speech from Acre; they were not merely Lion-Heart, or Barbarossa, or Saladin, or Baibars; they were not merely St. Bernard's rabble, the Assassins of the military orders; and they were not merely the salvation of holy places, the war between cross and crescent. They were instead the necessary and inevitable jostling-together of peoples and cultures, the almost indiscriminate trials of strength and ideals, in a central, almost ventral, area of a world which was casting off its darkness and was fighting to emerge into light and self-determination. The crusades were the keystone of that arch of human development on the one side of which lay what was to become the modern. So it might be said that almost everything which has happened to Western men or to nations since the crusades is in some degree attributable to them.

It is conceivable that America was discovered because Western Europeans, having developed the techniques of shipbuilding and navigation during the crusades and having found the Eastern seas largely closed to them after Acre, felt the need to expand commercially and territorially in step with that wider outlook which the New Learning from the sacked and distributed libraries of Constantinople brought to Northern and Western Europe.

Free movement of peoples away from the feudally-held land since the time of Clermont may have been responsible for the English Peasants' Revolt in 1381. After which, it becomes almost a commonplace to suggest that the further emancipation of man during the English Civil War, the French Revolution, the Commune of 1848, the 1917 Revolution in Russia, all in some degree spring from the same initial source.

This is not to say that the men who were in later ages to demand freedom were *conscious* of their original sources of thought—any more than the prince regent was, in ordering minarets to be raised above his marine palace at Brighton. It was something to which man had become conditioned.

Only the scholars with their "new" books, or the magnates with their Byzantine statuary or Turkish rugs, were aware *for a time* what they owed directly to their contact with the Near East. To the great mass of European mankind who possessed no tangible reminders apart from a village inn called The Saracen's Head, the brightening dawn of liberation which flared before them was of their own doing, they imagined.

It must be remembered that the diffusion of Moslem and general Arabic culture in European life had been produced by contact in many other spheres than that of the simple Syrian coastline. For centuries before the first crusading ship set sail, *ideas* had fed westwards from Byzantium, itself in close touch with the East. Later they came from the Norman kingdom of Lower Italy, established on a Saracen basis—and for perhaps 800 years the Iberian Peninsula with its interpretation of Arabic and Christian Roman ideas had produced a peculiar amalgam of culture which was to persist even after the crusades had long been forgotten. So it is difficult to prove whether the Arabic civilising influence in the West came in any individual instance through Spain, Italy, Byzantium or Syria. The crusades themselves may be assumed the general purveyors, if only because of the constant contact of West with East over a period of more than 200 years.

European languages show an unusual abundance of Oriental borrowed-words such as *cotton*, *muslin*, *damask*, *sofa*, *mattress*, *alcove*, *carafe*, *bazaar*, *barracks*, *magazine*, *arsenal*, *admiral*, *amulet*, *elixir*, *douane* (customs), *tariff*, *algebra*. In the Romance languages, and especially in Spanish (which had the longest and closest contact with Arabic), the loan-words are extremely numerous and very often give a clue to the institutions and phases of culture which came from the East.

Of plants with an industrial significance, perhaps cotton is the most important. It first came into use in Europe through Syrian commerce and astoundingly brought with it the Arabic invention of cotton paper, in place of parchment. The importance of this one item cannot be over-estimated. In his *Outline of History*, Wells says on the matter: "This the Arabs seemed to have learnt from the Chinese by way of Central Asia. The Europeans acquired it from the Arabs. Until that time books had to be written upon parchment or papyrus, and after the Arab conquest of Egypt, Europe was cut off from the papyrus supply. Until paper became abundant, the art of printing was of little use, and newspapers and popular education by means of books was impossible. This was probably a much more important factor in the relative backwardness of Europe during the dark ages than historians seem disposed to admit. . . ."

Other typical exports included fabrics, cinnamon, cloves, mace, musk, galangal and nutmeg. Among the herbs and spices exported, perhaps the most important was that balm which was grown in Jerusalem in the twelfth century and which was used in the services of the Christian Church. Indigo and ivory were also mentioned frequently in trading schedules. It should be noted here that the crusading Franks themselves, being more concerned with war and administration, did not play much part in trade, but left it to the Moslems or those *native* Christians of Syria, such as the Greeks or Armenians. Moreover, the Italian merchants, who were largely responsible for the flow of goods and materials into the Western world, did most of their bargaining directly with Moslems.

The cultivation of sugar cane, together with its name and that of syrup, became known first to the crusaders on Syrian soil. Sugar became the principal foodstuff to enter Europe from the East, and it might be said that all the sugar used in Europe during the twelfth and thirteenth centuries came from Syria. The same source provided the sesame lily, the carob tree, and saffron. Pistachio nuts and lemons still bear their Arabic names. Apricots were for a long time called Plums of Damascus; damsons are Damascenes; the little shallot onion is really the ascalonette—

that is, the onion of Ascalon. Even the water-melon, now so common an article of diet in Europe, came in with the crusades from Syria.

The crusades had an immense influence on food in Europe. True enough, the Romans had done much to educate the tastes of those primitive peoples with whom they came into contact, but exotic dishes disappeared when the legions left Gaul and Britain. The rough Saxons contented themselves with a gruel of ground beans and field-herbs; they ate dark bread, soft cheese, and drank a thin weak ale. On rare occasions they rose to venison pottage, roast duck, bacon and cabbage, all flavoured with a coarse grey salt which they obtained from boiling sea-water in iron cauldrons. The Saxon and Norman nobility fared hardly any better—though as privileged hunters they had a greater choice of flesh to eat.

By the time of the first crusades, diet had become a little more varied. For the peasants, there were bread, ale, beans, peas, wheat and rye; soft cheese, onions, mead made from the honey of wild bees, leeks, cabbage soup, dried cod, and salted flesh once a week. At Michaelmas there would be a goose, and at Christmas a roast pig. No doubt rabbits would be poached from the master's warren and even deer from the king's forests. Folk of the land-holding classes, however, took full advantage of the variety of foods which were now coming from the East. They ate fig pie, flavoured with pepper, ginger and mulberries. Their fish-pie was cooked in verjuice, the liquid strained from crushed crab-apples, and then flavoured with currants, raisins, dates, cinnamon, mace, ginger and cloves. Iced pears and peaches such as Saladin once sent to Richard Lion-Heart were impossible in the mild, damp English climate; but their counterparts stiff with honey syrup and flavoured with cinnamon were well known. A sort of blackberry jam was created by squeezing the fruit in a cloth bag until the pulp ran into a dish, when it was mixed with salt, sugar and vinegar.

At the high table of the lords, hands were washed in perfumed water, after the manner of the Saracens; while the board would be garnished with a model, in sugar, almond-paste and rice-flour, of a castle. Even the native roast rabbits would be spiced in the Syrian fashion; and wine was no longer drunk in its natural form, but heavily flavoured with cinnamon and sweetened with sugar. Every man of any substance at all placed his order regularly with the merchants, for pepper, ginger, mace, nutmeg, cloves, raisins, currants, dates, saffron, and rice, as a matter of course.

Some of the Eastern recipes of the times are worth quoting in detail: strawberries were first washed in red wine, strained through a fine cloth, mixed with almond paste, and then stiffened with rice-flour. After this, raisins, saffron, pepper, sugar, ginger and cinnamon were added. The whole was sharpened with vinegar and finally decorated with pomegranate seeds before serving. In 1390, a recipe for a "Saracen sauce" was recorded, consisting of rose hips, almonds fried in oil and then ground to a fine powder, the whole covered with red wine, to which had been added sugar, pepper and ginger. After this mixture had stiffened it was mixed with rice flour and garnished with pomegranate. It seems that there was no dish and no country into which Moslem flavourings did not penetrate after the eleventh century.

Syrian exports to Europe were numberless: silk, from silk-worms cultivated at Tripoli and Beirut since the sixth century, was highly popular among the Western nobility.

Flax was grown in the plains of Palestine and made into linen in Nablus. Samite (velvet) was woven at Acre and Beirut, while the purple dye which coloured it was manufactured at Tyre, a city which also shared with Antioch the production of glass and pottery, under Jewish supervision. Most of this material came westwards.

The customs tariffs of Acre, which have been preserved, record that this port sent to Europe rhubarb from East Asia; musk from Tibet; pepper, cinnamon and nutmeg; aloe wood from Assam; camphor from the Sunda Islands; Indian and East African ivory; incense and dates from Arabia. The port of Beirut seems to have contributed mainly pepper, incense and pearls.

For the first time Europe came to value and to cultivate the arts of carpet-making and embroidery. Persian carpets were first hung on the walls, but as the Middle Ages wore on they found their rightful place on the floor.

Our knowledge of dyeing came almost entirely from Syria. "Crimson" and "lilac" are Arabic terms, as are also "azure" and many other shades of colour used on the escutcheons of crusaders. Ironically enough, much in later heraldry is owed to the East.

Extensive changes in dress and fashion came in with the Saracen trade. It is likely that the voluminous *houpelande* of late Plantagenet times was based on the Arabic robe, and it is almost certain that the turban which was so popular during the reign of Richard II was a Saracen borrowing. So were slippers, or to use their Eastern name, *pantoufles*.

The noble ladies of Europe benefited from this traffic of ideas. Such cosmetics as rouge for the face and henna for the hair now became common. The last is of ironic interest since, originally, it was used by Saracen women to give them something of the appearance of the Franks, whereas later it became identified in the European mind with the more exotic East.

Of more practical importance was the glass mirror, which came to the West through Constantinople and replaced polished metal discs. It is likely that the more discerning mirror of glass, together with the salves, rouges and unguents of the East, both drew the attention of European ladies to the ravages which smallpox had made to their charm, and also gave them some means of disguising them. Certainly the mirror and the cosmetics must have induced in men and women a higher degree of self-consciousness with regard to physical appearance.

Lords whose shaven chins had been the subject of Byzantine and Syrian mirth began once more to wear the beard and, curiously, at this time the handkerchief was introduced, some say by fastidious Richard II, others by Edward I, who himself conducted a crusade. Use of steam-baths, or "Turkish" baths, was now made by crusaders who had once despised washing as an effeminate custom, but whose contact with the insects and climatic necessities of the East had taught them better. Aromatic scents for the dress and body came in at the same time from Syria. Perhaps it is in such matters of the "luxury trade" that the East had its most far-reaching effects on Europe; and this great change in domestic and social customs was not long in passing over from the nobility and clergy to the more successful members of the new moneyed class—the merchant citizens of the town.

In the arts themselves there was considerable traffic from East to West—though Spain and Constantinople were the routes by which much of it came. Poetry and romance were stimulated by strange lands and adventures among a different people; even in the fourteenth century Chaucer in *The Squire's Tale* still describes the tumultuous court of Jenghis Khan, with its wild and luxurious feasting and all its magic contrivances. In 1378, during the reign of Charles V of France, plays and pageants were still devised to represent certain episodes from the early crusades; and even in the modern times of Elizabeth I of England, the poet Spenser chose as his three villains for *The Faerie Queene*, the Saracen brothers, Sans Foy, Sans Joy and Sans Loy. The commonly accepted stories and pantomimes of "Sinbad the Sailor" or "Ali Baba and the Forty Thieves," even "Aladdin," in our own times are an extension of this interest in or borrowing from the East. And how many drawing-rooms or parlours have resounded to the cadences of that Persian Assassin-poet, Omar Khayyám, whose *Rubáiyát* was published in 1859 by Edward Fitzgerald!

From Constantinople the use of figured brocades was borrowed, as was the art of sculpture in its ecclesiastical forms. Mosaics from Constantinople, though formal and ritualistic, were vitally and dramatically lit, as though their creators wished to produce a third dimension in their picturing. This "stereoscopic" concept was something new to appear in Western art, which had previously existed "in the flat." The illumination of books had much of the same sense of colour, light, shade and depth. Though immense destruction of pictures and manuscripts happened at this time, a great number of these must have found their way back through Europe, and it is from this time that English decorative art, both in stone and in paint, cast off its rigid Saxon or Norman formalism to become rich and brightly coloured in the Eastern manner. Byzantine artists borrowed from Persia, India and even China, and often took as a subject for their frescoes or illuminations that exercise which was a necessity to the medieval world, hunting; but which now became a cultural obsession with European painters and weavers of tapestry. Many objects of Byzantine art, like the four bronze horses which Henry Dandolo stole from the Hippodrome of Constantinople for St. Mark's in Venice, came westward after the sack of Constantinople by the crusaders in 1204.

The influence of the Arabic East on Western music is limited perhaps only to the Mediterranean, Spain and its colonies in Latin America. Moors, Berbers and Jews lived long enough in Spain to impose their indelible imprint on the folk-music of the southern provinces and, more recently, on the serious music of such composers as Albéniz, de Falla and Tárrega. Even today one can hear Arabia speaking through the Latin-American music of Villa-Lobos, half a world away from its origins.

The principal instrument which the Moors left behind them was the *vihuela*, a direct ancestor in most details of the present-day, and ubiquitous, guitar. It is from this instrument that one can now hear the rhythmic, crackling and filigreed music of the *flamenco* style in half the cities of Europe and America. I believe that the Arabs also gave us the violin, through their model for the rebeck, a three-stringed instrument with a peculiarly nasal tone, played with a bow. The quality of its sound is amazingly like that produced by Arab or flamenco singers with the voice.

There is no doubt about the debt of the West to military architecture in the Near East, and especially to that of Byzantium. The Normans who first went into the Near East carried with them the concept of a castle as being little more than a single stone tower, square in shape and encircled by a single or double wall, closed in by a natural or artificial moat. Such of them as returned to Europe brought back a much elaborated architectural pattern, in which castles were set high upon a crag, the towers rounded to prevent mining at the angles, and in which wall after wall enclosed a series of turrets, each providing a line of fire upon the other and each therefore protecting the assault of the other. Furthermore, these new Eastern-style castles had a projecting upper section, or machicolation, which enabled the defenders to lean over their opponents and to counter-attack them with such refinements as molten tar and Greek fire, another product of the crusades. In Britain, such castles were first set up against the Welsh at the order of Edward I, by an architect who had served all his apprenticeship in the Near East. He created citadels so reminiscent of Antioch as Harlech, Caernarvon and Conway.

Syrian influence on domestic architecture in the West is more difficult to assess—except in Spain, where Moorish styles came in with the first occupation and, especially in Granada, still show their mark in arches, colonnades and mosaics. In most of Europe, however, Arabic modes of building found no foothold. Arabic borrowings in domestic architecture were to be seen in carpets, cushions, wall-hangings and perhaps glazing, rather than in the buildings themselves, though certain elements of Victorian "Gothic" show more than a mere trace of Saracen influence.

Here one might hazard a guess that the Spanish window-grid, or *reja,* meant to keep inmates from straying outside, or outsiders from making their way in, was an architectural result of the Arabic insistence on the polygamous subservience of womankind. Moslem women were closely guarded from seduction and elopement, and the harem system was strong wherever the Arabs set up their communities. A trace of this protective and proprietary attitude towards women still exists in Spain, though today a different, protectively Catholic, reason might be given for it.

Eastern influences on ecclesiastical architecture in the West are almost as indefinite as those on dwelling-houses. Certainly Romanesque and even Byzantine forms are seen here and there through Europe, but the average parish church owes little to the East, unless it be the pointed arch, the decorative cusps, or perhaps the stained glass in its windows. The typical church of the crusading states was a building of stone, using little wood in its interior, largely because Syria was prone to earthquakes. Windows were small so as to keep out the blaze of the hot Eastern sun. Domes were used instead of towers. Such churches, with their intricate mosaic floors, their many courtyards and their geometrically-decorated capitals could hardly accommodate themselves to the European climate or custom; and the tradition of the Church is in general the oldest of all our traditions. Certainly there are contemporary exceptions to this; the Roman Catholic Cathedral at Liverpool or the Basilica of the Sacré Cœur in Paris are obviously of exotic origin; but they are not typical of Western building habits.

There is no doubt, however, about the influence of Arabic and Moorish studies on European intellectual discoveries. In fact so anxious was the Western world to learn as much as it could from the Arab that Raymond Lull (1235–1314), the son of a Catalan nobleman, persuaded six European universities to institute schools of Oriental languages within their walls without delay. Nor were these centres short of the texts from which to study, for as early as the tenth century the Arabic language had been made available to scholars in a number of grammar-books, dictionaries and philological treatises, most of them produced by the book-copying "factories" at Alexandria, Damascus, Cairo and Bagdad.

The extent to which the Arabs themselves contributed to European learning may be assessed by the fact that in the year 970 (a century before the First Crusade) there were nearly thirty free schools operating in Córdoba alone, for the education of poor Moorish and Spanish students. Moreover, there were efficient universities at Basra, Kufa, Bagdad, Cairo and Córdoba at which students from the furthest West were made welcome at any time, and always irrespective of religious wars. Scholarship for the Arabs stood outside political or religious dissension. Christian students flocked particularly into Spain, and carried back their findings to the less liberal universities of Paris, Oxford and Italy. Professor De Burgh notes wryly in *The Legacy of the Ancient World* that in the Western centres of learning the works of Aristotle were studied "in Latin translations of Arabic translations of Syriac translations from the Greek."

At Córdoba the Arab philosopher Ibnrushd, or Averroes, who lived 1126–1198, lectured on Aristotle to vast audiences, pressing forward beyond the bounds of localised religious observance towards scientific rationalism. For him neither Islam nor Christianity was allowed to obscure logical thought. And slightly before this, Ibnsina, or Avicenna, lectured on medicine so expertly as to gain himself the title even among Europeans of "the Prince of Physicians."

Taking their foundations from the Greeks, Arab

scholars developed mathematics, evolved from India the numerals which we use today and, by the twelfth century, discovered the decimal notation. Though they added little to the Euclidian system of geometry, they *created* algebra, developed spherical trigonometry and went on to invent the sine, tangent and cotangent.

In their studies of physics, they were the first to use the pendulum and to make progress in the science of optics. So the telescope came into being, to be used in the various observatories which the Arabs set up in their study of astronomy. At a period when to most European men the heavens were a mumbo-jumbo of goats, bulls and fishes, the Arabs calculated the angle of the ecliptic and the precession of the equinoxes.

Their advances in the field of medicine were no less spectacular. European medical knowledge had always been hampered by the Church, which considered that treatment by ritual might only be performed by the clergy and that men and women had a duty to suffer Christ's agony. The Arabs broke through this barrier to study physiology and hygiene and to evolve a materia medica and a system of treatments which are in many cases still used today. What is more, in their practice of a highly-developed surgery they used anaesthetics such as opium and myrrh for which the too-stoic Christian world was to wait almost until our own times.

As chemists, they discovered potassium, silver nitrate, corrosive sublimate, and nitric and sulphuric acids; as workers in such metals as silver, gold, bronze, copper, iron and steel, they led the world. Their pottery and glass excelled that of any other country or people; their paper, leather-work and enamels were of the finest quality.

In all departments of agriculture and of irrigation

they were superb. They had early learned the use of fertilisers and had made a careful study of the chemistry of the soil. Their practice of crop-rotation, a necessity in their own easily exhausted soil, was not to occur to European thought for another 700 years.

In accounts of the crusades there are many references to orchards, which were normally situated in a belt on the outskirts of the populous Saracen towns. It was in such places that the Arabs cultivated fruits of exquisite varieties and also practised the art of grafting, which had never been known in Europe until the amazed crusaders saw the enemy at work and so learned their secrets.

In all it might be said that while the Arabs learned little from the land-hungry Franks, Europe absorbed from Syria almost *every* art and science which was necessary to raise medieval man from the condition of peasant subsistence towards a "modern" awareness of what life had to offer him.

It should be firmly stated at this point that the crusading states themselves did hardly anything to expand or contribute to that body of learning with which they found the Saracen already possessed. Europe obtained its information almost entirely from the scholars and merchants. It is ironical that almost the only element of Eastern culture which the crusaders themselves brought back to their countries of origin was the concentric castle —a piece of apparatus which prolonged but could not finally preserve feudalism. Cannon, the invention of which may also have come from the East, played a part in ending this.

It might be said with truth that the first Latin kingdom resulted in a freezing-up rather than an expansion of intellectual interchange between East and West. Certainly Christian intolerance there had the effect of producing a similar intolerance among Arabs, who by the eleventh century had become the most liberal and enlightened thinkers in the world.

Nor can it be overstressed that to most crusaders Constantinople was as much "the enemy" as was Islam. The peculiar nature and past history of this great city was never properly understood by Westerners who saw it as being strange, and therefore wrong, evil or deserving destruction. In this matter the Christian Church and the papacy did not do much to educate its soldiers. Conversely, it often seems that the popes were more anxious to gain power over the patriarchs than to "save" Jerusalem; which leads to the inevitable if cynical view that the crusades in general were to become an instrument less for the salvation of Christendom than for the expansion of the Roman Church.

An unavoidable result of this situation was that the native Christians of Syria or Armenia found themselves trapped between the two political or doctrinal millstones of East and West. They who were born and who lived where Christ himself was born and lived were the *real* victims of the holy wars, not those stubborn foragers of Hattin or Acre. And sadly these native Christians were left to suffer on, as slaves of the Turks who had invaded as far west as the Balkans, when the European urge to go crusading had long died away.

It has to be admitted that the crusaders of almost every nation and shade of belief were primarily marked by greed and intolerance. With the opportunities of absorbing a rich way of life which their own places of origin could not offer them, they could hardly ever bring themselves to look beyond the immediate moment of aggression and material acquisition. Even the famous military orders, splendid as they were in courage and tenacity, were bedevilled by a material envy of each other that in the end became almost suicidal.

Each crusade cost its country of origin dearly. What the West gained religiously or territorially from those centuries of exhortation, travelling and massacre was negligible; what it gained in science and in general culture from Arab literacy can never be fully assessed.

Yet it is difficult to see how else the average Western lord might have behaved than as a warrior, in a Europe which had not yet fully awakened to the value of its scholars, and which by its code of chivalry prized the fighting man above all others? In the persons of Saladin and Ousama we have seen that the Saracens held learning in high respect and that even the most greatly occupied warrior was also required to be a man of letters; but the West until the Renaissance (which had its origins in Constantinople) thought literacy to be the sign of a meek or debilitated disposition, and the man of peace was only too often despised. Frederick II is a typical case, at the highest level. Even the Church itself seemed to give praise to the warrior above other men, and as early as the ninth century Pope Leo IV declared that the warrior who died in battle for the Church should be the first to receive the joys of heaven. A little later Pope John VIII seemed to give sanction to violence by classifying all dead warriors as holy martyrs, provided that they died fighting for the Church and had been pure in heart.

To the Byzantine man of culture such martyrs were more to be feared than the Turk himself, and at the beginning it is probable that Constantinople was less afraid of Saracen invasion than was safely-distant Europe. At least the average Greek had a basis of intercourse with his Moslem near-neighbour, the Seljuk Turk, whereas the Frankish modes of thought, speech and behaviour, as expressed by the Normans, were entirely foreign to him.

In any case, such Saracens as first swept west as far as Spain were as much the descendants and sharers of the ancient Greek and Roman glory as were the Byzantines themselves. It is likely that the Byzantine felt more at home at Cairo or Bagdad than he would feel at Paris—or even at Rome.

Between the Greek Empire and the Caliphate there lay tolerance and no attempt at conversion after the first Moslem sweep; but between Byzantium and the Catholic West there lay an eternally unsheathed sword.

Nevertheless, the crusades had certain salutary and educational effects on the politics and economics of the West. For instance, at their close they tended to stabilise frontiers. By about 1453, the Moslems held Constantinople and the Danubian provinces, and thereafter Europe began to learn what its own limitations were. The end of the crusades marked the end of any concept of the illimitable power of Rome, for example; for while the crusades had begun with the Seljuk Turk uncertainly holding Nicaea, they ended with the Ottoman Turk firmly and irrevocably entrenched along the Danube and *containing* Europe in a way that had never before been known.

And within that new Europe the crusades also hastened many changes. The baronage itself was undergoing a metamorphosis; in many cases the smaller estates were broken up because of the heavy scales of pledging by the nobility who wished to go crusading, but either could not redeem their land from money-lenders, or who died in the East. Often the fiefs passed into the hands of remaining daughters, and so, by marriage, into other families. Only the greatest barons, the magnates with numerous male offspring, continued much as before; the smaller ones tended to disappear. And those barons who still held land and political power were no longer quite the same in outlook; they had had time to become familiar with Oriental ideas of nobility and statecraft—a more cultured and fluid system than their own—which had the effect of producing, to some degree, a liberal frame of mind in the West. Liberal, that is, in the sense of the barons becoming more tolerant to new ideas. From the Greeks they had learned something about the art of war—about fortification, sapping, mining, the use of siege-engines and Greek fire. They had also found to their cost that an army composed of small territorial or jealously feudal units was no match for a large and determined army under a unified command.

After the crusades, the old concept of feudalism was for ever undermined. Men tended to be seen now as individuals, each with his own capabilities and rights, and not as nameless slaves. So began the great period of civic charters, which allowed many men to achieve a freedom from the land to which their grandfathers had been tied. Richard Lion-Heart openly sold municipal charters to raise money for his eastern expeditions; and between 1100 and 1300 a multitude of peasants bought documents which raised them to the comparatively independent position of burghers, or free townsmen.

And just as each village community now began to see itself as an independent unity, so did each country. The crusades quickened the growth of nationalism, principally in England, France, Germany, Italy and Spain.

In matters of religious administration, the crusades were not initially responsible for causing disunity. The conflict between East and West, between Pope and Patriarch, had become a Christian duty long before the First Crusade. However, illustrating the newly developing dissensions in crusading Europe, both in Church and State, Pierre Dubois, writing in 1300, said: "Let the Pope sell his rights to the French King, who will then become undisputed sovereign, and the peace of Europe will be settled. For it is the peculiar merit of the French to have a surer judgement than other nations, not to act without consideration, not to place themselves in opposition to right reason."

The Abbot of Prémontré, striking out at another enemy, once more emphasises the disunity which did not begin, but which grew during the crusades: "We cannot find in history that Germans and French were ever at accord in any great common enterprise," he says. Even during the Hundred Years' War an Englishman, Walsingham, expresses rather more picturesquely the divergencies of European opinion: "Now is the Pope a Frenchman," he says, "and Jesus is English; let us see who hath the stronger arm, the Pope or Jesus. . . ."

There was one matter of state, however, in which the crusades had a similar unifying effect throughout Europe—that of direct taxation. The early kings had no income for the needs of government, beyond that raised from their own landed estates and the feudal dues which could be exerted on the holders of royal fiefs. In time for the Second Crusade, however, Louis VII of France imposed a direct tax on all his clergy, while in 1188 both Philip

Augustus and Henry II of England decreed a Saladin Tithe on the Church. The Popes followed their example.

At the beginning of the crusades there was no gold coinage in Western Europe, except in Moslem Spain and Sicily. Silver was largely used for the higher denominations. When the crusading states became established, however, gold dinars and bezants, named after Byzantium, became widely coined, the metal from which they were minted coming from the Sudan by way of Moslem traders. In effect, the crusaders put Europe on a "gold standard" which persisted almost to our own times.

At this point it is perhaps of interest to consider the finances of the crusading states themselves, more especially with regard to the average attitude towards money of those Europeans who set themselves up in Outremer. In general, the Franks of Syria were incompetent in most matters of finance. Daring feudal warriors, incorrigible plunderers, they were naïve when it came to the administration of a whole country's economic system. Certainly, the princes exacted a ten per cent toll on all goods passing through the customs of Outremer—but they farmed out the collection of this tax to their vassals, the Church and to the military orders, which resulted in an inevitable confusion and wastage, since no efficient check was kept on the activities of the tax-gatherers.

Superficially, it appears that a number of Franks made great use of the iron-mines or sugar-factories in Syria, yet here again appearances are deceptive since the average Frankish magnate tended to produce only enough for a purely local consumption and had little interest in building up an export trade outside Outremer. The Franks contented themselves by being merely well-do-do, whereas with more effort they might have become, like their Moslem, Italian or Genoese counterparts, positively rich. Furthermore, they relied chiefly on that sort of labour which was unlikely to produce for them any great output—natives, slaves, prisoners-of-war—among whom there was no concerted effort to create and to develop an efficient or even an economical production of goods. The gulf between inexperienced Frankish magnates and disinterested slave labourers, was immense and unbridgeable. The conquering Franks were trained as fighting-men. They captured the land, but then did not know what to do with it, apart from setting up their castles.

The result was that the government of Outremer was always poor in wealth. Customs duties were invariably both inadequate and difficult to collect. It is ironical that finally Outremer came to depend mainly on taxes levied on Christian visitors or pilgrims to the holy places. The Franks began to prey upon their own kind rather than upon the Moslem enemy. Even the offerings made at the various shrines became subject to Governmental taxation in this blind and desperate attempt to raise money.

The Church itself in Outremer, being deprived of much of its income by the government, had to rely largely on its estates in the West for economic survival. The same situation applied in large measure to the military orders, who drew revenues from their holdings throughout European Christendom. There is, however, an exception in the case of the Templars, who were also able to finance themselves on the spot by their Eastern banking activities. Indeed, this order soon became so financially secure that during the Second Crusade the knights were able to feed money back to Europe, at an extortionate interest, to enable France to set forth once more against the East.

This much must be said of the Templars, that though they outdid even the Jewish and Armenian money-lenders of the time in avarice, they were utterly reliable. There was about them a certain realistic logic which, divorced from false patriotism or emotion, caused all men to trust them in business matters without necessarily liking them. This tended to separate the Templars from the faith and the Frankish political system which they had come into existence originally to serve. Their financial success welded them into a cosmopolitan force of cynical and often insubordinate mercenaries.

The Italian merchants were much like the Templars in that they set personal profit above religious unity. It is obvious then that Outremer could never be financially stable while it depended on so many divergent and profiteering forces. The survival of this state which had been founded on a mixture of religious fervour and land-hunger ultimately depended on what amounted to gifts from the West—and when these were cut off, Outremer naturally decayed.

The peculiar nature of commerce in the Holy Land is worth consideration. What must be emphasised is that Europe in the Near East did not act with a unified purpose. Whereas the First Crusade, of Franks, uncommercial and religious in its origins, caused the growing Italian maritime cities to fear that any crusading success might mean the ruin of their trade with the Moslem Levant, when those Franks proved themselves militarily successful and set up settlements in Syria, the Italians sensed the prospect of extended or even new markets and so gave that support to the crusading movement which they had previously withheld.

The issue is complicated at this point, for while certain crusaders were obviously prompted in their actions by religious fervour, many others, including the lesser nobility of France and the Low Countries, were impelled by sheer land-hunger. This grew from the system of primogeniture, by which the eldest son came to hold the fief in the mother-country, leaving the younger ones to make their own ways elsewhere. Such men would snatch whatever came to their hands, without considerations of stable trade or even religion.

Furthermore, the vast army of foot soldiers who constituted the earliest crusades did so for almost entirely mercenary reasons; they were in the main peasants escaping from lives of poverty and famine towards lands of almost legendary wealth and riches beyond the bounds of the limited European imagination. For them, Jerusalem was literally a golden city.

The reality was naturally much less desirable than the dream. Those peasants who reached the Moslem world found little for themselves in lands which needed careful tending and in which a rigid discipline of the self was required from anyone wishing to live entirely off the soil. The average European, unaccustomed either to the Syrian climate or its soil, found life in the East unrewarding. It was not long before news of this disappointment was passed back to Europe, after which the ordinary peasant began to look on Outremer not as a Heaven on earth but as a harsh battleground, to be visited only under necessity, and then to be looted and left as quickly as possible.

The Frankish younger sons, more expert in fighting than in husbandry, carved out estates for themselves in the Latin kingdom and soon came to depend on the territory *beyond* the coastal strip, beyond the Jordan, for their food-supplies. Outrejourdain it was that grew the corn and commanded the trade-routes from Damascus to prosperous Egypt; though, of course, as the European taste for spices, silks and fine porcelain increased, the Franks tended to profit by customs duties on any such luxuries as passed through their territory of Outremer.

However, the volume of this trade varied from crusade to crusade. Under Islam, goods from the farthest East had originally come up the Persian Gulf to Bagdad; but after the disruptive effects of the First Crusade this route was changed and merchandise from China and India passed over the Indian Ocean and thence by the Red Sea to Egypt, so cutting out Syria and the Europeans who might profit from Islamic enterprise. By the time Nur ed-Din and Saladin had brought a new order to the busy Moslem world in Syria and Egypt, the Far East once more landed its goods in Persia, from which country they travelled overland to Aleppo and Damascus, and so to the Mediterranean. It was only at this period that Tripoli, Acre and Tortosa began to grow in mercantile importance, not before.

It is important to note here that any trade with the West depended almost entirely on the Italians. It was their shipping which ultimately carried the luxuries of the East to the bowers and tables of the West; and these Italians were not hampered by any inhibiting concepts of religious duty. Until the end of the twelfth century, these Italians sailed directly to Alexandria for their Egyptian trade, ignoring the Frankish ports of Acre and Tripoli. The result was that, at this time, the trade-starved Franks of Outremer were compelled to raid and to forage in the countryside round about them simply to keep alive in a foreign land.

But as time passed the Italians became more tolerant and wide-seeking, and at last began to conduct uninterrupted business with the Frankish-held Syrian ports. The only problem which disturbed the men of Genoa and Venice was what they could bring from impoverished Europe to barter for the luxury goods of the East; and the answer was, at first, slaves. In the early days of this trade, these kidnapped peasants were usually Hungarians and Slavs, but after such Balkan peoples became Christians in the tenth century this traffic became increasingly difficult. However, the Italians were opportunists and soon their ships began to be laden with Turkish or Tartar slaves, destined for sale in Egypt, on the grounds that neither Pope nor Patriarch could object to their selling heathens to Islam.

There were other supplies which were necessarily clandestine, such as the wood and metal which were exported from Europe to the East, to be made into weapons of war for use against the crusaders. Spanish merchants joined with those of Genoa and Venice in these dealings—though such merchandise was prohibited by law. It was argued by the Spanish and Italian traders that if they did not supply the Saracen in such materials, then the Danes, Saxons or Flemings would step in and steal their contracts from the Turks.

So the chaotic situation arose that while half of Europe seethed with fury at Saracen military victories and trembled for the final religious outcome of the conflict, the other half continued to run vast quantities of war-materials into the Turkish ports. In fact King James I of Aragon dared openly to promise state protection to the shipwrights of Barcelona when they shipped planks of wood to Egypt—a military commodity which the Egyptians had exhausted in their own country. This farce finally became so highly developed that commercial ambitions swamped religious feelings, and by the time that Frederick II, "The Marvel of the World," became the titular head of a crusade, his relations with the sultan had become so amicable that German merchants were always allowed to travel through Egypt to the East Indies, often in the company and under the protection of their Moslem fellow-traders.

In present-day nationalistic terms, it seems incredible that the great European trading families should have had wharves and jetties in most of the enemy Saracen ports, as well as in Constantinople. That the Venetians and Genoese should have their settlements along the Eastern Frankish-held seaboard is not surprising—especially when one recalls that their trade made Acre the safest and most prosperous port of the Levant for a while and when one reflects that these traders also transported pilgrims, and so were in a measure assisting the crusades, though at a great profit. But that in the uncertain period even before the First Crusade the city of Amalfi should have owned factories in Constantinople, a street in Antioch, and a hospital in Jerusalem is an outstanding tribute both to Italian acumen and Moslem liberality.

At Acre and Jaffa by the twelfth century there were entire Genoese *quartiers*, and in Jerusalem one occupied entirely by the shipping magnates of Marseilles. When we remember that the children who sailed in 1212 with Stephen of Cloyes, did so from Marseilles, the ease with which the slave-ships ran in to Bougie in Algeria to make a sale becomes more understandable. It is equally true that Saracen slaves were a commonplace in the thirteenth-century markets of Southern France and Italy, and were to remain so until the Renaissance, and even later. By 1250 even the commercially backward English had a trading-street of their own in Acre; and along the four hundred miles of the North African coast there were twenty-seven ports into which almost any European merchant could run his cargoes without being in any way impeded by the current crusading wars.

This indiscriminate free enterprise was somewhat curtailed with the expansion of the Mongol Empire in the thirteenth century, especially goods coming from the Far East. The old trade-routes were changed and merchants were encouraged or forced to take the overland route from China. Moreover, Chinese junks had their terminus settled by their Mongol overlords at the Indian coast. Thereafter, Indian merchants, wishing to avoid Mongol levies, came up the Persian Gulf to deliver their wares at Damascus, often under extra difficulties from Egyptian competition. But though this new obstacle between the Far East and Syria was set up, trading between Europe and the Moslem world still persisted. The final stage of cynicism was reached when the Saracens, finding that the crusaders were badly in need of supplies of plumes for their helmets, began ostrich-farms in Egypt to meet the growing European demand.

In the middle fourteenth century, Mediterranean sea-trade reached its climax—after which the slower northerners of the European seaboard began to compete ever more strongly with the clever and experienced bargainers of Italy and Southern France. Before the crusades began, the northern peoples had traded largely along the Rhine and so into Central Europe, or across to England or the Baltic; but after the crusades had opened up new trading horizons, there was hardly any limit to the routes which became available to courageous merchants. Soon Bruges became the great central meeting-place of the Western shipmasters, who formed themselves into a mercantile union called the Hanseatic League, allied with the Teutonic Knights and the money-lending Lombards. From Bruges and later from Antwerp, a merchant-prince might deal with all the then-known world to the East as far as China itself.

In 1260, when the Baltic ports of the Hansa formed their first Parliament in Lübeck and became a maritime republic under an elected Grand Master, rather like that of the Templars, the nature of future developments in trade became apparent. Such a republic could and did defy kings and even popes. By the fifteenth century, eighty-four cities had joined this merchant-league. In 1488, as a sign that the merchants could look after all their own affairs, they beheaded 150 pirates in the market-place of Hamburg alone. Never before had commerce openly shown itself to be so strong.

This Hanseatic League, the result of early Italian successes in the crusading Mediterranean, had depots in London, Boston, York, Bristol, Ipswich, Norwich, Yarmouth and Hull. The merchant-princes, soberly dressed and dour, had become a more powerful force than the armour-clad lords of the manors. Despise commercial Dandolo as we may, he set the pattern of the future, though he did not live to see it. It was not until 1641 that this Hanseatic League was dissolved, and only then because, by that time, the development of the New World across the Atlantic had diverted the more lucrative trades from the old, easily-controlled northern routes.

As a co-founder of the modern age of commerce, Prince Henry of Portugal, "the Navigator," must be included with such free-thinkers as Dandolo and Frederick II. Henry's deliberate policy as a royal prince was not to win land-wars but to extend and control sea-trade, and hence to stimulate discoveries of new routes and markets. At Sagres he systematically built up a great merchant fleet and personally cultivated the company of mariners and mathematicians, whose practical advice enabled him to draw up maps and charts of a more accurate sort than had ever been known before. Soon his vessels explored Madeira, the Azores and the Canaries, all of which were made Portuguese colonies. They then sailed on down the west coast of Africa and returned with slaves and exotic food cargoes.

Henry, a true child of the crusades, died in 1460; but Bartholomew Diaz, a Portuguese captain, continued with these explorations and in 1486 reached the African Cape of Good Hope. Less than ten years later, and strongly influenced by his two Portuguese predecessors, Christopher Columbus struck outwards to the west and discovered America.

Obviously, this new and nationalistic movement upon the sea demanded a code of behaviour every bit as stringent as that which prevailed among armies on the land. As early as 1190, when Richard Lion-Heart sailed from Gascony for the Holy Land, sea-laws had been announced to the sailors and put on record by chroniclers. This crusading sea code, severe as it sounds today, seems to have had the desired effect of keeping rough men at peace with each other over long and arduous voyages, for it was taken as a model and extended later in the laws which governed all sea-going traders—such as the Laws of Oleron, of 1266, which were obeyed throughout Europe, the Laws of Wisby and of Jutland, and the Mediterranean Consulate of the Sea.

The results of the crusades on Western concepts of

religion should perhaps be the most obvious of all the legacies from the East; yet this is not so. It is unlikely that doctrine or ritual within the Roman Church itself changed at all merely because of contact with the Moslem world. What effects Islam had may have been on congregations rather than on priests, and on social understanding rather than on doctrine or ritual.

Possibly by contact with other religions, crusading Christians acquired a better understanding of their own and a greater tolerance towards the faith of others. Certainly, in Spain, where there had long been many generations of intercourse between Christian and Moslem, by the year 850 the southern provinces had come to prefer both the Arab speech and their scriptures to their own. A commonly-used exclamation in Spain even today is "*ojála*," which is an invocation to Allah. While in Sicily, under its Norman masters, the two great religions enjoyed mutual tolerance and respect for many generations.

It must have come as something of a shock for the average conservative Frankish baron to find himself regarded as an idolator by those Saracens he had been taught to think of as Anti-Christ; and much that happened in the Holy Land must have upset the preconceived notions in many a docile Christian mind.

For instance, Saladin once gave a reception to the Western lords in a tent, the floor of which was covered by a carpet embroidered with crosses and Christian emblems. While the Saracen emirs made their way carefully round this carpet to their appointed seats, the arrogant Franks strode across it without a second thought. After a time, Saladin shook his head sadly and said, "My own emirs would have been less careless of the symbols of their religion, my lords."

It is true that whenever a new army of crusaders landed in Outremer, they observed how easily their predecessors had settled and how pleasantly they fraternised with their Arab neighbours. Certainly, Moslem tolerance and sympathy were such that, after one Christian defeat, Joinville reports certain Saracens as saying, "If Mahomet had suffered such mischief to be done to us as has been done to King Louis, we would never have kept our belief in Him." The frequent discovery of good in the enemy's heart did much to modify Christian thought, so that by the time of Frederick II the dominant feeling to emerge in the East was one of easy tolerance as between Christian, Jew and Moslem. Conversion, where it was attempted, was made by persuasion rather than by force or torture. As early as 1219, St. Francis of Assisi went to Palestine to convert the sultan, who greeted him in a friendly manner and listened to his preachings with all courtesy, though a violent war was being waged about them at the time. Afterwards, although the sultan persisted in his own beliefs, he allowed Franciscans to settle unmolested wherever they chose in Syria.

It is from such examples that gradual reassessments of the enemy and of the world at large are made. The crusades tended to break down the medieval assumption that there was only one code of religious belief, and so, in their own peculiar way, helped to prepare the European mind for what was later called the Reformation.

Perhaps the finest results of the crusades, in their effects on the previously restricted European mind, lay in the wide and exciting horizons at last opened up by the journeys not only of soldiers and merchants, but also of priests and scholars. Early and often semi-pagan merchants who followed their trade to the Holy Land, first "saw the light" there and returned to tell their stories and even to take holy vows in small European country towns. Many who went abroad to make their fortunes spent all at the blessed shrines and ended by becoming inveterate pilgrims.

The merchants of Italy and Flanders fared further afield than most others, and, after the pioneering work done by Franciscans, opened up the Far East to other travellers between 1250 and 1400. It is probably true to say that though the crusading armies themselves stimulated the mobilisation of great fleets and the development of navigation, it was the friars who often showed the merchants how best to make use of such fleets. Such friars often travelled immense distances trying to make Christian treaties with the infidel wherever they found him. In 1346, Friar John de Carpine walked far into Turkestan, hoping to convert the grandson of Jenghis Khan.

Friar William of Rubrouck, sent by St. Louis as an envoy to the Tartars in 1253, describes how he met Buddhist priests on the plains clothed in sacred yellow vestments; and how in Tibet "were men who were wont to eat the carcasses of their dead parents, in order that, for pity's sake, they might make sepulchre for them in their own bowels. Howbeit, of late, they have left off this custom, because that thereby they became abominable to other nations. Notwithstanding, unto this day they make fine cups of the skulls of their parents . . ." This indefatigable friar travelled on foot or in the saddle over five thousand miles to be at the Great Khan's court at Karakorum.

But it is not to Friar William that we look for the best description of the great world beyond the Mediterranean. It is to two Venetian merchants, the brothers

Nicolo and Maffeo Polo, who in 1260 took the overland route to the Far East, on a journey which lasted many years. Kublai Khan, who was then on the throne of China, greeted them warmly, since they had taken the trouble to learn the Tartar language and so could bring him accurate news from the West. He then ordered them to return to the Pope with a request that a hundred missionaries should be sent out. The brothers got back to Italy in 1269 to find the Pope dead. They waited for two years, hoping for the election of a new Pope and at last in desperation went East again, taking with them this time Nicolo's son, Marco, then about sixteen years old, and two Dominican friars who were to act as missionaries at the Khan's court.

This expedition started from Palestine but before it even reached Armenia, the two faint-hearted friars turned back, unwilling to face the hazards of the nightmare journey. Unabashed, the three Venetians went on alone through Mosul, Bagdad, across the salt desert of Khorassan, and so up the Oxus valley and into Pamir to "the roof of the world." They reached the Great Khan's court in 1275—a journey which staggers the mind by its length and its hardships. Young Marco, by this time twenty-two, knew many spoken languages and could write accurately in four of them. He seems to have been a youth of such good presence and quick wits that the Great Khan Kublai became immediately impressed with him and employed him as his ambassador to countries as distant as North Burma, which was not again to be visited by a European until 1860.

Marco's success did not stop there. For three years he held the post of Governor in Yangchow with twenty-four towns under his rule, during which time his father and his uncle went trading in jewels throughout the Far East.

After seventeen years of this exotic but tiring life, they expressed the wish to return to Venice—only to be told that the Great Khan had become so attached to them that he did not wish them to leave his empire. Thereupon Marco Polo was sent on an important mission to India so that he would be kept occupied by other thoughts than homesickness. Nevertheless, the Venetians got away at last, via Java, in a fleet of thirteen vessels, and carrying letters from Kublai Khan to the kings of France, England and Spain. They reached Venice once more in 1295—that is, *thirty-five years* since they had made their first journey to the distant East!

They were true Venetians—of the Dandolo breed; there is little need to remind ourselves of the care which they must have taken, in all respects, to get that cargo back home and into the markets of Europe. Their coats were stuffed with precious jewels and their heads with the most incredible information ever to come out of the Far East. Marco Polo lived until 1344, and had much to set on record. This he did largely in dictation to the writer Rusticiano, as a means of passing the time while he lay in a Genoese prison, having been captured in a sea-fight between Venice and Genoa. His influence was enormous, not only in teaching European travellers what they might expect to find beyond the plains of Tartary, but also in giving vivid instructions to those map-makers who were later to fire the imagination of Henry the Navigator or of Christopher Columbus himself.

One can well understand the incredulous laughter of certain cautious Italian tradesmen when they first heard the Polo version of the Far East. At last, however, through the mouth of one man the superiority of the infidel in matters of trade, travel and wealth became accepted.

Christianity itself stood at the cross-roads of indictment in every counting-house and tavern in Europe for a while.

It is not surprising that Marco Polo was disbelieved when he first tried to introduce hard-headed Venice to the ways of the Far East. Yet no wonder he beguiled the Venetians in the next breath when he spoke of the Mongol trading-folk who knew nothing and cared nothing of the so-called arts of war, but whose main interest was in the bargain they were conducting and who, when the day's trading was done, went out in their pleasure-boats, accompanied by their dark-eyed mistresses, to sail the incense-laden stream, in a purple night of coloured lanterns and softly-twanging lutes.

This was the birth of the legendary, mystic and exotic East; the dream which was soon to bemuse the European imagination, to turn it away from the Holy City and the Palestinian sea board, and to redirect it towards China, India, the Spice Islands. It was in his attempt to reach this fantastic East by an unusual route that Columbus gave America to the world.

Appendix

CHRONOLOGY OF MAJOR CRUSADES

The First Crusade : 1095

After Pope Urban II had appealed for a crusade, during the Council of Clermont, bitter feeling against the Seljuk Turkish Moslems ("Saracens") arose. In some ways, this was the greatest and most successful of the crusades, for it united Christendom as never before, and perhaps never since.

The first wave of "crusaders," under Peter the Hermit an Walter the Penniless, consisted of an undisciplined rabble of common people—Provençals, Italians, French, Germans and Normans. In the Rhineland, many of them committed excesses against the Jews; others massacred Hungarians, who seemed like Saracens to them. The main route taken was along the Danube valley and so to Constantinople. On arrival there, the Greek Emperor, Alexius, dismayed by their conduct, shipped them across to Asia Minor, where they were massacred by the Seljuk Turks in 1096, without ever reaching the Holy City of Jerusalem. Their numbers dwindled from perhaps half a million to twenty-five thousand.

The organised forces of true crusaders, headed by gre nobles, arrived in Constantinople in 1097 and, after fierce fighting, captured Antioch. In July, 1099, the Belgian Godfrey of Bouillon led a victorious army into the Holy City, where he was elected as the ruler, but not the king of this new Latin Kingdom of Jerusalem. Other nobles ruled Antioch, Edessa and Tripoli, prominent among whom were Bohemond of Otranto and Raymond of Toulouse.

Once beyond the territorial limits of Asia Minor, which was claimed by Emperor Alexius, these crusading noblemen had as their chief object the carving out of kingdoms for themselves. The "Latin Kingdom" which they created was a narrow strip of coastal territory, stretching from Edessa and Antioch down to Ascalon and Jerusalem. It was, in fact, a long line of fortresses with some ports, including Acre (captured in 1104), and was largely protected by a small permanent garrison mainly consisting of the two new orders of military monks, the Knights of St. John the Hospitaller (1100) and the Knights Templar (1123), whose creation had grown from the military necessities of this First Crusade.

As time went on, this Latin Kingdom and the Eastern Empire of Constantinople became more and more antagonistic towards each other. As early as 1101, the mercantile republics of Venice and Genoa began to give aid to the Kingdom of Jerusalem, so increasing its power in the East.

The Second Crusade : 1146

The kingdom of Jerusalem held its own for forty-five years after its first creation, under its elected kings, Baldwin I, Baldwin II, and Fulk of Anjou. But by 1144, the Seljuk Turks had reorganised themselves once again and had captured the northern outposts of the kingdom, Edessa.

In 1146 St. Bernard preached the need for the Second Crusade, which started out in the following year, led by King Louis VII of France and the Emperor Conrad III. It was much more stately—but infinitely less successful—than the enthusiastic

First Crusade. For one thing, its aims were now divided and uncertain: one large division of Germans, for example, instead of going to the Holy Land, turned aside to fight against the pagan Wends, who lived east of the Elbe. This they counted as a legitimate crusade—as did the Flemish and English contingents who made their way to Portugal and set up a Christian kingdom, with its centre at Lisbon.

In the meantime, the situation in the kingdom of Jerusalem was becoming desperate. In 1169, a Kurdish adventurer named Saladin, of great intelligence, culture and strength of purpose became ruler of Egypt. He was a Saracen of great military skill and devotion to his religion. Soon Saladin began to unite the Moslem world, from Cairo to Bagdad, and, when his armies were ready, preached a Holy War, or *Jehad*, against all Christians. This Jehad so inspired the Saracens, who now looked on themselves as holy warriors, that in 1187 they recaptured the Holy City of Jerusalem.

The Third Crusade : 1189

Saladin's capture of Jerusalem in 1187 provoked the Third Crusade, which was a very grand affair led jointly by the Emperor Frederick I ("Barbarossa"), King Philip Augustus of France, and King Richard ("Cœur de Lion") of England who, at that time, still owned many of the richest French provinces.

By 1187, the papacy was in an enfeebled state so the conduct of the Third Crusade was left almost entirely in the hands of the kings concerned who were, at this date, obsessed by the ideals of courtly chivalry and knightly behaviour. For the common people, however, all the glamour had gone out of crusading. From bitter experience they had learned that only kings or barons straggled back after a defeat: the common soldier was beheaded or left behind in slavery. Moreover, in order to pay their ransom money to Saladin, monarchs and noblemen exacted such heavy taxes from their subjects that ordinary men always lost more than they gained in these "holy" wars. Furthermore, it now became obvious that even the popes used the idea of crusading for their own purpose—to weaken dangerous monarchs, or to put down heretical sects.

The Third Crusade was a failure. Barbarossa died suddenly in Asia Minor; and although Antioch was saved for a time, Jerusalem was not retaken from the Saracens. True, the Christians remained in possession of the Palestinian coastal-strip, but Saladin's basic power was not shaken. King Richard of England, gloriously heroic on the field of battle, acted with blind stupidity when it came to dealing either with his allies or with Saladin, at the council table. With the failure of Richard and Philip Augustus, it can be said that the great days of the crusades were over.

The Fourth Crusade : 1200–1204

After Saladin captured Jerusalem in 1187, all the heart went out of crusading. The election of Pope Innocent III, eleven years later in 1198, certainly brought vigour back to the papacy, however. Under him it reached the height of its power after generations of decadence: uncompromisingly, Innocent claimed more than any other pope had dared to claim—a divinely ordained supremacy over all monarchs. As the guardian of the infant Emperor Frederick II of Germany (later to be acclaimed as "the Wonder of the World"), Innocent ejected the German overlords of Sicily and Naples; he deposed King John of England, and then reinstated him as his own vassal; he imposed himself as the feudal lord over the Kings of Portugal and Aragon; he even organised that war against the Saracens in Spain which ended in their decisive defeat at Las Navas de Tolosa in 1212.

The Fourth Crusade resulted from Innocent's exhortations—but also from the fact that Constantinople was politically insecure and tottering. This fact, more than the Pope's fiery words, stimulated such leaders as Boniface of Montferrat and Henry Dandolo, the business-like Doge of Venice, to profit by the Byzantine weakness while, at the same time, *appearing* to go on a crusade. Of course, the Venetians, as Christians, were bound to support *any* crusade: but by this time the Moslems were such good customers of the Italian merchants that the Venetians hated the idea of injuring their trade with the East. In fact, they had only recently struck a new gold coin, inscribed with extracts from the Koran, for the use of their Saracen customers! Constantinople seemed a more sensible goal for this "Crusade."

The French nobles under Boniface of Montferrat, dependent on Dandolo for their sea-transport, were easily persuaded to agree to the Doge's first scheme—which was to attack his commercial rivals in the Hungarian city-port of Zara—and then, in 1204, to commit the shocking crime of besieging, sacking and burning Constantinople itself.

This Fourth Crusade did not reach the Holy Land at all. Instead it gave mercantile Venice much of the coasts and islands of the Eastern Empire. The reigning Greek dynasty was deposed and the Greek form of Christianity was declared abolished. Dandolo elected his own Patriarch, the Venetian Morosini, who at that time had not even taken holy orders. The Frankish crusaders then elected Baldwin, Count of Flanders, as "Greek" Emperor. In this way, it was thought, Catholicism and a Latin Empire could be established by Byzantium.

This act was a great blow to Christianity in the East, for if the Greek Empire had been weak, the new and feudal Latin one was weaker! In fact, it lasted only half a century, after which the long-suffering and exasperated Greeks rebelled against it. In 1262, Michael Palaeologus recaptured Constantinople from the Latins, from which time a Greek dynasty and the old orthodox faith were re-established, to endure almost for another 200 years.

The Children's Crusade : 1212

"The very children put us to shame," declared Pope Innocent III, when in 1212 the boys and girls of France and Germany moved southwards to the Mediterranean, expecting to walk dry-shod across the sea, as Moses had once done, to the Holy City. Of 30,000 French children only one returned. The rest were auctioned off in Algiers, or sold into slavery in Cairo. The German boys and girls were more fortunate; of their 20,000, a tenth straggled back across the Alps, taunted or enslaved by the ironical peasants who had watched them set out.

Index